BEFORE THE FLOOD

BEFORE THE
FLOOD

Destruction, Community, and Survival
in the Drowned Towns of the Quabbin

ELISABETH C. ROSENBERG

PEGASUS BOOKS
NEW YORK LONDON

BEFORE THE FLOOD

Pegasus Books, Ltd.
148 West 37th Street, 13th Floor
New York, NY 10018

First Pegasus Books cloth edition August 2021

Interior design by Maria Fernandez

ISBN: 978-1-64313-644-8

10 9 8 7 6 5 4 3 2 1

Printed in the United States of America
Distributed by Simon & Schuster
www.pegasusbooks.com

"For Gx4"

—ECR

CONTENTS

They love the land because it is their own,
And scorn to give aught other reason why;
A stubborn race, fearing and flattering none,
Such they are nurtured, and such they die.

—W. K. Northall, *Life and Recollections of Yankee Hill*, 1850

Prologue

April 28, 1938

To all former Town Officers of the Towns of Enfield, Greenwich, Dana, and Prescott:

You are hereby formally notified that the corporate existence of the aforesaid towns ceased at 12 o'clock midnight, April 27th.

In view of this fact, the town's officers are to carry on no municipal function on and after April 27th and shall do only such acts as are necessary to affect the transfer of properties of the municipalities to the Metropolitan District Water Supply Commission and to affect the commitment of taxes to the town to which the respective territories are annexed.

—R. Nelson Molt, Commission Secretary

April 27, 1938
Enfield, Massachusetts. Night.

Town Hall was built to hold three hundred people. This evening, one thousand crush into the old brick building. Twice that number, many of them reporters from across the US, stand impatiently outside, scribble notes, and aim their flash cameras at anyone going in or out. Cars are parked for a mile on either side of what was once Main Street, in front of stone-ringed ditches that were once grand Victorian homes. Inside, the wooden floorboards shake.

Old Dr. Segur, physician, town selectman, and volunteer fire chief, who has delivered many of the attendees and the attendee's children and comforted their parents in their last days, gives a brief, emotional speech, bidding farewell to the professional life he has known for the last half century. He and his wife strike up the band and take their front-row places in the Grand March.

In the winding march across the town hall floor, engineer Norman Hall and his wife, Wilma, known to the press as "The Valley's Most Popular Couple," have the position of honor as the Grand March's second pair. Engineer Jerome Spurr, who, after a decade as a state surveyor and scientist, has become a community leader, and his wife, Anna, follow. Some women wear their first-ever formal gowns. Others, their handmade wedding dresses. Still others wear black, in mourning. Black bunting covers the walls. The volunteer fire department serves free beer in the town hall basement.

Dance cards, with tiny pencils attached, are bordered in black, like a funeral invitation. But on the floor, there's forced gaiety, at least for the cameras. Norman Hall, beaming in a tuxedo, serves cake and ice cream. One of the orchestra members accidentally sits on a cake-filled dish abandoned on a chair, and the reporters swoop in to photograph a pretty young lady dab the ice cream off the back of his pants. McEnelly's Orchestra plays jazz and swing, with a smattering of old-time barn dancing.

In the balcony, the black-suited old-timers—the wealthy Howes, Zappeys, and Doubledays—whisper unsmilingly between themselves. The children, in their best Sunday short-pants suits and white dresses with Shirley Temple hair bows, doze in the overheated balcony and try to figure out why everyone is so upset, because isn't moving to another town an adventure? The valley's poor—some of whom sit on their rotting front porches with shotguns in hand, waiting for the Commonwealth of

Massachusetts to come take what little they own—are not present. Tickets are fifty cents each.

Just before midnight, Dr. Segur motions for the band to stop. The packed hall falls silent. Onlookers outdoors grow quiet. Photographers prep their flash bulbs. The town hall clock strikes twelve. Dr. Segur lifts his arms. The orchestra plays "Auld Lang Syne," and then "Taps." The audible waves of sobbing—women and men, young and old, native and newcomer—begin.

After more than two hundred years, the towns of the Swift River Valley have ceased to exist.

INTRODUCTION

'A Well-Watered Place'

Boston needed water. Since 1630, the city on the salty, silty Shawmut Peninsula had been on a perpetual quest for sources of clean, pure drinking water, and there was never enough. Pipes had been laid, reservoirs built and filled—first in Boston proper, then the suburbs, then far outside the metropolitan area. By the early twentieth century, Boston's thirst had outstripped its water supply yet again, and the city was growing fast.

Sixty-five miles to the west, a group of small, self-sustaining farming and industrial communities in the Swift River Valley had all the clean water they needed. The water was so good and abundant that in the 1700s their forebears had forcibly taken the land from the Nipmuc Indians, who called it "Quabbin," or "well-watered place." The Commonwealth of Massachusetts determined it had one final option to sate urban demand: impound the Swift River and send the water to the city. Were the state to turn the Swift River, the valley's local ponds and lakes, and overflow from the nearby Ware River into a giant reservoir, the second biggest in the US at the time, Boston, and the millions in its orbit, would have fresh, pure water in perpetuity.

The catch: The four towns of the Swift River Valley—Enfield, Dana, Greenwich, and Prescott—along with sections of surrounding towns and villages, would be destroyed. Every last home, barn, business, wooden fence, tree, flowering bush, and blade of grass would be sold off or taken by eminent domain; graves and coffins disinterred and relocated; topsoil removed. The valley would be destroyed by fire and then flooded with more than 400 billion gallons of water to a depth of 150 feet. Historic county boundaries would be moved. The four towns would be removed from maps as if they had never existed.

The Commonwealth convinced itself this grand plan was justified, noting that time had not been kind to the valley. New industrial and farming practices hamstrung the small mills and dairy farms; the valley's remoteness and difficult topology delayed the arrival of electricity, telephone, and radio. Rumors that the state might take the valley for its water had circulated as early as 1895, a disincentive for new industry and an incentive for people with financial means or without deep roots to move on.

Journalists around the region quickly realized the Swift River Valley's impending demise made a piquant topic. Articles were written about it as early as 1920, even before official decisions had been made. The state printed a proposed map of the reservoir in 1922. Valley residents and their lone state representative fought the plans, but had little political or social capital. The Ware River Act and Swift River Act passed the General Court of Massachusetts in 1926 and 1927, with only one vote against them. The reservoir and the massive fifteen-year project it entailed was unstoppable.

Automobiles packed with surveyors arrived in the valley to photograph and document every acre and standing structure. These young men were mostly recent college graduates, chiefly from the Massachusetts Institute of Technology and Northeastern University in Boston—quick talkers and thinkers, fancy dressers.

The engineers came, armed with building designs, and the state hired laborers to carry out the literal dirty work of digging giant shafts deep underground and lining them with concrete to build gravity-fed water tunnels. The grand plan would culminate with one of the largest earthen dams ever built, constructed from the valley's own stones and dirt and ultimately rising as high as its gentle mountaintops. The Swift River itself would be redirected from its riverbed through a tunnel dug into bedrock. In 1937, one year before the valley was evacuated, construction began to proceed twenty-four seven—a never-ending cacophony of drilling, rock crushing, klieg lights, air- and bullhorns, and rumblings of the earth.

"They were known as carefree fellows," said a 1938 article in the Springfield, MA, *Union* about the engineers, "toying with an instrument, stringing tape across the road, or riding in state cars, driving perhaps a little too fast, noticeably about 5 P.M., headed in the direction of the Metropolitan Commission office. They were not accepted by the residents. Only the poorest houses were available to them as rents. To get into an established group was almost impossible. They were looked upon as foreigners, sent to wrest the land from the natives, and were generally referred to by those whose language was more picturesque than refined as 'those damned engineers,' expressed with as much vehemence as that of a good Southerner when referring to the Yankee . . . This quiet valley . . . contented and all abiding, heard rumors of the great project which would deprive them of their homes, businesses and associations—and here were the men actually at work doing just that."

It was easier to blame the faces they saw every day than the shadowy figures in Boston.

Then, gradually, something happened. The engineers were treated less as heartless invaders and more as members of the community—men who increasingly brought out their wives and young children—and who were equally anxious to find work in a desperate Great Depression economy. The valley residents' resentment of the Boston pols and the Metropolitan District Water Supply Commission did not abate, but the individual engineers, with whom they interacted daily, functioned, for a time, as a replacement for the young people who had left the valley. By day the engineers directed the destruction of the only home most valley residents had ever known. After hours they became pillars of those same communities: school and church board officials; volunteer firefighters; heads of local civic organizations like the Masons and the Grange. Their wives became schoolteachers, de facto social workers, and members of ladies' social clubs. Several engineers and young valley women even got married. When everyone, local and engineer alike, was forcibly evacuated, just before the flood, some friendships remained for decades afterward.

Popular regional history structures the Quabbin story as a binary. The "victors" are the state government and the population of metropolitan Boston, who have Quabbin water to drink and the large and nearly pristine watershed around it for hiking, fishing, and wildlife spotting. The "losers" are the members of the valley diaspora and their descendants, who have made every effort to keep their history alive, and a large number of whom still actively resent the taking of their ancestral homes.

Left out of the historical equation are day-to-day designers and builders of this great testament of twentieth-century civil engineering, men whose college educations never prepared them for their ultimate day-to-day job duties. They literally worked hundreds of feet underground. They fought fires and persevered in the midst of floods and hurricanes. They built buildings, elaborate engineering contraptions, and artificial lakes. They grew the forests that now cover the Quabbin watershed. They took more than ten thousand photos, pored over rocks and sand and water in makeshift labs. They presided over the dead and brought them to their new resting places. And yet they have remained, like the designers and builders of medieval cathedrals, anonymous and communal.

No longer. For the first time, the engineers have names and photos and biographies. They were people who honed a trade, fell in love, learned to live among people not like themselves, suffered in their labor, and learned to feel grief that was not their own. Every engineer felt differently about the death of the Swift River Valley and his part in it, and repressed or commemorated all that had happened to him accordingly.

How did the engineers live among and befriend people whose lives they were destroying? And how could they have been befriended in return? Why did a few remain loyal to the Quabbin project throughout their lives, even choosing to be buried at the new Quabbin Park Cemetery; why did others refuse to acknowledge what had happened in the Swift River Valley, never even telling their families about their work?

Even today, the majority of Bostonians and the residents of the more than fifty communities that drink Quabbin water don't know where their water comes from, let alone the story behind it. But as ongoing climate and water crises throughout the US continue with no resolution in sight, more and more Americans will be driven from their homes and livelihoods, abandoning depleted or destroyed resources, or else relocated to re-allocate what scarce resources remain. Will those Americans be treated more fairly than the residents of the four drowned towns a hundred years ago?

The story of Quabbin is a parable of everything that has gone, and continues to go wrong—and sometimes right—with American public works planning. The Quabbin was both a triumph of engineering and a feat of forward-looking environmental stewardship, yet the most vulnerable humans were disregarded in the process.

Climate change increasingly will affect how humans interact with their water supplies. Federal and state governments should expect and plan for more water-based human displacement, either from drought or flooding. Both the public and private sectors should evaluate the extent to which disruptive technologies benefit the many versus the few. Nor can we anticipate a stable future economy.

On a community level, that Swift River Valley society functioned for as long as it did is a testament to disparate groups compelled to rise above suspicion and prejudice to create a community of necessity. American, and global, society must learn these lessons before we face the inevitable extreme economic and cultural challenges created by environmental changes and devastation.

Birth of a Valley: Prehistory—1900

T en thousand years ago in what became the Commonwealth of Massachusetts, Ice Age glaciers retreated. In their place they deposited the riverbeds of the Swift River, three fingerlike branches that flowed southwest to the Connecticut River, west of the geological divide separating the two halves of the state. Had the Swift River flowed east into the Atlantic Seaboard, this story probably never would have happened.

The glaciers cut two parallel valleys: The Connecticut (colloquially known as the Pioneer River) Valley to the west and the Swift River Valley to the east. The Connecticut Valley was broad and fertile. The Swift River Valley was narrow, and lay in shadow.

The native Nipmuc tribes found it, nevertheless, an ideal place to live. They flourished in valley settlements beginning in approximately 1000 B.C.E., primarily along the banks of the Swift River, which was known, even then, for its plentiful fishing.

By the mid 1600s, Massachusetts Bay colonists had established settlements in the central part of the state, outside the Swift River Valley, up to the Connecticut River. These settlements traded with the Nipmuc and their leader, Chief Quabbin, and the neighboring tribes with whom the Nipmuc intermingled. Settlers and Nipmuc were pulled onto opposite sides in the drawn-out colonist–Native American conflict usually called King Philip's War (1675–1676). After the colonists' victory, the local Nipmuc not killed were scattered and absorbed into other tribes; arrested and sent to prison or labor camps; or sold into slavery in the West Indies. As a reward for their service, the Massachusetts Bay Colony gave captured Nipmuc land in the Swift River Valley to veterans of the war. This land grab was the first act of defiance against the government, in this case the British—a sign that the colonists could handle affairs by themselves, without any help from the bureaucrats far away.

The settlers, largely Calvinists of Scottish descent, were homesteading in the western part of the state because much of the good land in the east was already being farmed. The colonists given the Swift River Valley were happy to take it for free; in their frugalness, they did not seem to care that the Connecticut Valley, with its superior growing abilities, was just one mountain ridge west.

The 1,200 acres taken from the Nipmuc became the town of Greenwich, the first white settlement inside the Valley, which gradually grew to 25,000 acres and split off into the towns of Dana, Enfield, and Prescott. The first white child was born in Greenwich in 1735.

Shays' Rebellion

The colonial settlers were fiercely proud of their self-sufficiency and independence from the rest of the state. Many twentieth-century valley residents were descendants of the rebels who fought in Shays' Rebellion (1786–1787), an unsuccessful uprising against the Massachusetts state government in response to high taxes and economic hardship. Daniel Shays, a Revolutionary War hero, led a brigade of 1,100 men to the city of Springfield, thirty miles south, where they attacked the Springfield Arsenal, protesting how the state government had unfairly locked up western Massachusetts debtors. Shays had made his plans in Conkey's Tavern, in the town of Pelham. The site of the tavern is now under water.

Animosity toward Boston was baked into valley culture in successive generations, reminiscent of how Southerners' views against the North further hardened after the Civil War. Valley natives always remembered that their forebears had fought the power, lost, and kept going, and the resentment only deepened.

Puritan influences were still visible in the nineteenth century, primarily a type of harsh spirituality that valued hard work and lack of worldliness. Two hundred years ago it was easy not to be seduced by progressive thought, when the valley's plentiful resources provided nearly everything. The Swift River produced the power for often prosperous mills and factories—in many places the soil was rich and farming profitable and easy. By the middle of the nineteenth century Enfield was the richest town per capita in the state. Enfield, Dana, and Greenwich all had hotels; Enfield's Swift River Hotel's elaborate dining room could seat three hundred guests.

Much of what we know about the intimate history of the valley is due to Enfield native Francis Underwood's 1893 ethnography *Quabbin: The Story of a Small Town with Outlooks on Puritan Life*. Underwood, along with a coterie of nineteenth century luminaries like Ralph Waldo Emerson, Henry Wadsworth Longfellow, Harriet Beecher Stowe, and John Greenleaf Whittier, was a cofounder of *The Atlantic* magazine. He was an antislavery crusader and temperance advocate, and, at the end of his life, US ambassador to Scotland.

As Underwood grew older he returned to the Swift River Valley to try to understand the place that had formed him, and to grasp to what extent it had moved beyond the Puritan, antiprogressive culture that had existed even in his childhood. Underwood's simultaneous disdain of and empathy for the valley's residents and a longing for the beauty of its hills and waterways were the same amalgam of emotions most reporters attempted to convey throughout their coverage of the valley during the Quabbin project.

Valley residents themselves were not particularly introspective. As in most New England towns, school, church, and town hall were the three pillars of community life. According to Underwood, they found their circumscribed world "cheerful; they knew no other. In the small houses there was no luxury surely, but no lack of wholesome food or seasonable raiment." This contentment without self-examination, Underwood suggested, caused the valley and its principal town, Enfield, to be "one of the most sluggish of rural communities . . . not poverty-stricken, but limp and lifeless."[1]

But the nature all around them was exceptionally beautiful. In his return, Underwood relives his childhood wonder about Great Quabbin Mountain: "It was a Delectable Mountain for children. The ascent was easy. To one looking back when half-way up, the village below, nestling under shade trees on both sides of the river, had a soft and almost unreal beauty . . . The upper region was alpine in its cool serenity, its airy pastures, sparkling brook and broad horizon."[2]

The center of the town was the oval-shaped common, half an acre long, and dominating the common was the Congregational church, which was the epicenter of public life for more than a century: "A steeple was set astride the roof; the building was painted white, furnished with green (outside) blinds, and turned with its end to the street. The vane, of sheet metal, gilded, was cut in the form of a man, the head cleaving the wind, and the legs extended for rudder. As it turned with a sharp cry on the rod which pierced its body, it needed but little aid from the imagination of a boy to become the image of some sinner transfixed in air, and held aloft to swing in lingering pain."[3]

Men of previous generations had Old Testament names like Hezekiah, Eliphaz, Hosea, and Ezekiel. They followed old Hebrew traditions, like beginning the Sabbath at sundown, not cooking or doing work on "Sabberday," and ending it when they saw three stars in the sky. These were "Sinners in the Hands of an Angry God" Christians, descendants of the parishioners who had listened to Jonathan Edwards preach in Enfield, Connecticut.

The valley's relative isolation was reflected in its accents; even into the mid-twentieth century, many of the rural folk spoke Old Yankee—not the dropped Rs and broad vowels of blue-collar Boston, but an accent similar to the traditional Down Mainers—slower and more nasal, with Southern-sounding hints. Recordings as recent as the 1981 documentary *The Old Quabbin Valley* reflect voices trapped, to modern listeners, in the amber of a lost world.[4]

During Underwood's childhood, Enfield was collapsing due to the staggering rates of alcoholism among the town men and even a few of the women; public drunkenness did not seem to be incompatible with twice-on-Sundays church services and a general contempt for secular learning. It took many years of the Congregational minister's patience before Enfield could dry out, and the years of rampant drunkenness were an influence on Underwood's temperance.[5]

What did the valley look like in its prime? Outside of town,

> Generally a couple of towering elms stood near each farmhouse of the better class, and not far away were apple trees in squares. Clumps of lilacs grew by the front door and by the edge of the garden; while along the neighboring road were rows of balloon-topped maples.
>
> The farms lying without the valley were and still are poor; their plain lands sometimes bore thin crops of rye, and then, lying fallow, were overrun with mullein; their undrained meadows were cold and wet, and infested with poison ivy and skunk cabbage; their hillsides rough and stony; their pastures gray and brown. The neighborhood roads were crooked, hilly, or stony and sandy.
>
> The houses of prosperous farmers were neat and comfortable, though invariably plain; but those of the poorer sort were miserable. Still, few farmers were educated beyond the 3 Rs, or

were in the habit of reading in hours of leisure, except for the
Bible and weekly newspaper.[6]

Everyone in the valley knew how to read and write. But like many rural
school systems, valley schools only went up through eighth and occasionally ninth grade.

During the first few decades of the twentieth century, despite tele-
graphs, telephones, electricity, and automobiles in the village centers,
country people still lived more like their parents and grandparents than
the radio-listening, train-traveling, shimmying townsfolk. The farmers'
furniture was "utilitarian, comfortable, serviceable—but nothing like what
you might call high-class furnishings." Men wore bib overalls and straw
hats. Women almost always wore aprons and long skirts.[7]

Outsiders, though, found it a restful and refreshing place to spend a
week on vacation. The back of a 1910 postcard of Greenwich Village reads,
"Mama and I walked to this pretty little village this morning . . . It was
perfectly beautiful. We picked berries coming back and had a lovely time.
You ought to see my mother climb a fence! Lovingly, Florence." On the
front, she adds, "This is Mt. Pomeroy, which rises right above the lake from
the hotel. I am watching the sun behind it now."[8]

Families were connected by complex marital and genealogical bonds,
and everyone knew by heart who had married into what families. When
University of Massachusetts at Amherst linguistic historian Audrey
Duckert recorded valley natives in the 1970s, they could rattle off lists of
marriages, remarriages, deaths, accidents, illnesses, successes, failures, and
personal eccentricities of people with whom they had second- or third-
degree connections. Family, like land, was paramount, and the work of
generations made the success of the land possible. Ancestors were always
visible, and the connection was strong.

Gradually—and not always happily for the natives—the Puritan influences were worn down, as they always are, and broader thought and culture
began to take their place. The lions in front of the New York Public Library,
for instance, were sculpted by Enfield native Edward Clark Potter. A few

men went to college; young women went to boarding or finishing school and then came back, only to leave again. Newspapers were delivered by the new train. But at the same time that expansiveness caused a brain drain. The population grew smaller and grayer, and those graying valley citizens had strong and settled views about political and religious differences, which were often one and the same: "A Massachusetts Federalist prior to 1810 was almost certain to be Orthodox [Calvinist] in faith; a church member was almost certain to be a Federalist . . . and it was generally the case that a Democrat was a Universalist, a Freethinker, or one of the 'otherwise-minded.' The wealthy, respectable and temperate people were Federalists, and supporters, if not members, of the Puritan church. Outside were Democrats, hard drinkers, and deists. For more than a generation the line of demarcation was invariable. The hostile feeling between the classes deepened often into malignant hate, and was felt wherever men came into contact."[9]

Many of their world views, which Underwood probably exaggerates, but probably not by much, are familiar even in twenty-first-century America:

The Quabbin man of the better sort believed the Bible to be inspired, in mass and in detail, from Genesis to Revelation; the Unitarianism and Universalism were doctrines of devils; that Methodists and Baptists were well-meaning people but blown about by the winds of doctrine; that the cross was a symbol of popery, and Christmas a superstitious observance; that the Federalists inherited the wisdom and virtues of Washington . . . that in a great city there were few honest men and fewer virtuous women . . . that the young men to be helped in 'gittin' college larnin'' were the ones intended to be preachers; that a lawyer was necessarily a dissembler and a cheat; that "old-fashioned schoolin'" was good enough; that a man who wore a beard was a Jew, or a dirty fellow, or both . . . that all the songs sung at church will be sung in heaven; and that the good old

7

days of samp, hulled corn, bean porridge, barreled apple sauce, apprentiship, honest work, and homespun clothes were gone, never to return. [10]

Ethnic and cultural homogeneity began to break down near the close of the nineteenth century. Smith's Village, as a de facto company town, hired many Northern Irish families as mill workers; the marketing materials for the mill advertised that they were Protestant, [11] but they were "clannish" and never assimilated. Then the Italians and French Canadians came to work in Dana's box and hat factories. Then the Poles came to buy cheap land and farm it. No open animosity existed between the old-timers and the newcomers; the newcomers simply didn't integrate, and the natives didn't bother, either.

Underwood died in 1894, aware that the valley was growing increasingly lifeless and sad: "It seems the crops have decreased; the great barns are no longer bursting with hay . . . all the people are fed with Western beef and flour. Many farms, though not abandoned, yield little return . . . The owners must pick up a living as best they can; the thin and stony soil can do no more for them. Their sons are away in the cities, or in the far West, and their daughters are teachers, or are married and settled, and not in Quabbin." [12]

A year later, the first exploratory engineers began to fill five-gallon jugs of Swift River water and take them back by carriage to Boston. Enfield's population had shrunk to less than one thousand.

The Towns

Even during the nineteenth century, "Swift River Valley," "Quabbin," and "Enfield" were popularly conflated. The valley was also called "Quabbin." Enfield was sometimes called "Quabbin." Because outsiders often never got past Enfield, the most conventionally "town-like" of the villages, "Enfield" also might refer to the valley as a whole.

The Swift River Valley was actually comprised of four towns—Enfield, Dana, Greenwich, and Prescott—and a number of villages associated with each.

Enfield was the largest of the four towns, with the greatest concentration of wealth and social capital. Enfield Center was arrayed like a standard New England small town, with a grassy common in the center surrounded by grand homes, the church, the school, agricultural Grange Hall, and the town hall. Main Street, the largest road in the valley, ran through Enfield Center, and the "Rabbit" train ran behind the town hall, near the Swift River and the water mill. Enfield had a small business district, which included a general store, butcher, post office, pool hall, café, hotel, and, eventually, a gas station. Enfield Center was the first area of the valley to acquire plumbing, electricity, telephone, and radio broadcast. Its residents had automobiles and domestic help. By the 1920s, it was the site of a de facto movie theater; the Howe family, oldest and wealthiest in the valley, rented movies from the larger towns and brought the reels to the town hall for weekend screenings.

Generally, Enfielders were better educated and more traveled than the valley population as a whole, and more involved in the churches, schools, and civic organizations. They were the most politically active in trying to block the reservoir, and also the most fatalistic about its demise. The Metropolitan District Water Supply Commission set up its headquarters in Enfield Center, and engineers who chose to settle in the valley lived in Enfield—resulting in more daily interactions between them and the Enfielders.

Smith's Village, while technically part of Enfield, had its own post office and school. The Smith family were the mill owners, and Smith's Village was essentially a company town. Residents were largely Northern Irish immigrants, poor and insular. The Smiths and a few others had large houses in the village, but the rest of the housing was poor. Photos and diary entries depict a grinding, almost urban poverty not seen elsewhere in the valley.

While Enfield Center and Smith's Village are now under a hundred feet or more of water, the borders of Enfield actually extended up the side of

Mount Quabbin—now the site of the public road that circles around from the Winsor Dam to the Quabbin Spillway, Enfield Outlook, fire station, Goodnough Dike, and back down to Route 9. Ruins remain in this part of the watershed, including foundations and retaining walls.

Dana, like Enfield, was divided into two main entities: Dana and North Dana. Dana Village was like a smaller version of Enfield Center, but more isolated. North Dana was the industrial center of the valley, with lumber mills and small factories. A number of well-off families lived in Dana, where the valley's Catholic and Universalist churches were located. Dana's many large ponds made it the site of summer homes for families from Springfield and Worcester as well as several summer camps, including the only Jewish camps in that part of the state.

The remains of the Dana town common are in the Quabbin watershed and publicly accessible. Dana Common was placed on the National Register of Historic Places in 2013.[13] North Dana is under water.

Greenwich (pronounced "Green-witch") was another small town with a railroad stop, hotel, town hall, and lumber mills. It is the only Quabbin town with nearly 100 percent of its land underwater, other than two mountaintops that poke out of the reservoir. Greenwich, more frequently turned inward rather than outward, was too small to have its own fire department, and many of its buildings were burnt down and not rebuilt prior to the arrival of the Commission. Greenwich also include a smaller section called Greenwich Plains, and while it had rich soil, prosperous farms, and lakes for fishing and camping, Greenwich never had electricity, telephone, or town plumbing. Despite this, it was the location of a spiritualist congregation in the nineteenth century, started by a wealthy eccentric who owned a piano-and-organ factory in Boston.

The closest visitors can get to Greenwich is to walk across the top of the Quabbin Baffle Dam, erected right on top of Greenwich Village, when reservoir water levels are low.

Prescott was the least populated, poorest, and most spread out of all the towns. It is also the town that remains most above the waterline. Prescott's remote hilliness and rocky soil forced most farms closer to subsistence than successful commercial enterprises. The Prescott Peninsula was used for training during World War II, and from 1969 to 2011 the top of the peninsula was home to the Five College Radio Astronomy Observatory.

The Prescott Peninsula is not open to visitors except on an annual tour given by the Swift River Valley Historical Society. However, what was once North Prescott, now bordering the town of New Salem, is partially open to the public.

Small hamlets existed on the peripheries of each town, usually populated by specific families, and boasting quaint names like Atkinson Hollow, Bobbin Hollow, Cooleyville, Doubleday Village, Puppyville, Millington, and Packardsville.

In addition to the four towns, sections of the towns of Barre, Belchertown, Hardwick, Orange, Pelham, New Salem, Petersham, Shutesbury, Ware, and Wendell were all taken in order to impound parts of the Ware River and to preserve the purity of the Quabbin watershed.

TWO

A Long, Slow Decline: 1880–1920

The Swift River Valley's gradual slide into economic irrelevance was precipitated by a number of factors beyond its control: westward expansion, changing industrial practices, and its geographical isolation in the face of technology that demanded connectivity and communication.

The valley had always been at a disadvantage compared to the Connecticut River Valley, which included the city of Springfield, thirty miles to the south of Enfield, and the Pioneer Valley, which included the towns of Amherst, Northampton, Hadley, Holyoke, and Chicopee, today all exits on north–south I-91. Exiting the Swift River Valley usually meant going over and around mountains. The nearest towns to the valley were Belchertown, five miles to the southwest, and Ware, seven miles to the southeast.

The Connecticut Valley, like the Swift River Valley, was a manufacturing and mill center, but on a much larger scale, with access to the Connecticut and Chicopee Rivers and the industrial city of Springfield, a powerful urban hub until the mid-twentieth century. The Pioneer Valley developed an early version of the "knowledge economy," with Amherst,

Smith, and Mt. Holyoke Colleges and Massachusetts Agricultural College (later UMass Amherst) developing as thought and research centers, and much cross-pollination via train, telegraph, and telephone between the Pioneer Valley, Boston, Hartford, New Haven, and New York. While in 1850 there may have been some economic parity between the Pioneer and Swift River Valleys, by 1900 that parity had been erased.

The fifty-five-mile north–south Enfield railroad opened in 1871. It allowed freer movement in and out of the valley, but was primarily an intravalley mode of transport, with six passenger stops and a flag stop in as many miles; valley residents nicknamed it the "Rabbit," supposedly because it stopped and started so often. Valley teenagers could now attend high school on the other side of the hills; on the other hand, education and the ability to see more developed areas outside the Swift River area encouraged them to leave.

The valley's hilly topology and limited infrastructure was not conducive to expanding industry. Existing small factories and mills made piano legs, boxes, brooms, bricks, soapstone, charcoal, buttons, nails, carriage wheels, palm-leaf hats, and three types of inexpensive fabric. In winter huge chunks of ice were brought out of the valley to cool the iceboxes of residents of the eastern half of the state. But there were far more people living in Massachusetts, and in the US, in 1900 than in 1850. Small-scale manufacturing in the dense confines of New England was no longer profitable, and large-scale industry was moving west. Carriage wheels were rolling toward obsolescence, and outsourcing the handweaving of palm-leaf hats to women and children in Dana began to look a little ridiculous. Most valley mills and factories shut down in the first two decades of the twentieth century.

Enfield and Dana were electrified in the 1920s and had telephone service installed decades before then. Greenwich and Prescott received neither electricity nor any paved roads, and thus fewer opportunities for commerce.

The valley was primarily agricultural, however—known regionally for its dairy farms, apple orchards, chicken farming, sheep, and berries. At one point nearly fifty varieties of apples grew locally. Centralized creameries and dairies were common until about 1890, after which local farmers began selling milk instead of cream. Farming families worked hard and ate well, and in their later years former residents recalled their childhoods as happy and satisfying, with a common refrain of "we didn't even know we were poor." In an interview from the 1980s, former Greenwich resident Walter King rhapsodized about his childhood breakfasts: "'Mother would serve up boiled potatoes, eggs or pancakes, some type of meat and home-made donuts, if I could talk her into it.' Of course, bread, butter, jelly and milk were always on the table."[1]

Farming success also depended on the location of the farm; Enfield and Greenwich had rich soil, while Prescott soil was arid and rocky. This was in part why Prescott ceased to function as a town in 1928, allowing itself to be taken over by the Metropolitan District Water Supply Commission rather than continuing to stagger on with diminishing returns.

In 1920, Massachusetts state regulators enacted "pure milk" laws. These included that cows and horses be kept in separate locations; no pigs or manure be kept under the barn; stables must be cleaned, whitewashed, and ventilated; milk must be strained and kept away from the barn; and all cows must be tested for TB.[2]

Valley farmers could not bear the costs of this regulation. Some larger dairy farms shipped milk to neighboring states that had not yet enacted milk purity laws. Most did not. Working around this required some thought: "Surplus milk was carried to town in 40-quart milk cans and hoisted on a platform for pickup. The cans were marked with the name of the farmer and the milk would be picked up by a Holyoke or Spring-field creamery for pasteurization. The farmer would receive a statement once a month detailing how much of his milk was purchased and what it was used for. A certain amount of money was deposited for him in a Springfield bank, making it necessary for him to travel to Springfield to withdraw it."[3]

Walter E. Clark was a Quabbin engineer who published *Quabbin Reservoir*, one of the first books about the valley, in 1944. "When we started work for the Commission in the Valley," Clark wrote, "it was surprising to see so many good farms capable of maintaining large herds of cattle, having no cows or perhaps one for family use. In many cases fences had been neglected and excellent pasture had grown up in weeds and brush . . . [T]he owners seemed to be reaching out for some other line . . . many settled down to the poultry business."

Some farmers began relying on gathering ferns, hemlock, and laurel to sell to florists. Others sold blueberries, blackberries, and raspberries. According to Clark, one man sold roadside produce, including potatoes, two days a week from a farm stand on the road near his house. The man lived alone, Clark said, and one farm stand day he left his produce to check something at his house. During his absence a truck drove up and stole everything. He never sold again. [4]

With so little hope for the future and with representatives from Massachusetts state interests showing up more regularly and more purposefully, people were migrating out of the valley at a faster clip. Some left their houses and farms behind, assuming that no one would buy them. A malaise settled over the gentle countryside. "Everyone was very much shocked and depressed, and they just didn't seem to care anymore," said Trudy Ward Stalbird Terry of Enfield in 1980. "All the ladies neglected housework, and they started playing bridge. They'd go play bridge any old time, I guess. And many of them didn't care if they improved their houses, or have them be papered, or things like that. They hadn't done any repairs or upkeep for six, eight, ten years. You get damaged chimneys, and everything was getting run down." [5]

"Letters from Quabbin" describes farms left to their own devices: "The grapevines are untrimmed, the fruit trees unpruned and shrubs and plants uncared for . . . No one climbs to the roof to replace a shingle . . . The steps sag, holes have appeared, and the vines are broken from the trellis . . . Barways topple, grates have fallen flat." [6]

Eleanor Griswold Schmidt, whose Prescott farm family was one of the very last to leave, described people while not maintaining their properties simultaneously not acknowledging their fate until far into the 1920s: "It was maybe just not for real. Maybe they'd go away. And there wasn't fear . . . there was just a heavy feeling."[7]

Horror writer H. P. Lovecraft, who was familiar with the valley and knew about the coming of the reservoir, even wrote about its despoliation in two of his stories. In "The Dunwich Horror" he describes traveling through a "small village huddled between the stream and the vertical slope of Round Mountain, and wonders at the cluster of rotting gambrel roofs . . . It is not reassuring to see, on a closer glance, that most of the houses are deserted and falling to ruin, and that the broken-steepled church now harbors the one slovenly mercantile establishment of the hamlet . . . it is hard to prevent the impression of a faint, malign odor about the village street, as of the massed mold and decay of centuries. It is always a relief to get clear of the place, and to follow the narrow road around the base of the hills and across the level country beyond till it rejoins the Aylesbury pike."[8]

And, more presciently, in "The Color Out of Space," which was published in 1927, before the reservoir and the new highways were anything other than design plans in the Commission's Boston office and a decade before the valley had been transformed into a moonscape: "There was once a road over the hills and through the valleys, that ran straight where the blasted heath is now; but people ceased to use it and a new road was laid curving far toward the south. Traces of the old one can still be found amidst the weeds of a returning wilderness, and some of them will doubtless linger even when half the hollows are flooded for the new reservoir. Then the dark woods will be cut down and the blasted heath will slumber far below blue waters whose surface will mirror the sky and ripple in the sun. And the secrets of the strange days will be one with the deep's secrets; one with the hidden lore of old ocean, and all the mystery of primal earth."[9]

Professions and family life in the valley were not at all poetic. Nearly everyone in Prescott was some sort of farmer; in Greenwich there were a few stores, an inn, and a tearoom, but mostly farming. Dana also had a hotel, but most people were employed by the box factory or the town. Enfield had more store owners and managers, but also workers for the woolen and lumber mills, the railroad, and the town. Every town had a postmaster and mailman, but Enfield also had people who worked the phone lines. There were three auto mechanics, a gravedigger, a meat inspector, and, in Smith's Village, a retired vaudeville acrobatic duo from Latvia, who lived on the same block as the Congregational minister and his wife. By 1930, many men had been reduced to being odd-job laborers; others were caretakers or gardeners. There was an insurance salesman and his daughter, a sporting-goods sales-girl, who presumably worked outside the valley. So did the young women who were nurses. Many people, especially women who were single heads of households, listed their profession as "None."[10] Bill Fielding Jr., son of an early engineer in the valley, recalls that "Some were farmers by accident after they lost their mill jobs—they just had a plot in the back yard or something." The Dickinson family had owned a trucking business when the mills ran, but according to Fielding, by the late 1920s "they had a couple of trucks over there, just rusted out from lack of use" and had to supplement their income by taking in the reviled engineers as boarders.[11]

There were few of what we think of now as "traditional" nuclear families except among the recent Polish immigrants. Adult children and their spouses lived with one set of parents rather than on their own. Older parents who were not farmers had no work; the adult children held down the jobs. They took in "wards of the state" for boarders, a primitive foster care system for which they were paid. The valley was largely devoid of traditional middle-class professions and the growing slice of middle-class nuclear families that existed elsewhere. When the married engineers arrived with wives and children, this family configurations must have just added to their general differences from the natives.

Beginning in the 1920s, New England residents with automobiles, more discretionary income, and a stylish longing for rural life began venturing as tourists into the valley. They built rustic summer cabins on the shores of Pottapaug Pond and the numerous other ponds. Several summer camps were established in Dana. Had these tourists, summer residents, and antique hunters arrived a decade earlier they could have improved the valley economy, perhaps staving off the state's decision to take the land—or perhaps their enthusiasm for the area could have led them to ask their state legislators not to vote for the Swift and Ware River Acts. By the 1920s, it was too late.

THREE

Boston's Thirst for Water: 1630–1930

B oston's history is inextricably bound with its need for water. Puritan settlers decided on Boston rather than other coastal locations north or south because the water was better. They purchased land from William Blackstone, the first British settler in Boston, because of his property's access to the "Great Spring," now near Boston's Government Center (and, ironically, near the location of the Metropolitan District Water Supply Commission's main office).

The city quickly outgrew the Great Spring and built a conduit, or waterworks system, in 1652, for drinking and firefighting. But the water was still not good, and there was not enough of it.

By 1699, Jamaica Pond, southeast of the existing city, was tapped for Boston's water, and private residences and businesses willing to pay for it directly piped water from the pond via hollow logs. Jamaica Pond did not serve the northern, wealthier neighborhoods of Boston, which had to rely on their own wells and cisterns. Pollution and disease continued to be issues; in one case, forty-three families were using a single well.

In the 1830s, engineers found it necessary to recommend Long Pond in Natick, twenty-four miles away, as a source of ample clean water. Natick was on higher ground, and engineers believed that a gravity-fed water supply would aid both quantitative and qualitative water supply problems. Long Pond was renamed the Lake Cochituate Reservoir—"Cochituate" being a Native word for "place of rushing water." Construction was completed in 1845; water flowed through the Cochituate Aqueduct into reservoirs in Brookline, Beacon Hill, and South and East Boston. Boston's population was rapidly reaching 125,000.

A "water celebration" was held in Boston Common on October 25, 1848. Author M. A. DeWolfe Howe, in his 1910 book *Boston Common: Scenes from Four Centuries*, describes how "the highly variegated procession paraded the streets, bringing its march to an end on the Common. There the Frog Pond became literally the center of the stage, for the Mayor and other dignitaries took their place on a platform over the middle of it. When the water was turned on and the fountain leaped high into the air, the school-children, assembled with representatives of every other element of the population, sang Lowell's *Ode*, written for the occasion, beginning, 'My Name is Water'; the bells rang, cannon were fired, rockets soared aloft; cheering, laughter and even tears paid their spontaneous tribute to the completion of a great undertaking."[1]

Smaller reservoirs were built and connected in the northern and western suburbs, out to Sudbury, equidistant to Natick from Boston. Still, it was not enough for the whole Boston area, and Boston's water was becoming unsafe again. The state board of public health proposed a "water district," which would include the development of a large water supply for not only Boston proper, but the communities around it, up to ten miles from the state house. Thirteen towns joined initially, then another sixteen. The metropolitan area's new source of water would be the impoundment of the Nashua River by the Wachusett Dam to create the Wachusett Reservoir forty-eight miles from Boston. Ground was broken in 1897. Boston's population was now 525,000 and the population of the rest of the water district was over a million.

The Wachusett was completed in 1905. Sections of the towns of Boylston, West Boylston, Clinton, and Sterling were taken to build it; residents fled west to where land was cheaper, including the Swift River Valley. When the reservoir filled to capacity in 1908 with sixty-five billion gallons, it was the largest manmade public water supply in the world.

Even as it was being built, state engineers knew that the Wachusett would not be big enough to withstand metropolitan Boston's rapid expansion. Projections by the Joint Board, made up of the Metropolitan District Commission and the Department of Public Health, determined that the Wachusett would be inadequate by 1930. There would have to be another solution—one that would give Boston clean water in perpetuity. And so, as early as 1895, the state began sending surveyors and engineers to the Swift River Valley.

"About 1895, two young engineers were surveying the land and testing the water of the Swift River and told the paper mill personnel they were students of Tufts College and that someday the City of Boston would take over the territory as a water basin for that city," wrote valley historian Donald Howe.[2] But to most people "in the placid country towns of the Swift River Valley, the invasion of the engineers was a matter of passing comment, perhaps worthy of discussion in the long winter evenings in the old General Store where, in the circle of the comfortable glow of a huge pot-bellied stove, men could decide the great issues of the day and the commonest incident of daily life with equal equanimity.

"But . . . it seemed that there was a shadow cast across the face of the valley—a shadow from a cloud hardly more than that in a summer sky—yet enough to create a foreboding that sometime this matter would be again heard of by the valley folk.[3]

"Six years later," Howe adds, "the matter was revived, and once again the shadows deepened, and the valley folks became a people of depressed and sorrowful mood."[4]

Enfield native George Boynton remembered that when he was a child in grammar school, "a man went by with a horse and buggy and some five-gallon glass jugs in the back of the buggy. That would be in about

1907 or '08. We were inquisitive and wanted to know what he had in the jugs. And our teacher told us that for many years before this, that they had planned to take the whole valley as a reservoir to supply Boston with water. And they went over to the west branch of the Swift River and gathered two jugs, which they did every 2–3 months to be sent to Boston to be analyzed to see if the water was pure, which it really was—you could drink right out of the river."[5]

By 1920, the state had created official maps of what the reservoir area would look like. Journalists began to come to the Swift River Valley in excited expectation of the pathos when these old Yankee folk were displaced. And in 1922 the Joint Board recommended the diversion of the Ware River and the creation of a reservoir to the Metropolitan District Commission water supply system.

This decision had not come without conflict. The Joint Board had also discussed taking the Ware River, east of the valley, for the reservoir, but that water would have to be treated, which was not necessary in the Swift River's case. The Swift River was conveniently upland, and thus could become a part of the state's network of gravity-fed water systems. Significant industry on the banks of the Nashua River ruled it out as a water source, whereas the Swift River Valley, far out of industrial areas, could protect the water supply via a large watershed.

Connecting the Ware River to the new reservoir, which would then connect to the Wachusett, was considered audacious in its boldness and scope. The so-called Goodnough Plan was named after its architect, X. H. Goodnough, who had worked on the 1895 water study. The Massachusetts General Court, even though it would have preferred not to side with Goodnough, was aware that another water shortage was imminent, and the Goodnough Plan was passed and adopted in May 1926.

Between 1895 and 1926, valley communities expressed fervent but sporadic opposition to the project. These protests were headed by state Representative Rev. Roland D. Sawyer of Ware, a former fire-and-brimstone preacher turned Thoreauvian philosopher who today might be considered a far-left "social justice warrior." Sawyer was seen as a kook and a curmudgeon by the other end of the political spectrum, which was comprised of "Boston Brahmin" state legislators. Sawyer sometimes wore sandals and a toga to the Massachusetts State House to remind fellow legislators of their political origins, but his acerbic and eloquent speechifying was no match for their political will. More committees were formed, more decisions made. The valley town halls were filled with angry discussions. The people didn't have the time or money to come frequently to Boston to lobby; politicians representing metropolitan Boston had little appetite for driving out to the middle of the state to negotiate with what they believed were hicks with little political clout.

Finally, the towns' selectmen and other senior officials, tired of being whiplashed from plan to plan when they were not being ignored, wrote a letter of surrender to the Massachusetts General Court:

> We folk feel that it is only a matter of time before we will be forced out, and for a decade . . . we have lived from day to day in anticipation of that time. If the Legislature is to act at all, let it be now, so that at least from now on we can plan the rest of our days elsewhere, taking with us what we can salvage of our life's work. We have rights and ask then that our rights be carefully considered by the Legislature, that we be made as whole as is equitable. But above all let it be swift and decisive action.[6]

The action was both swift and decisive: the Ware River Act was passed almost immediately, and the Swift River Act on April 26, 1927.

One of the tenets of the Swift River Act was to create a new board, called the Metropolitan District Water Supply Commission, generally referred to as the MDWSC, or, more commonly, the Commission. The Commission had the power to hire the chief engineer of the project and his deputies, who would then hire direct employees and bid out contracts.

Frank E. Winsor was appointed as chief engineer. Winsor held the first PhD in engineering from Brown University (specializing in hydraulics), and had worked on a number of large civil engineering projects including the Scituate Reservoir in his native Rhode Island; in New York State; and in Massachusetts, including the Wachusett Reservoir. Winsor was much beloved and respected by both peers and employees for his geniality and human touch as well as for adhering to honest and just business practices in a milieu where graft, favoritism, and shoddy workmanship were normative.

Winsor's judiciousness was reflected in his hard work and personal life. Winsor took almost no time off during the project. A chauffeur drove him into the valley two to three days per week, but according to his son, Edward, neither he nor his mother were allowed to ride in it because it was against Commonwealth regulations.[7]

Joining Winsor's initial team was X. H. Goodnough of the Goodnough Plan; J. Waldo Smith, formerly chief engineer of the Board of Water Supply of the city of New York; riparian engineer Charles T. Main; and geologist Charles P. Berkey, of Columbia University.

This team in turn hired R. Nelson Molt, a young Worcester County assistant district attorney, as commission secretary. Molt was completely out of the Boston political loop, but Worcester had to be represented in the Commission, as the city would benefit from the reservoir as well. In fact, Worcester County backed right into the proposed reservoir watershed; the town of Dana, which only recently had been slated for destruction, was in Worcester County.

In his recommendation letter, Molt was described as "loyal, thoroughly industrious, honest, fair-minded, and dependable, with no definite 'outs,'" but at the same time "lacking somewhat in personality, particularly such that would make him more desirable in trial work," and it was said that he focused too much on the minutiae of a task. However, the Commission noted, "not the least of his qualifications is that he is able to get along with country people."[8]

It was clear to the "country people" early on that this last qualification was wildly inaccurate. As the face of the Commission's administrative branch, Molt was loathed and mocked. "We used to say that that 'R' stood for 'Rat,'" said Herman Hanson, originally of North Dana. "He was in the North Dana Post Office one day, bragging about what a beautiful body of water this would be: 'Why, up on this side hill in a few years, there won't be a human being up there!' I says, 'Now, Mr. Molt, do you really believe that?' 'Why of course!' he says."[9]

Molt drove in to the valley from Worcester, more than an hour away, often with his wife, Olive. Olive, who had been a school art teacher, had contracted tuberculosis some years earlier, and at the sanatorium the doctors had recommended rest and outdoor time in the country. The Molts plainly despised each other; many of the photos of the Commission she eventually gave to the Swift River Valley Historical Society had his face cut out of them. But Olive was willing to spend time in her husband's company in order to take her Brownie camera, colored pencils, and oil paints and memorialize the valley in photography and art. A tall, big-boned, bespectacled woman with a face suggestive of *The Wizard of Oz*'s Miss Gulch, she also had a reputation for flirting with the young engineers.

But the Commission was not going to dwell on personality, for good or ill. There was work on a huge scale to do. The primary engineering jobs, roughly in order, were to:

1. Dig seven to eight shafts at a depth of two hundred to six hundred feet, starting east of the proposed watershed in the village of Coldbrook and moving west, in order to build the tunnels between the Ware River and the proposed reservoir.
2. Once the tunnels for the aqueduct were completed, build a "diversion tunnel" for the Swift River so that it would move toward the proposed dam. When that tunnel would be sealed, the valley would flood.
3. Build a large dam and dike (a dam but without a spillway channel), a smaller "baffle dam" for the Ware River, and a spillway channel for when the reservoir would be full.
4. Create new roads and highways around the valley.
5. Build an administration building atop the dam.[10]

Meanwhile, property would have to be purchased or taken by eminent domain and destroyed, new forests grown from millions of seedlings, and, eventually, the reservoir basin stripped of topsoil so that no living thing was left or could grow when the reservoir was flooded.

The Commission planned on this gargantuan enterprise taking approximately twelve years to complete.

The fact that the valley towns had asked the Commonwealth to hurry up and get it over with did not mean that they rested meekly once the Acts were passed. People were hopping mad. There were lawsuits. Mill owners below the dam wanted to know whether they could stay in business and what would happen if they could not. Valley shop owners and workers demanded to be reimbursed for their loss of business. Some of these lawsuits continued for years, with varying degrees of success. [11]

More important to some than the needs of the living was the concern over the dead. What would happen to their ancestors once the churchyard cemeteries were flooded out? The result of this last outcry was the creation of the Quabbin Park Cemetery and the Commission's reassurance that all remains and tombstones would be dealt with expeditiously, sensitively, and at no cost.

The Reservoir Goes to the US Supreme Court

After the passage of the Swift and Ware River Acts, the State of Connecticut filed suit against the Commonwealth of Massachusetts. Connecticut claimed that diversions from the Connecticut River—even though the river would not be diverted directly, only through the stream flows of other rivers—would have adverse impacts in areas as diverse as power generation, fish life, and agriculture. Valley people were hopeful that as *Connecticut v. Massachusetts* moved up the court system, it would be decided in Connecticut's favor, thereby preventing Massachusetts from being able to finish the reservoir project. In fact, the case went all the way to the United States Supreme Court, which ruled in favor of Massachusetts in February 1931, long after the project was fully underway.

For the new engineers, this was an exciting opportunity to be one of the first workers on one of the largest public works projects in US history. For the natives, there was nothing to do but live through what came next.

Plans for the Reservoir and New Experiences for the Engineers: 1926–1930

The Nuts and Bolts of the Reservoir Project

Probably the young engineers hired in 1927 had only a vague idea of the enormity of the state's undertaking and what it involved. This is a simplified version of what they were probably told:

The Swift River Valley was like a bathtub. Small ponds and lakes north of the Swift River flowed into the three branches of the river, which then flowed back out of the valley toward the south. For drinking water to reach Boston, the bathtub had to fill up and stay full. A massive earthen dam would hold the water in place. But the river had to be bent in the direction of the dam, and so a "diversion tunnel" would be dug in the valley bedrock, literally moving the waterway. When the dam was finished, the tunnel would be blocked, thereby plugging the bathtub and allowing it to fill.

How would the water get from the new reservoir to the Wachusett Reservoir? Before the dam and diversion tunnel could be constructed, a huge twenty-five-mile-long aqueduct would be dug between the dam site and the Wachusett. Another parallel tunnel would be constructed to move overflow water from the Ware River back east to the Swift River, where it would be circulated and sent in the tunnel back east. That east–west tunnel would require its own dam, in this case called a dike because it would have no spillway, on the side of Quabbin Mountain.

Just like bathtubs have holes at the top to make sure the tub doesn't overflow, the reservoir would have a spillway where excess water from the reservoir would fall down into the dry riverbed on the far side of the dam. When the spillway was flowing for the first time, that would mean that the Quabbin project was completed. The filled reservoir, it was estimated, would hold 415 billion gallons of water.

That was the future. What about the present? What would an engineer arriving in Enfield for the first time in 1927, right after the passage of the Swift River Act, have witnessed?

He (and it was always "he" during these years) would have seen what engineer Jerome Spurr called "a typical sleepy New England town,"[1] already fraying at more than the edges. Even Main Street in Enfield was unpaved, although by around 1929 workers were starting to spray blacktop—not for benefit of the residents, but because the Commission needed roads that were safe for their vehicles to drive on.

Religion and Race

The engineer would have seen a town still very much centered around religion and especially the Congregational Church, itself a relic of the Puritan era. "The churches had quite a lot of feuding between different Protestant factions," said Bill Fielding Jr. "There was another small church further up the main street and it wasn't used, so in the long run they all became

Congregationalists."[2] Nearly everyone in town was a member of the Congregational Church, which some engineers themselves gradually joined.

In addition to actual church services, many aspects of Enfield life had religious overtones.

The Congregational Church owned a chapel building between the town hall and the main square where it held social activities such as "strawberry suppers." The Congregational Church building also had a social hall or meeting room where members put on slideshows and so-called "pageants," or religious theatrical presentations. The church even paid for the upkeep of Enfield Common itself.

Catholics, who, until the engineers' arrival, were mostly Polish and French Canadian immigrants, had two choices: somehow get to Dana for services, or attend Sunday Mass in the Enfield Town Hall every fourth week, where a portable altar was rolled onto the town hall stage. Dora Foley, Catholic town clerk, was occasionally harassed. Fielding and his brother were also harassed: "My father was a Democrat and was for Al Smith in the 1928 presidential election. My older brother and I were beaten up by Republican kids because he made us wear 'Smith' buttons to school. One lady drove really slowly down the side of the road, let her son get out of the car, and let him beat up my brother. 'He's a dirty little Mick!' she said. 'Hit him again!'"[3]

Greenwich Pond and Quabbin Lake were the two "summer ponds." The Jewish campers had one side of Quabbin Lake, and the Dickinson family had the other, where they built up a beach and sold "soda pop and cheese sandwiches."[4] The two sides of the lake did not mix. The campers and their families came very rarely into Enfield Center during the summers, but when they did, they "would scandalize people by wearing shorts downtown."[5]

Even the engineering corps itself was not immune to prejudice. A young Bill Fielding once heard an engineer brag about the Commission's ethnic purity: "he says, 'you'll never find a Jew on the civil service list in Massachusetts—never.'" But in fact, "there were no Jews in the civil service at that time. There wasn't a lot of noise about it—they simply didn't hire them."[6]

Other than the campers, probably the only Jew in the valley was the peddler David Ronsky. An older man with an unfashionable "Moses beard" and a big black hat, "Big Dave" and his horse-drawn wagon made the rounds across the valley every six weeks or so, selling mostly fabric, sewing notions, and kitchen knickknacks to people in remote parts of the area who lacked transportation not only to leave the valley but even to come into town to shop. Ronsky had a bunk in a stall in the Dickinsons' barn. His horse slept one stall over. People paid very little attention to his presence, but the story was that his peddling had put his children through college.[7]

One farmer, Charles Smith, who was mixed-race, was the only non-white person in the valley. According to Ruth Ward Howe, the ascent to his property was called by valley children, quite matter-of-factly, "N***** Hill." When he was bought out by the state he moved to Montreal, where he thought he would be better accepted and perhaps even find a wife.[8]

Businesses and Education

An engineer would have seen a number of traditional small-town businesses, including a doctor, barber, meat market, one family-owned and one chain supermarket, and the Howe family's combination post office/general store/ice cream bar, which served Moxie soda and Fro-Joy ice cream and sold items as varied as underwear and chocolate by the pound.[9] Around the corner was James Lisk's pool room in a converted house, plastered with ads for Velvet and Model tobacco, Whitcomb's Tel and Tel Cigars, Peter Schuyler cigars.[10] The Pickwick Ale signs would have been taken down for Prohibition. The Swift River Hotel had been closed, and was not yet reopened for Commission guests. But even before Prohibition, it was the only place in Enfield with a bar.

The engineer would have had grudging respect for the valley schools, which, although they only ran through eighth grade, delivered a solid education to the valley's children. In 1930, every adult born in the valley knew how to read and write. And while not every valley child finished or even went to high school, those who went through the grades one through eight school system had a solid background in reading, math, and history, and could write clean, engaging essays that occasionally won regional or even state awards.

In Enfield, small classes (combined grades one and two and grades three and four in the town hall, and combined grades five and six and grades seven and eight in the schoolhouse next door, plus one unofficial "ninth grade" for fourteen-year-olds not planning to attend high school, which was eventually phased out) allowed teachers to easily promote or hold back children on either end of the learning curve, including for single semesters, and provide them with work more closely tailored to their academic levels. Bill Fielding Jr. was promoted halfway through sixth grade.[11] Trudy Ward Stalbird Terry, who claimed to be "a devil in school," would "cut up all year and then I'd have to stay back a grade. Then I'd buckle right down and I'd jump a grade!"[12] (While Trudy never went to high school, she married an engineer from MIT.) Teachers, however, never stayed more than a few years before they were cycled out. Some were closer to valley culture and understood the students' backgrounds and needs; others were bursting with energy and progressive educational theory. According to Bill Fielding Jr., a teacher from New York "separated out a number of us, so we would not be impeded by the general ignorance. It sounds pushy, but some of those people got to fourth or fifth grade and they couldn't read the Bobbsey Twins."[13]

Starting in the late 1920s, a school bus ran to Belchertown High School, about five miles from Enfield Center, so that students could attend high school full-time. Prior to that students had to take the Rabbit Train north to Athol High School, where they didn't arrive until 10:00 A.M. and had to be back on the afternoon train south at 2:00 P.M.

Someone had donated funds for a playground set at the Enfield school for the younger children, while the older ones played informal games or sometimes volleyball or baseball in the big field behind the school, so long as no balls broke the adjoining town hall windows—an event that occurred more than once. The more sporting teachers joined in the games during lunch period.

The eighth grade girls, for a while, had their own basketball team, and there was a basketball court in the town hall. But the boys did not have enough people for a full baseball team that could play kids in other towns. They called the loose gathering their "scrub team."

"They Weren't All Hicks"

Contemporaneous newspaper pieces liked to focus on the valley's supposed backwardness or Puritanism, but the engineers discovered early on that the reality was much more nuanced. People knew the latest dances and popular culture. The valley had no newspaper of its own, but papers were delivered twice per day. It had no radio station and extremely poor reception, but in 1930 at least a quarter of Enfield households owned radios. There was no movie theater, which was why the Howe family brought in equipment to show a popular film in the town hall each month. George Boynton remembered the first movie he saw there: "It was a train coming down the track, and it seemed like the people were on the track, and the train got larger and larger. I yelled. I know a lot of kids did."[14] Many people were well-read. Every town had a post office that sent out mail at least twice a day. Bill Fielding remembered the adults as having "a great deal of what you might call 'Jazz Age'—they were up with the times. There was a lot of social give and take. They were lively."[15]

For people who liked action, the Indian Motorcycle Company of Springfield held summer races up the side of Mount Quabbin for cash prizes. Tony Mason's Trotting Park was in Dana.

The valley had access to two newspapers from Springfield, the *Republican* and the *Union*, and a local weekly, the *Ware River News*. Iola Downing was both the town librarian in Enfield's surprisingly well-stocked library—a number of wealthier valley residents of previous generations had willed money to the library—and the society columnist for both the local edition of the *Union* and the *Ware River News*. "She must have been paid by the inch," said Norman Heidel in a 1980s interview. "She'd write about anything—if someone left town, or if someone came back into town. I got into the *Union* because she took a photo of me with my homemade sailboat."[16]

It was Downing, via the *Ware River News*, who announced the return to Enfield of Miss Nellie Brown.[17] Brown had retired from her teaching position in Maine, where she had established a system of progressive state-funded kindergartens, and, with Miss Grace Glass, her companion from Bangor, had moved back into to her grand Victorian home on Enfield Common to participate in polite society—more or less, because as a women's rights advocate and a Universalist who also owned a large car driven by a chauffeur, she was a thorn in the side of the valley's particular social hierarchy.

Social Structure

What might not have been apparent to young engineers—to their detriment—was the valley hierarchy. Common to any set of small towns, valley families had complex domestic and social relationships and strong cultural codes inculcated while the valley was still a Puritan outpost that continued into the twentieth century.

The Ewing family lived out of town, high on Ewing Hill, and had a stable of horses they rode for pleasure rather than hitching them up for work. There was intermarriage between the Ewings and the Woods family, which owned property on top of Quabbin Mountain and which had lived in the valley since 1718. The Howe family had lived there nearly as long, and as he aged, patriarch Edwin Howe Sr. flaunted his status by wearing a swallowtail coat long into the 1930s, along with a stovepipe hat and a cane.

Then "you had your tradespeople," explained Bill Fielding. "Even though the mills weren't functioning, the former manager class—I wouldn't say they looked down on the workers, but they were distinctive . . . I believe the Walter Browns [Walter Brown was Nellie Brown's brother] were at the management end of it . . . There was also a lot of bias—although it was perhaps not apparent to everybody—these were largely Northern Ireland people, the mill workers."[18] But the Protestant mill workers were higher in the hierarchy than the more recently arrived Polish immigrants.

The Polish families lived outside the town, tended to be farm people, and mostly interacted with one another. The town people didn't have too much familiarity with them. The Jelskis and the Gurskis lived up Hill Street, away from Enfield. Mr. Jelski was a barber and his children were "bright, active people," according to Bill Fielding, who went to school with them, "but I don't think they really meshed with the town social activities."[19]

More difficult to place within the social hierarchy predating the engineers were the old, eccentric families of Prescott Ridge like the Wilders and the Newburys, who had lived in the valley since at least the American Revolution. By that definition they should have been at the social pinnacle, but they were so odd and antisocial, with long hair and big beards, that no one knew what to do with them. Bob Wilder said that that the older Newbury brother "carried a black crow on his arm when he went to town. Big bushy black beard. He also had the reputation of being a 'barn burner' of the people who crossed him."[20] The younger Newbury brother, Robert, known as "Unc," came down from the Newbury hilltop farm, pushing a wheelbarrow, to buy groceries. Technically, the Newburys' road was a public road but they had installed a gate. (Unc was nearly arrested by the state police for pulling a gun on a surveyor.) Other than the wheelbarrow grocery trip, the Newburys raised their own food; the Commission photo of the Newbury house shows a very old, weather-beaten property with a cow, some chickens, and a rain barrel in the yard, and the forest pressing up from behind.[21]

Greenwich engineering contractor Walter King told a story about Unc's eccentricities: "Every Saturday night, about quarter to nine, he would show up at Harry Hess's market in Enfield, to get the leftovers. And he'd come in, and he'd look at the stock of bananas hanging on the wall, and he'd say, 'How much, Harry?' and Harry would say, 'Four cents a pound.' And he'd say, 'Can I get them for less?' and Harry would say, 'Come back at 9:00.' And he'd come back at 9:00 after Harry had closed, and they would make a deal—2 cents a pound. For bananas. And it wouldn't matter if it was four bananas on that rack or four dozen, Unc would take those bananas and sit on the steps and eat every goddamn one of them. I guess he was an idiot savant, because in mathematics he was an absolute genius, but anything else he was completely out of it."[22]

Perhaps a young engineer would have been amazed by the decades-long dedication of Dr. Willard Segur, who, despite being a transplant from Ohio via Dartmouth College (where he wrote the official school song, still in use, in 1892), had become an embedded presence in the valley. He was also a town official and volunteer fireman, but most importantly he was trusted and beloved by everyone.

"He used to spend hours with his patients, stay overnight if necessary," said his son, Bill. "I used to go by sleigh and carriage, and then by car, on calls with him starting when I was about eight."

Young Bill helped his father out in the office. "On Saturdays I'd sweep and clean out the office after my father saw patients." When the Segurs finally bought a car, with solid tires and a high carriage suited for back-country roads, "at age fourteen or so I'd drive my father . . . with a pillow beneath and a pillow behind to prevent jostling, on roads that were just two small ruts, so my father could sleep between patients."

Sometimes Dr. Segur was paid in cash. Other times, he was paid in produce: "Garden produce. Native trout. He accepted it. He created good will by accepting it because he knew they didn't have the money."[23]

The Segurs, like almost everyone else in the valley, grew their own vegetable and flower gardens; Bill's maternal grandmother lived with them and tended the bursting hydrangea and tomatoes. They also had the advantage of living at the base of Mount Quabbin. Their water "came from the spring up on the hill and I think several other families had pipes connected to that same spring down to their homes." That was the thing about Quabbin water; it served almost everyone. Even in the poorer Enfield and Greenwich homes Segur visited with his father, "there would be a pipe from the family spring on the hill, and there was a steady stream of pure, cool water coming in year-round."[24]

Far above everyone, literally at the top of Mount Quabbin, where the Quabbin fire tower now stands, was the Woods estate, looking down its nose directly at Enfield. Almost no one saw the Woods family face-to-face—they were missionaries to India and came back to the valley only in the summer. For those children who sneaked onto their property in their absence, the Woods' fields were blooming with acres of peonies and violets, just begging to be taken back down the hill to their mothers. On Independence Day, the Woods held a fireworks display, and everyone would watch the top of the mountain as Roman candles rained down.[25]

The engineers descended into this world fresh from college and city living, with no previous understanding of the subtleties and textures of this community, and no one to explain it to them. It's no wonder they initially got it wrong.

The Engineers Arrive: 1926–1930

The Commission began scouting local engineering colleges for talent even as the Swift River Act was being signed. MIT, and to a lesser degree Northeastern and Worcester Polytechnic, were the top Massachusetts schools graduating young, eager engineers with solid educational backgrounds and potential leadership skills.

Harvard was not a school for engineers. Engineering was still considered a "trade," and in the 1920s students at MIT were, fundamentally, being educated for a trade.[1] So Winsor came to MIT in person to interview members of the Class of 1927.

Among the graduating seniors interviewed was Jerome Lyon Spurr, a civil engineering major. Spurr was fascinated by power dams and had taken one geology class at MIT and a couple more classes in soil engineering with Dr. Karl Terzaghi, who is considered to be the father of modern soil mechanics. Those qualifications were good enough for Winsor, who not only hired Spurr on the spot but asked him to suggest other 1927 MIT graduates who might fit the Commission's engineering profile. Around seven students, young men only passingly familiar with either rural life or dams, packed their bags immediately after graduation and were hustled down to the valley for what became months of slow, mostly uninspiring work.

The MIT group started out as a surveying crew, whose first job "was setting a triangulation station down in the valley, where the local surveys would be run from the main triangulation station, which controlled the entire project."[2] The supervising engineers drove into the valley each day, but the junior engineers lived in Enfield—boarding with whoever would take them in—and then were fetched by a state touring car to each day's job.

They were viewed suspiciously not only by the locals, who perceived them as a second, louder wave of invaders, but also by the existing on-site engineers and surveyors, some of whom had been working and planning for several years prior to the passage of the acts, making maps and models, and then, in 1926, supervising the first contract. At least one of them, William Fielding Sr., had worked on the Panama Canal.[3] When those older, mid-career engineers had arrived, there had been no Commission, no engineering board. Now they found themselves having to supervise a boisterous group of recent graduates.

"Some of the older men had backgrounds that I don't recall too well; they'd been in the surveying game for a while," Spurr said in a 1987 interview. "I think one was supposed to have been in a boundary dispute in South America. The rumor unfortunately got around among some people that we—the MIT grads—had come up to take over the job, so there was a little amount of opposition among some of the older fellows who'd already been hired. It looked like a bit of a possibility that their jobs would be taken from them."[4]

The MIT group appeared a little cliquish to the outsiders, a perception that took many years to dispel, especially after the laborers, men with no or technical college educations, came on board. The MIT grads, were after all, working aboveground. The less privileged were sent below, to start digging the shafts and tunnels that eventually would become the Quabbin aqueduct.

Downward Dig

The shafts, descending hundreds of feet below ground level, were largely constructed west to east—Shaft 1 was right at the Wachusett Reservoir, while Shaft 12 would be drilled at the eastern edge of the new dam holding the reservoir in place.

Engineer "camps" were set up near the shafts. According to the Chief Engineer's Report of 1928, the camp site at Shaft 1 was located "about 350 feet south of the shaft and at a considerably higher elevation. The camp buildings include dining room and kitchen, two bunk houses, an emergency hospital, cook's quarters, drying house and storeroom. Wash water and other liquid wastes were disposed of in septic tanks, the effluent leeching into porous ground located in the drainage area of the settling basin." Meanwhile, at the shaft itself, buildings included a general office, engineers' office, compressor house, garage, blacksmith shop, and cement shed. This setup was duplicated at all the shafts, and then, eventually, at the dam and dike sites.[5]

The shafts, of course, brought humans and their biological and industrial waste to the groundwater, and the Commission was insistent on showing how dedicated it was to the fundamental premise of the reservoir: clean drinkable water from the source, no treatment required.

Initially, garbage was removed by local farmers, sink wastes disposed of in septic tanks, and "human excreta" incinerated. The construction of the sanitary works began in early July 1928: "The embankment of the settling basin was constructed of earth with a compacted soil core, most of the material being obtained from excavations for the shaft and outlet channel. All water pumped from the shaft and other excavations flows into the settling basin. Chlorinating apparatus for treating the overflow from the settling basin was completed ready for operation on July 20."[6]

The 1928 Chief Engineer's Report proudly includes a photo by young engineer Charles "Chet" Chetwynd of the "settling basin" at Shaft 2, a raw 100-foot-square ditch, filled with sludge, in the middle of the countryside.[7]

Thousands of Photos, One Camera

The Commission hired a couple of professional photographers in 1927 and 1928, although there was no job title called "photographer." Both men left within a few months, and thus it was left to the lower-level engineers to continue the massive project of photographing everything in the valley.[8]

Every piece of property to be purchased by the state had to be surveyed and photographed. The surveying engineers would drive out in teams of two to each building. One engineer would prop a portable chalkboard near the property line, indicating the street, owner name, date, Commission ID number, and location of each building on the plat. A two-foot-long wooden arrow was set along the chalkboard, pointing north.

The other engineer set up the camera. On the negatives the photographer would duplicate some of the information on the chalkboard—whatever fit on one line—as well has his own name. The photographers' first subjects were buildings or land the Commission wanted to purchase for its own use; these had lower ID numbers. Other low numbers were allotted to property owners who wanted to sell quickly to the Commission and get out. By early 1930, more than 1,200 properties had been photographed.[9]

Surveying engineers had to move quickly to take as many photos as possible on a given day. As a result, the photographs sometimes have charming, unprofessional details: groups of curious children; a grandmother sitting on the porch rocking a bassinet; a suspicious, gathering flock of turkeys; a girl reading a book underneath a tree; much laundry hung out to dry; and, in one case, a dog and cat sniffing each other's noses on the side of the road.

In other cases, the sights were much bleaker. By the late 1920s a significant number of properties had been abandoned. Particularly outside the town centers, houses and barns had broken windows, sagging doors, and missing shingles. In a photo after a 1927 nor'easter, two children stood in the flattened ruins of what had recently been their house.[10] Regardless, every piece of property, no matter the condition, had to be documented for the state's eventual "taking."

Site, Rod, Ax

Each surveying team dispatched to the woods and swamps typically consisted of six to eight people. Following the crew chief were the chief's second-in-command, the instrument man (who literally carried instruments), field equipment, hammers, stakes, and nails; draftsman, who drew the surveying plans; rodman, charged with transporting and setting up surveying equipment; axeman, responsible for blazing "witness trees" and "bearing trees," erecting posts, digging pits, and building mounds to mark the section corners; and gauge keeper, to ensure accuracy of measurements. The party inspector sometimes went out with the team, and sometimes stayed back in the office; the stenographer, the only position that sometimes included women, did not go out in the field.[11]

In 1928 the Commission had not set up any permanent offices in the valley. Most paperwork, including hiring personnel and drafting contracts, was drawn up and signed in the Commission's offices at 20 Somerset Street in Boston, just a few blocks from the Massachusetts State House. Rented office space in the valley was located in Enfield Center above Harry Hess's meat market; the laboratories were near Shaft 1 and in Springfield. The Commission, however, was in the process of determining which of the many splendid properties in Enfield to purchase for its own; the prize was the former Chandler mansion at the edge of Enfield Center—a house the size of a small hotel, with a turret, cupola, and grand wraparound veranda, on a lot of several acres. In better days it was described as "a dream of wooden pilasters, wreaths, and scrolls, with a fretwork balustrade of wheel patterns upon the eaves, and an arched and decorated gateway, all in glittering white."[12]

The Commission had also purchased the Randall farm on Blue Meadow Road on the Enfield-Belchertown line, the site of the future Quabbin Dam. Former Enfield resident and historian Donald Howe, in his book *Quabbin: The Lost Valley*, describes how "the two hundred and fifty acres of farm land owned by D. L. and Ethel Randall was absorbed for two principal purposes, first, to form part of the eastern approach highway off the Ware

Road on Route 9 and, secondly, for the stripping of the rich soil to form a section of the topping of the Dam. The [farm's] upper section was used as a permanent nursery for the growing of pines."[13]

The Randall property had been owned by that family since 1824. "The former Blue Meadow had for many years . . . been the scene of scores of gatherings of people of both Belchertown and Enfield, as well as the site for many picnics arranged by three generations of the Randall family." In 1951, the publication year of *Quabbin: The Lost Valley*, the farm was, "naturally, unrecognizable to any of the latter group."[14]

Engineer Carl Remington's photograph of what would be the dam's apex is taken at the top of a rocky, gentle slope dotted with Queen Anne's lace, cut by a barbed wire fence and stone retaining wall. It's an early September afternoon in the country; you can almost hear the cicadas breaking the warm stillness. The Swift River runs unobtrusively nearby. Nothing has been cut down, built up, diverted, dug, or in any way altered. But the arch of the hill is also the arch of the dam, and the view of the hills is familiar to anyone who has stood atop the dam and faced south, toward the Quabbin Administration Building and Route 9. In fact, a Blue Meadow Road still exists in Belchertown, on the state's Department of Conservation and Recreation's Quabbin administrative property; based on the road's location it once ran down the hill and across to Ware, rather than into the water and back out again.

The young engineers apparently weren't interested in the "big issues" of history and ownership, though—or at least they didn't discuss it. There wasn't time. The work was mostly exhausting and occasionally exciting, and after working hard all day, like other laborers and farmers around the valley, they came back hungry and tired.

There were few places for them to live. Early in the reservoir project, the valley people saw little difference between the Commission officials, who were designing and deploying the valley's demise, and the state hires who did the day-to-day work: Even if the engineers had never personally signed a land deed or knocked down a house, they were still malevolent outsiders. They were college boys in a valley with almost no young men left. They looked, spoke, and dressed differently than the natives. They were living day-to-day reminders that the end was coming, and with every photograph they shot or woods they penetrated, they were the perpetrators of destruction. According to the authors of the 1938 newspaper series "Letters from Quabbin," they were not always sensitive to the concerns of the residents, either: "The younger engineer, anxious to make good, was often thoughtless in his approach to the residents, and antagonized them almost from the first."[15]

Few people would accept them as boarders, so much lodging recommendation was done by word of mouth, and engineers didn't stick around in one rental for very long. At this point the Swift River Hotel had been closed (it was later reopened by the Commission, for use by the state) so engineers lacked the opportunity to become acclimated to the valley by staying as a hotel guest for the first few nights on-site.

Jerome Spurr, for instance, initially found a room at a house about a quarter mile out of Enfield Center, but stayed there less than a month. He then heard about an open room at the Dickinson house in Enfield, where at least half a dozen other young surveyors were staying. The Dickinson house was not big—the surveyors were probably sleeping at least two to a room—but Mrs. and Mr. Dickinson and Mr. Dickinson's brother, who also lived with them, kept a full pantry. Spurr said that the young men "ate at a common table, served family-style, with the Dickinson family," with roast pork on Sundays, their only day off, and vegetables grown from the Dickinson garden.[16]

After almost a year the six engineers moved out of the Dickinsons' and tried renting their own house in Enfield. One of that "bachelor pad group" was Carl Remington, a recent Worcester Polytechnic grad and early real estate photographer.

In the late 1920s there was still not much interaction with the locals, but a small amount of mingling with the contractor employees took place at a carriage house between Enfield and Smith's Village, which the owner called Linda Vista and where bands sometimes played. It was the only nightlife available in the valley and also functioned, apparently, as a speakeasy. Quabbin contractors Ken Cross, from Ware, and Walter King, from

Greenwich, said that the engineers would try to bond with them by giving them construction photographs with pictures of the contractors in them, and then, in return, the contractors would connect them with people who sold alcohol. According to Cross, that alcohol was mixed with rye: "It was like drinking kerosene!" Those in the know "had to go down there and ask for a specific person, and then usually we'd get a pint of hard cider. Or we could ask for another person and we'd get turkey moonshine . . . it gave you a good go—you just didn't feel that good when you got up the next morning."[17]

N. LeRoy Hammond, the division engineer, was himself, according to his obituary, a graduate of MIT, and his son, also named N. LeRoy, also attended MIT in the 1930s. Hammond didn't do the direct hiring, but he encouraged Winsor to go back to MIT later in 1927 for another crop of engineering recruits.

The MIT/Northeastern/WPI group, with a few out-of-state stragglers from Dartmouth and the Universities of Rhode Island, New Hampshire, and Vermont, did become "cliquish," and a little insular. They had their own newspaper, the *Backsite* (a play on "backsight," a surveying term for a reading looking backward along the line of progress).[18] They called themselves the "Enfield Engineers Club," and one cold night in January 1928 the whole crew—around forty in total—gathered in chairs around the big stove in the Commission offices above the meat market, and chemical engineer and photographer du jour Ben Burbank, who graduated from Bowdoin College in 1926 and who would leave the project shortly afterward, took a group photo.

The men are young—most are in their mid-twenties. Most exude confidence, and the kind of cocky privilege that got them into and through top colleges. It could be a group photo of a fraternity, with a few older chapter alumni sitting in for fun.

Had this not been Prohibition, they probably would have been photographed with beer bottles. As it is, there are a number of pipe-smoking poseurs. Many wear knee-high lace-up boots and puttees. Nearly all of them look like they washed up before the photo shoot, cleaned their gear, and came in looking "business-casual."[19]

Even this early on, a couple of engineers had already gotten married to young local women they'd met as part of their work. Homer Briggs had married Muriel Feindel, daughter of Dana's town doctor. Chet Chetwynd had married Rosalind "Bud" Sawyer, daughter of Ware-based state Representative Roland D. Sawyer, the man with the toga and sandals and the only member of the state legislature to vote against the Swift River Act. Other engineers were slowly bringing their wives and children to the valley—a difficult choice between family unity and moving to an alien place with relatively few resources, scant education, and much animosity.

The "Enfield Engineers Club" is a portrait of the surveyors, who were a combination of junior engineers and engineering aides. But just as there was hierarchy within the towns, there was hierarchy within the engineering ranks. The Commission members did not socialize with any of the engineers, period. The senior engineers seldom socialized with the junior engineers. And Commission employees rarely socialized with contract employees and local laborers—unless there was liquor involved. As time passed and as people moved up the engineering ranks these boundaries became more blurred.

"Engineer" was a dirty word in the valley for the first few years. Bill Fielding said that locals "called everybody from the axman to the Chief Engineer 'engineers.' It was a generic rather than a professional term," and a sign of local resentment that people did not bother differentiating between the groups. But there was a flip side; when valley workers lucked out and found a job with the Commission, they were proud of their fortune: "When Joe Wilder was hired as an axman," said Fielding, "he showed up at a Grange meeting and announced he was now an engineer, and wore his swamp boots to evening events."[20]

Because everyone on the engineering side had to get along, tensions seldom surfaced, but they were felt. There was antipathy on all sides against engineers who had been "let in" too easily for whatever perceived reason.

Those reasons could include political affiliation. "Hammond was a civil service type from Boston, like a 'professional Republican,'" said Bill Fielding, "and he was always coming up in conflict with the more liberal ideas of the people who worked for him. 'Union' was a dirty word. Equivalent to 'Bolshevik,' or 'Industrial Workers of the World,' or whatever. Franklin Roosevelt was supposed to be a communist."

It wasn't quite a meritocracy, either, according to Fielding:

> You had after the First World War these guys who were veterans who got veterans' preference. [Clifton] Wells was from Providence; [Fred] Farley was from Lexington—they were able to call themselves engineers because of the fact that they had been in Army Engineers in the war. They were not MIT men by any means.
>
> On the other hand, there was a lot of resentment toward the younger engineers who *were* from Northeastern or MIT. They were the smart-ass paper workers who didn't get their hands dirty. You had all these internal tensions that don't show up in the history.
>
> Homer Briggs was the nephew of the architect Austin Briggs. Spurr had connections. Tillinghast's mother was the head of the immigration commission in Rhode Island. It was really hard to separate politics and science at that time. The tie-in between college people and upper-class jobs—even technical jobs—was total. You didn't get to be a prominent engineer unless you were part of a prominent family. And they took great care to keep whoever they could out of the colleges and universities. If you weren't socially suitable, you wouldn't last long on any campus.[21]

Particular mockery, apparently, was saved for Jerome Spurr.

> He was a "paper man." No one listened to him too much. He was just an egghead . . . He got up on the side of the hill there, on a Sunday morning, and—"Hut Two Three Four!"—all by himself in the pine woods. You could hear him all over the valley—"leading his troops." He was in the National Guard at

the time. On Sundays he would go up there and practice the vocal part of the thing—make sure that the boys in the back row could hear him, I guess.

If anyone says this Commission thing was all hearts and flowers, don't believe 'em. [22]

Jerome Spurr had actually enjoyed the outdoors and physical labor of surveying, and so he was disappointed when he was referred by Hammond for a desk job. "The early years, as I look back," he admitted, "were not very exciting, and they were, a lot of times, marking property boundaries or locations that had been submitted to the Commission for sale. And other times, working on topographic surveys to develop the capacity of the reservoir, and of course the flow line which was all-important for the clearing and property taking."

After the bulk of the surveying work was completed, the results were sent to the Boston office, which would determine if any property lines were incorrect. The Enfield office would have to make its own independent determination.

Soon after that, Spurr was shifted from the field surveying operations to the Chandler House. Determining the actual property boundaries was initially unpleasant work for Spurr, "but it turned out to be quite interesting from a historical viewpoint. We attempted to obtain, for each line on the property that we were surveying, a corresponding line in the adjacent properties so that we could tie one line in one to another line in the other. In a good many cases, we went back almost to the Revolution, when quite a few settlers came to the valley as a result of the land options offered by the state. We ran into all kinds of interesting descriptions, such as going to 'a pile of stones in the dingle,' or a 'stake and stones in a swamp,' or an 'old chestnut saddle.'"

The deed engineers "utilized the experience and knowledge of some of the old settlers who went out with us to point out corners as they remembered it—their fathers or grandfathers, in some cases" and also gleaned information from aerial surveys, which indicated historical lines of demarcation. [23]

Generally, when there was a property dispute the Commission brought the parties together at the Chandler House or at the site to hammer out an agreement. The parties were usually agreeable, as the differences in monies received from the state would be small and the properties were all to be destroyed in any case.

Spurr confirmed stories of gun-toting property owners refusing surveyors access to their land, even if he never experienced hostilities personally. Nevertheless, "It was a warning to be on our good behavior. We always announced to the property owner when we were checking out their property lines."[24]

The surveyors were usually followed by the real estate appraisers, who were local and respected by the community, as the Commission found that property owners were more likely to trust their own people. Generally, three appraisals were made before the state made an offer; the state decided early on it was in everyone's best interest to be fair to the residents.

But Spurr didn't stick around with the appraisals; he was moving up yet again: "Mr. Hammond, the division engineer who reviewed all the correspondence going to the Boston office including my deed analyses, said I had an 'analytical mind,' and as a result of that I was selected in the next stage of my career up there to head the laboratory for soil testing and determining the quality and quantity of soils that might be available for the earth dams." Spurr would keep this job for eight years in Enfield, and then continue it as the aqueduct moved closer to Boston.[25]

SIX

"Human Moles": 1929

The Swift River was pure. The Ware River, twenty-five miles east, was not. The Commission needed both rivers to flow to the Wachusett. So a two-way tunnel was designed; surplus water from the Ware River would move into the new reservoir, where it would mix with Swift River water and then flow back through the main aqueduct to the Wachusett.

Meanwhile, the Swift River itself would have to be moved toward the direction of the dam, by way of what was called a "diversion tunnel." This meant a lot of breaking rocks.

A reporter for the Sunday *Springfield Republican/Union* (the newspapers gave up their rivalry on Sundays to print one large issue) described the early construction milieu:

> Drills whirr. In the hot summer air blasts of dynamite detonate even more loudly than usual. Derricks swing clumsy wooden forms high above the ground. Rubber-clad workmen clamber in and out the jagged orifice yawning in the earth's surface. A tiny truck runs along a narrow gauge way and dumps "tunnel

muck" . . . man's conquest of Nature is subterranean, taking place underground, where few can see and none but the hardiest venture.[1]

These unlucky contractor teams were building the tunnel shafts, about forty feet in diameter with depths ranging from about 250–650 feet. Two parallel tunnels were being constructed, one to carry water from the new reservoir east to the Wachusett, then ultimately to Boston, and the other to carry the overflow water from the Ware River west to the new reservoir. Once the tunnel shafts were dug, workers were sent down to the bottom to blow out the tunnels. It wasn't quite like digging your own grave, but for the squeamish and claustrophobic, it was close.

The Commission set up temporary camps at each shaft site. Unpainted board buildings that housed dynamos and air compressors also served as bunks. Old roads through the woods, previously disused, were freshened up and now served as throughways to each site. Engineers erected handmade signs with directions from one shaft to the next. "The site here is lovely," wrote the Springfield reporter, "and makes one believe for a moment the romance of great construction feats. In a pine wood trees have been sewn down to clear a space where a camp has been built large enough to house 60 men, although only about 45 workers are on the job at Shaft 5 now. A narrow cut has been made through the trees where the tight tension wires of the New England Power company are stretched, and through this lane one can look toward the shaft mouth, a hundred or more yards distant. Over a board walk, one plank wide, one takes his way to the workings. A brook, which once ran clear and cool through this swampy undergrowth is now cloudy and muddy. No wonder: Forty gallons of water a minute are being pumped out of the shaft and into the brook."[2]

Each horseshoe-shaped tunnel opening had to be large enough to "fit a small house,"[3] as one writer put it—blueprints show measurements of twelve feet and nine inches from top to bottom and eleven feet at the widest point. Once the tunnel was drilled, wooden "forms" were snapped into place to prepare for cementing.

Pneumatic drills powered by compressed air helped construct both the shafts and the tunnels. The engineers drilled nine feet into the rock and filled the holes with dynamite. The dynamite exploded, and the shattered rock was removed until the work crews dug all the way down to the tunnel floor. The air compressors were powered by a high-tension line installed aboveground along the length of the tunnel. It required two ten-hour shifts (each work day had two shifts) to drill, blast, and excavate six feet. Those six feet required one hundred pounds of dynamite.

The tunnel workers did not have to breathe compressed air, but it was still noisy, smelly, and dangerous:

> The great quantity of powder necessarily used, the chance of falling segments of rock loosened by the blasts were dangers always present. While there was plenty of light (electric) and the temperature was 50°F, winter and summer, the men who worked at the rock and those who removed the shattered soil welcomed the daylight on return to the mouth of the shaft. [4]

Commission promotional film shows workers rising from the shafts in groups of about five, standing around the lip of what looks like a giant well bucket, holding onto the hoisting ropes. As the bucket rises above the surface, they jump off and grab their lunch pails like nothing has happened.

Later, after the start of initial work on the dam and dike, when workers were laboring under pressure, the Commission built two "decompression rooms" meant to hold two workers each. [5]

The engineers mixed the concrete on-site with materials on hand, part of a process of material conservation that continued up through the completion of the dam ten years later; conservation both sped the construction process and lowered the cost. The engineering teams pulverized the discarded tunnel rock to provide the sand and the crushed stone, and used the available aquifers for the water to mix it. They shot the mixture down the shaft and through a pressurized pipeline that sprayed it into the giant wooden forms inside the tunnel until the concrete set, about twenty-four hours later.

It was romantic work—to outsiders.

In late 1929, Nason H. Arnold, a *Worcester Telegram* reporter who also wrote children's books, including a series called *Rusty's Travels* about a globe-trotting dog, was allowed deep underground to watch the engineers at work. He wrote, with nerdy breathlessness:

> The huge pile of sand is constantly receiving a small stream of more sand from a spout at the top. Just beyond another huge cone of fine crushed rock receives its steady quota. At one side a huge cylinder of steel, filled with holes, revolves with a tremendous clatter as masses of rock come tumbling down into it to be sorted by the holes, the smaller pieces going into a crusher that can handle them, the larger ones tumbling down into a crusher that modifies their dimensions, dumps the smaller fragments onto a moving belt that whirls them around into the smaller crusher where the sand goes on one belt to eventually reach its proper cone and the fine rock takes a ride on another belt to its temporary resting place on the top of the other cone.
>
> All this is heard and seen without evidence of human hand to be responsible for it all. Far up above from a shed comes the whine of machinery. Cables extending down into an unseen spot move and stop and move again.
>
> In that shed is an engineer, hauling up from the original pile of debris by means of an inverted steel snow blower . . . Back goes the plow, hauled down the slope, this time with its nose to the front, even if it is upside down. And down there is discovered a helper whose business it is to see that the plow gets a proper start in the debris. [6]

After two years of twenty-hour days of drilling, 364 days a year—the team got Christmas off in 1927 and 1928, and that was it—the first of the tunnels was on the verge of connecting, a just cause for grimy, fatigued, perpetual-night celebration. Arnold was invited back to witness the festivities.

At around 3 A.M. on October 24, 1929, a crew of young engineers who had been in charge of the operations at Shafts 6 and 7 "held a war dance in the water and dust and electric torch-lighted depths of the tunnel."

The Shaft 6 team was digging west; the Shaft 7 team, heading east. Early that morning the tunnel headings met "on the nail": witnesses were a number of young assistant engineers, including Robert Moir and Bernard Ford; the heading foreman; a few workmen; Commission photographer Chet Chetwynd; and Arnold. (Chetwynd also brought down his friend Ellis Barbier from Ware. Barbier was so impressed with the scene—and so out of work during the Depression—that he began working for the Commission himself in 1936.)

"As the machine gun rattle of the 16-foot steel in the compressed air drill on the other side seemed to sound all over the face of the heading, the engineers were nervous; no denying that. It was their first big job of this kind," Arnold wrote. "The torch of Peter Brisbois, superintendent of the contractor at Shaft 7, picked up the point of the drill as it shot through squarely in the center. The picture then was of a hilarious double quartet of college students celebrating a victory with an Indian dance in the darkness of a very wet tunnel 400 feet underground."[7] They had connected through a distance of 1.75 miles.

This was the first of many tunneling victories. Shafts 5 and 6 (2.1 miles apart, at one point 650 feet down), headed by engineer Frederick Gow, met on New Year's Day 1930. Directed by engineer Herb Spink, headings between Shafts 4 and 5, 7 and 8, and 3 and 4 were opened in the following few weeks—and then Shafts 1 and 2, and the tunnel was complete and ready for concreting.

Chetwynd's photograph of some of the Shaft 6 and 7 group taken underground, however, doesn't show a celebration; instead it reveals a group of very tired men covered in dust, sitting uneasily on giant rocks, and looking blankly at the sudden bright lights of the camera. [8] Now that they were done, they would have to endure the ritual of coming up, slowly, in the bucket, and immediately getting back to work. They were no longer the cocky engineers of the Enfield Engineers' Club, but workers without regular access to sleep and daylight, risking their lives for the water they would someday drink when they returned to the city.

SEVEN

Poverty and Wealth

Former residents recalled their childhoods as being happy and satisfying, with refrains like, "We were like one big happy family"[1] and "We didn't even know we were poor."[2]

But poverty certainly was present. Every town had an "overseer of the poor." Greenwich was home to a literal "poor farm," where residents grew their own food and contributed extra to the surrounding communities. Established families, and the churches they belonged to, regularly contributed to its upkeep. Also in Greenwich was the Hillside School, which, until its move to Marlborough, MA, in 1927 (it still functions as a private boys' boarding school for grades four through nine), provided "deserving" boys from poor local families with a "well-rounded" education that would allow them to be able to attend college.

Community leaders J. Frederick Zappey and his wife, Marion Thayer Zappey, both deeply involved in the well-being of the valley, became heads of the Hillside School in its last ten years. Zappey came to Greenwich from Boston in order to lead the school. According to Donald Howe,

Zappey was "active in both Greenwich and Enfield town affairs," serving as "past master and secretary of Bethel Lodge of Masons; past district deputy of the 19th Palmer District; past Patron of Zion Chapter, Order of the Eastern Star; was a trustee and treasurer of Enfield Congregational Church, and superintendent of the Sunday school."[3] Later, he "was tax collector and chairman of assessors in Enfield, and served as an appraiser for the Metropolitan Water Supply Commission." Marion Zappey was the last secretary-treasurer of the Enfield Library Association, the organist at the Enfield Congregational Church, matron of the Order of the Eastern Star, and a president of the Quabbin Club.[4]

But other than a family or two, no one was rich, and there was much poverty. "'Most people never saw more than $100 a year,'" said Walter King. "They may have earned wages in other forms, but rarely in cash. The men who worked at Mr. Walker's sawmill and grist mill [in Greenwich] got a slip of paper entitling them to groceries at his son's grocery store." One dollar bought three bags of groceries.[5]

According to Warren "Bun" Doubleday of Dana, in the first two decades of the twentieth century, a grocery salesman would come around with horse and buggy—he would take orders on Mondays, and on Thursdays he'd bring the goods, and people would pay in eggs or milk.[6]

People in clothing factories worked twelve-hour days, six days a week, and made do with what they had within the narrow valley economic ecosystem. Ruth Ward Howe's and Trudy Ward Stalbird Terry's father, Bill Ward, worked at the Smith's fabric mill and brought home remnants for the family. "We didn't have money to buy clothes," Ruth said, "but I made my own clothes starting at about age 12–13 and was among the best dressed teenagers in the valley."[7]

The small industrial town of Ware, just to the east of the valley, was considered a city. According to George Boynton, "Ware is where people did their banking. Went a couple of times per year. People bought bananas from Ware." And Springfield was the "big city": "We went wandering and window shopping, came back on the last train at night. Money was scarce—if you had a quarter in your pocket you were considered wealthy."

According to Boynton, people cooked "squirrels, rabbits, and partridge for pies. A lot of people depended on that for meat. Meat was local. People brought in flour and staple foods, salt and pepper. People baked their own bread."[8]

Some of this poverty was grinding and oppressive, particularly far outside the towns and in industrial Smith's Village, where many residents lived in rented multifamily houses with thin windows and walls. Income in Smith's was dependent on mill and factory work, which, by 1930, had essentially ceased.

A 1934 diary written by fifty-two-year-old Smith's Village resident Flora Wilder, grandmother and sometimes de facto guardian of local historian Bob Wilder, describes managing finances down to the penny in a rented two-family house, taking in laundry, not enough baby bottles, broken-down cars, unwanted pregnancies, domestic abuse, odd jobs, barely enough food, and the sense that nothing mattered because the life they lived, however meager and often miserable, was to be uprooted regardless.

The men in Flora's life worked as day laborers for the Commission or for contractors—not even full employees, although her son Joe was hired by the state and thus was proud to call himself an "engineer." Flora did wash for more affluent people in the valley, including her neighbors the Zappeys, and Marion Zappey and other well-meaning women often came to the Wilder home for informal "welfare checks."

Wilder had once owned her own two-family house, but in in 1928 sold it to the Commission for $4,300. She lived in one half of her rented two-family with her toddler grandson, Joseph, son of Beulah, her wayward daughter-in-law; her niece; and two boarders, one of whom was her live-in romantic partner. On the other side of the two-family was her son, also named Joseph, and his wife and child. Beulah lived nearby with her husband, Dick, in another half of a rented two-family, where Bob Wilder was born.

Flora Wilder took care of Joe and infant Bob when Beulah, who was twenty years old and in an abusive marriage, was unwilling or incapable. She also gave Beulah laundry to do, and often food, but did not consider her a good mother.

The inside front cover of Flora's 1934 diary includes the following chronology:

> *Feb. 14—Bad Dick (Mar. 3, 8, 13, 19 (Birthday)) [dates when Beulah's husband abused her]*
> *Feb. 28—Fred's [Flora's ex-husband's] new Nash*
> *Mar. 6—Fred's new Nash Repossessed*
> *Mar. 14—Kale House burned*
> *Apr. 28—Last Evening Train*
> *May 18—Kelly House being torn down*
> *June 9—Ed Randall Murdered*
> *June 12—Ed Randall's funeral (murdered)(covered up)*
> *Sep. 30—Trip to Maine to steal Bobby*
> *Oct. 1—Bobby's kidnapping at 2:20 pm from Still Water Park, Bangor, Maine* [9]

Dick had ordered Beulah to take Bob up to Maine to stay with Flora's sister because he did not want either Beulah or Flora raising him.

Flora and her son Joe drove up to Bangor together. According to her diary entry from October 1, "Went to Still Water Park at 1:30. Joseph got Robert at 2:20. Started for home. Wonderful trip home—went through White Mountains and Crawford Notch then through Bretton Woods and National Forest. We stopped for two hours to sleep on the side of the road at Concord, NH." The next day they drove to Palmer and sued for child support from Beulah. [10]

Bob Wilder's own annotations in the diary say that after the kidnapping, he did not see his mother again until June 1952. [11]

Periodically, Wilder and his siblings were officially wards of the state, or "dollar-a-day kids," so Flora Wilder was not raising her grandchildren purely out of filial loyalty. Still, she did what she could, even if it seemed primitive for the mid 1930s. They were still being bathed, for instance, once a week in shared bathwater heated up on the stove in a copper tub—outside.

The Wilder family "wore bib overalls, and we'd wear 'em and patch 'em and wear 'em and patch 'em until there was nothing left." When they went to church, they had to sit in the back of the sanctuary with newspapers on the seats and on the floors, because people thought they were dirty. The first time they visited Ware, young Wilder watched the mill employees leave for the day, and marveled at how well they were dressed. And then it struck him: "We were actually poor."[12]

Brushes with Wealth

Some valley residents, like Trudy Ward Stalbird Terry, remember going into "every house in Enfield" during their childhood. In their old age, many of those same people remember feeling that everyone in the valley was essentially economic equals. This was untrue.

When Trudy Ward married Quabbin engineer Jim Stalbird in 1933, Marion Smith, heir to the Smith's Village fortune, who had a Rolls-Royce and servants, gave them a set of china. "She gave Jim and I the most beautiful pattern," Trudy said in 1979. "Now in those days it was bridge parties and things. They'd give you a set of eight—you know, two tables. And I said, 'She has enough money to buy us a whole set!' and Jim says, 'Don't be a mercenary person.' Of course," she added, "when you're kids you make a different opinion than you do when you get older. We used to think she was staunch and stiff, but she was really lovely when you got to know her. And she had money—That's why I said she should give—oh, aren't I terrible!"[13]

Trudy described Howe matriarch Annie Howe as a "Tartar" and a hypocrite "sitting around all day" while other people worked for her.

Trudy's cousin worked as a housecleaner for the Howes, and according to Trudy, "she found two or three magazines underneath Mother Howe's mattress . . . she said, 'What do you want done with these magazines? I found them under your mattress.' 'You did not! Somebody must have put them there!' She said, 'Well, I imagine you did.' She didn't want anyone to know she read those 'true stories' and 'true romances' magazines!" Meanwhile, "Father Howe" was ordering books about sex from a Boston publisher in order to accomplish "scientific research."

Marion Smith had gone to school with Norman Heidel's maternal grandmother, and she was particularly fond of his mother, Geneva. Smith also gave a great deal of money to the Enfield Congregational Church. So it made sense that in the late 1920s, when Norman's father, Emil, took over the management of Enfield's chain supermarket, Smith was able to "grease" the system. According to Norman, Smith negotiated with church officials to have the Heidels move into the old church parsonage, which had a chandelier-like overhead light, wood paneling, and a sweeping central staircase.[14]

Time could not keep all the grand houses intact, though. The parsonage was two houses away from the old Underwood mansion, where Francis Underwood had grown up and where he had written the book *Quabbin* sixty years later. Adolescent Norman Heidel used to sneak into the empty Underwood house sometimes and marvel at its detail and size.

Depression Prices

For many people, their land, and sometimes their small business, was their only asset. Having the Commission pay a Depression price for farms that had been tended for as many as two hundred years felt like a plunge into poverty. Almost no farmer was able to start afresh anywhere outside the valley—they moved into other employment, often at low wages. Sometimes that employment was working for the Commission or one of its contractors. People did it when they had to, but either blocked out its significance or were filled with resentment at its necessity.

"I hated to see it done," said Bun Doubleday, who left the Commission in 1937 to start his own business, "but this was still back during the Depression time, and jobs were hard to find, so you just took what you could find."

The extended Doubleday family had lived in a section of Dana informally known as Doubleday Village. "My father owned a booming business," Doubleday recalled, "and two houses—the house where I had been born, and the house where I was brought up—and he also owned a couple of timber lots, and he figured that he either got a fair price—perhaps even a good price—for his real estate, and nothing for his business—or he got something for his business and a low price for his real estate. With hindsight, I can see that my father should have gone on the offensive and should have started legal proceedings, and sued the state for loss of business for the store. But he felt that he was a small person fighting against the State of Massachusetts, and they would undoubtedly drag the case along through many years . . . So in the long run he felt that he was just as well off to accept—to get as much as he could from them—and let it go at that."[15]

"The majority of the people in the valley were the working people," said Eleanor Griswold Schmidt, formerly of Prescott, "who owned their homes but didn't have much of anything in the bank. They didn't need it. These people were the ones who didn't have the millions—most of them—to fight, to pay a lawyer the thousands of dollars that would be necessary. They just felt, 'Well, we'll take what we can get, and go.'"[16]

Herman Hanson "had a little garage that I run on what they call the Monson Turnpike, and I did pretty good then. All of a sudden I'd lose a customer. They'd move out of town because they sold their property—somebody bought the house to take it down. Well, in another few days somebody else would move out. It got so I couldn't make a livin', so I had to get out."[17]

Even the Howes, who could trace their roots to pre-Revolutionary Enfield and who owned the general store and managed the post office and the phone exchange, worked long and brutal hours, as did their employees.

Ned and Ruth Howe did have enough time and money to take the train to Florida in the winter and, one summer, they bought a new car and drove out to California and back to visit friends who had moved away.

Neither were the engineers rich. Engineering was a well-paying job, and as college graduates they usually came from middle-class families. But most of the engineers who lived in the valley were right out of college and drew recent-college-graduate salaries. Later, as they married and had children, their salary increases were commensurate with their increased expenses. And they were living in the unfancy homes purchased by the Commission and rented back out at what were probably below-market but not exceedingly cheap rates.

Because many of the engineers did or at least supervised hard manual labor along with the hourly wage laborers, they also wore practical, unfussy clothes. But engineers also dressed distinctly differently than laborers. They wore chinos and sweaters, with ties for office work instead of overalls or coveralls, and they wore fedoras instead of caps. So while it was possible to identify an engineer from his clothing and probably his way of speaking, the differences between valley natives and engineers were not nearly as great as the differences between the engineers and the pinstripe-suited, homburg-hatted, topcoat-wearing members of the Commission, who swooped into the valley, criticized or praised, and fled again for the safety of Boston.

Similarly, engineer wives were not fancy dressers. It was true that valley women did not have the money or the opportunity to wear formals—Ruth Ward Howe wore her first formal—"a sleeveless green silk"—to the Farewell Ball in 1938. ("In the country you didn't dress up," she explained.[18]) Presumably the members of the Quabbin Club wore their Sunday best for their final 1938 meeting and group photo. In this case, it's hard to tell the difference between a local and an engineer's wife (the younger women are mostly engineers' wives; the middle-aged women are a mix; the older women are locals), because so many of them are dressed the same: in dark flowered dresses that look homemade and little round-brim hats that had been considerably more fashionable a year earlier. In fact, two women look like they have dresses made of the same pattern, with the same fabric, probably purchased at the same fabric stores in Ware. The 1937–38 Quabbin Club president Anna Spurr, engineer Jerome Spurr's wife, is wearing an ivory-colored silky dress with an unusual soft hat—a distinctive look that probably cost some money and sets her apart from the rest of the Quabbin Club members. The older women wear respectable dark wool suits that are probably not new. Only Geneva Heidel wears a fur stole, perhaps a gift from Marion Smith, and a pillbox hat with a veil.[19] She is absolutely overdressed for the company and the event.

Progress Not Always Wanted

Alice Twible Phillips's[20] father owned a tenement house in Smith's Village. Every apartment had its own "backhouse," with, according to Phillips, "Daddy Bear, Mama Bear and Baby Bear–sized holes."

The Twible family lived outside of the main part of Smith's Village, also with no plumbing. They were considered fairly well-off, or at least indifferent to whether or not they were poor. They used leftover clothing patterns and Sears, Roebuck catalogues as toilet paper. Four of Twible Phillips's siblings worked at the mill in Smith's—her brothers were weavers and her sisters were seamstresses. They had a cold cellar where they stored two butchered pigs a year, grew root vegetables in the cellar dirt, and had a water barrel and "a pump, I remember, because we used to go to the pump and throw water on each other."

Twible Philips herself married a British lawyer with degrees from Trinity College and Harvard Law, but she didn't enjoy living in Hartford, Connecticut, an hour or so away from the valley, and asked him to move back to central Massachusetts with her. The Philipses bought a home in Gilbertville, the same town where Twible Philips and her family had moved when they left Smith's Village, at the time an enclave of Polish immigrants ("We were the only Protestants!"). Her husband traveled through the area and into Connecticut to work. But she thinks of her childhood in the valley as the most joyful time in her life.

The Commission bought the Twible tenement house for $6,000 (a very low price—about 2.5 times an engineer's yearly salary) and renovated it. According to Phillips, "They used it there when they made the reservoir, for their boarders and roomers. And my father went over there one time and he cried his heart out. Because they had put the whole lower floor as a dining hall, and the kitchen and everything, and it made my father heartsick. And they put a furnace in there—they did a lot of things to it that we just didn't have."[21]

EIGHT

Exams and Promotions—and, Finally, a Name: 1931–1932

B y the end of 1932, surveying was largely completed. The Commission broke ground for the new Quabbin Park Cemetery on Route 9, just south of the proposed watershed, where the bodies from the old cemeteries would be moved, and broke deep into the ground with "exploratory caissons" for the dam and dike. The diversion tunnel was almost completed, as was the aqueduct between the Swift River and the Wachusett. Laborers and engineers—and the Commission photographers who documented them—had spent more than enough time underground and were eager to move to the surface.

These were also the hardest years of the Depression, and yet both workers and valley natives were surprisingly untouched—the Commission was spending hundreds of thousands of Depression-era dollars on contracts, and each of those contracts employed many people. Despite both the psychological and physical difficulty and frequent unpleasantness of some of the work, they were jobs, and people took them.

Engineers aspiring to work permanently for the state took Massachusetts state engineering certification exams in 1931. In spite of the Commission's preference for graduates of top engineering programs, the exam itself could be passed easily by someone with a high school education, as long as they knew the technical terms involved.

An assistant sanitary engineer position paid about $1,200–$1,500 per year to start, the equivalent of about $25,000 today. Exam questions included: "A sewage plant consists of coarse screens, pumps, mechanical sedimentation tanks with separate sludge digestion tanks and intermittent sand filters. What is the purpose of the coarse screens?" and "Discuss advantages and limitations of chlorination in the treatment of water supplies."

One General Knowledge question—relevant to the task at hand—was "What is the difference in quality of water from a stripped and unstripped reservoir?" Someone who apparently pilfered the exam wrote in, "No difference after about 12 years (color, algae)."[1] This is the wrong answer, at least as far as the new reservoir was concerned; a primary job of the Quabbin sanitary engineers was to ensure that no compound that could hold life existed on what would be the reservoir floor.

The 1931 Massachusetts civil engineering exam was more serious business. Grade I entry-level junior engineering aides, whose qualifications were either a high school diploma or a year of practical experience, were paid $1,560 per year; senior engineering aides could make between $1,680 and $2,160 per year (an average of about a $35,000 per year salary in today's money) and had to have a high school degree and one year's practical experience. Most if not all new Commission engineers were hired at these two levels. "Many men fail this examination because they apply for grades for which they are not qualified," the exam warned. "Therefore, if there is any doubt about the quantity or quality of your experience, take both the grade for which you think you are qualified and the next lower grade."

Exam takers had to answer correctly 70 percent of the questions each in the following categories: General ("What are slope stakes, and where are they usually set?"); Chemistry (general and lab demonstrations);

Mathematics; Hydraulics; and Design, each with a "classroom" and a "Practical Application" section, with word problems like "An ascending grade of 6% intersects with a descending grade of 8.4%. In order to have visibility over the summit at not less than 200 feet, what length of vertical curve will be necessary for a connection between the two grade lines? (Assume any additional data which you may think you need, but state your assumption clearly.)"[2]

This last question was highly relevant to surveying work.

By the time new engineers were taking the exam in 1931, the surveyors of 1927 and 1928 were performing more sophisticated work in water or soil analysis.

Soil and water samples had to be taken daily. As the dam and dike were built, it was crucial that the soil that made up their cores remain "impervious," or unable to be penetrated by the millions of gallons of water that would rush against them. The soil engineers would take "borings" of different parts of the soil and rock, first as they sunk the caissons into bedrock and excavated them, and then into the interior of the growing dam and dike embankments, often using diamond-tipped drills to penetrate the rock.

The engineers discovered that there were around nine different types of soil in the area, from powdery "rock flour" to coarse sand. They took the soil samples back to the lab at the Chandler House and examined it with a soil testing machine developed by MIT professor and Spurr mentor Karl Terzaghi. The engineers loaded the soil samples through the weights placed on a hanger and tried to duplicate the pressure of the soil at any given elevation and determine its potential consolidation and seepage. Soil left to its own devices could take years to settle, so even though the entire dam structure was dependent on the solidity of the soil, some accuracy had to be sacrificed for speed.[3]

By this point Spurr had been moved up yet again, from deed analyst to the head of the Enfield soil testing lab. Enfield division chief Hammond said the promotion was because of Spurr's hard work and "analytical mind"—something an MIT graduate would be pleased to hear. In the soil lab Spurr had two MIT graduates, John May and Charles Fenno, working on his team, along with Bun Doubleday and Norman Hall, who was not part of the MIT clique but had worked with Spurr as a surveyor and was handsome, personable, and ready to handle almost any task in a pinch. Spurr also partnered with Frank Fahlquist, an engineer whose specialty was geology rather than soils and one of the few men who Frank Winsor had brought over from Brown.[4]

Like surveying, the soil job was both monotonous and had very high stakes. The technology was new, and being used at an unprecedented scale. Spurr's team tested the dam core materials "at the rate of several hundred samples a day. Those samples, after being tested, revealed whether we had the right samples in the right places. The main problem was having the sand form little spits into the core [of the dam]—we had to test on a daily basis to make sure it didn't happen, and when we discovered it—we did this through test results which were plotted on regular forms—normally at 50' intervals along the line of the dam—and from those results the resident engineer on the job could determine what corrective action was needed. Copies went to Boston for information of the engineers there."[5]

As long as the material at the dam core remained fluid, Spurr added, "it was dangerous . . . it had no stability in itself anymore and was like a gallon of molasses." Too much molasses-grade soil and the result could be similar to the 1919 Great Molasses Flood in Boston, which Spurr certainly remembered and which killed twenty-one people; a collapsing dam, even one under construction, was far more catastrophic and expensive.

"Our $65,000,000 Baby"

Finally, the project unofficially referred to as the "Swift River," "MDWSC," "the dam," or just "the reservoir" was given an official name on October 25, 1932. The Commission's Chief Engineer's Report announced: "The

Metropolitan District Water Supply Commission . . . gave the name Quabbin Reservoir to the reservoir to be constructed in the Swift River Valley and previously referred to as the Swift River Reservoir. The commission also gave the name Quabbin Aqueduct to the tunnel which will connect Quabbin Reservoir and Wachusett Reservoir. The commission gave the name Quabbin Park Cemetery to the new cemetery established in the town of Ware."[6]

The name was obvious, and it made sense. It incorporated the original Nipmuc name of the location, which literally means "well-watered place," and of Chief Quabbin himself. Francis Underwood himself had called the entire area "Quabbin," the "Quabbin Valley" was nearly interchangeable for the "Swift River Valley," there were mountains and lakes named Quabbin, and even the venerable Powers mansion was called "Quaint Quabbin." The nature preserve watershed around the reservoir would be called Quabbin Park.

The *Boston Post* was a little nonplussed by what it perceived as lack of public input. In its article, "Our $65,000,000 Baby Has Been Named Quabbin," the *Post* acknowledged that while the "name is appropriate," "some persons may feel that the official naming of such an important State domain should have been accompanied by some ceremony similar to that which attends the launching of a battleship, [while] others are convinced that this quiet adoption of a new term is the surest and in the long run the quickest way to bring about the natural use of such a strange name."[7]

Certainly the Commission deemed that the people in the valley would find this an acceptable name, given that the word "Quabbin" appeared in so much valley nomenclature. But there are no records of whether the towns were ever consulted, or whether the name was foisted on them like everything else.

NINE

"The Bends": 1932–1935

The six-day week of labor was punishing, but on the seventh day, there was baseball. The 1932 Enfield Engineers team had nine men willing to play, uniforms, a coach, and some competition in Ware and other Commission sites closer to the Wachusett. Dick Jackson, Homer Briggs, Chet Chetwynd, Stuart Beach, Bill Potter, Preston Putnam, Carl Crawford, Joe Bruce, and Harold McLeod, along with their coach, Russ Snow, suited up for a July 4 weekend game in a field near the Chandler House and posed for the photographer on a wooden bench plopped down in the middle of the grass and with the word "Engineers" sewn onto the front of their uniforms.

Russ Snow is sunburnt from tending to the seedlings that will one day reforest the Quabbin watershed. Chet Chetwynd is smiling winsomely, as he does in all his photographs. Stuart Beach and Bill Potter are super-casual with their catchers' mitts.[1] Who cared if it was uncomfortably hot in their gray wool uniforms and high socks, and the next day they'd have to go back underground, wrangle with the bosses, lug large bags of soil or jugs of water from their source back to the lab, stop lazy contractors from loafing, or take more photos of the destruction du jour? Today they were regular guys.

In the fall of 1933, engineers set up shop next to the abandoned mill in Enfield, on the west side of the river, with the backs of the Main Street buildings facing them on the opposite bank. In the raw November air, in the shadow of the empty-windowed, sagging-roof brick mill, they began digging a pit to experiment with a "sluicing test bin," developing techniques that would help them build the dam. They constructed what looked like a twenty-feet-by-fifty-feet sandbox over the pit, threw the dirt they'd dug up into the bin, and sprayed it with hoses to make mud. Two workers with "batter boards" redirected the mud until it was solid, with water dripping into the pit. Once it dried, they did it over again. This was the miniaturized "proof of concept" for building the dam and dike: excavate the fill; mix it with water; drain off the water until the fill hardened. Eventually four million cubic yards of fill were used for the dam, and 2.5 million for the dike. But for now, this was high-sweat engineering experimentation. The engineers and the laborers wore layers of clothing: shirts, sweaters, jackets, coats, gloves, scarves, and hats, and then took off each layer as the digging got intensive. They smoked pipes to keep warm and stave off the stress. [2]

But again, they were aboveground, and that was better than below. Two miles away, and then again on Little Quabbin Mountain, the teeth of giant caissons chomped down into bedrock.

According to Donald Howe, a "huge block of concrete was constructed, 16 feet high, 9 feet wide and 45 feet long and it was reinforced with steel rods. It was constructed on the surface of the ground. But first a steel cutting shoe was laid and incorporated in the lower edge of a hollow chamber 6 feet high, and the width of the caisson, where men would dig the material which would be removed by buckets to the top of the caisson. As it settled into the earth, due to excavation of the material and its weight, it disappeared, and another section was added until finally there was a barrier 135 feet deep. On reaching the ledge, it was concreted and grouted to the rock." Rows of these caissons had to be laid next to one another, which, when completed, "formed a concrete wall 9 feet thick down to solid rock and insured as much as human ingenuity could, an underground core or watertight wall at the dam and dike." [3]

Unlike in the Quabbin aqueduct tunnels, these workers breathed compressed air, pushed through the locks on top of the caissons. As the water level was lowered, the need for pressure was lowered as well. This was intended to prevent "the bends," but Dr. Segur, who had taken yet another job as chief medic for the reservoir project, kept an eye on anyone who had the bad luck of having to enter one of the two "decompression rooms"—nicely furnished but claustrophobic cylinders big enough for two men to change out of their dirty clothes and lie down.

Contractors Ken Cross and Walt King, with more than a half century between them and the caissons, remember their time as "sand hogs" as something of a hoot:

> You could only work down there for about 55 minutes. Big buckets were lowered down. You filled them up with muck. And you had to "lock in" before you could get in there. All of us were in a chamber. You had to go in there so you could take the amount of air you needed to go in there. So you were sealed off from down below and sealed off from inside, and they started letting the air in. and you had to keep your ears open by yelling or yawning or something. And if you couldn't clear your ears it starts to hurt. If you couldn't do it they might let the air down a little lower and they tried again, but if you couldn't do it the second time they couldn't slow down production so they'd ask you to get out and you'd have to come back again on the next shift.
>
> We'd go down the ladders, and we used to have bales of hay in there to absorb the water—28 pounds of pressure would keep the water out, so when you're diggin' because not only would you lose the pressure you couldn't pick up anything in the shovel. Gradually, as you went deeper and deeper you had to use more pressure to keep the water out.
>
> At one point it was -65°F down below and no one believed it, so the state measured. There was one week where it never got higher than -45°F. But you're hot. You sweat. It gets cold. It's hard.

73

You had to decompress when you came out. Everybody's come up, and it would be, let's say, 28 lbs. of pressure, and they'd let it out very, very slowly and hold it at 5–10 lbs. and slowly let that go. No one had any problems. But there was one guy—we'd go to the coffee shack after we came up, and he did a blind stagger, just like he was drunk. Sometimes people were stricken 4–5 hours after the job was over. [4]

According to Cross and King, the caissons caused the death of a contractor, one "Stubby" Bean: "The muck lock came down—it filled one—the other one came down somehow—he got hung up at the bottom one—and then he started takin' it up. But he didn't realize—he got three quarters of the way up, and the bottom one came off. Landed on top of him and killed him. He was a big rugged guy, too. A bull. No one else was hurt. But it knocked him flatter than a platter." [5]

The Commission paid one dollar per hour for this work, and none of the contractors were union shops.

Chet Chetwynd, who had already photographed decrepit real estate, "sanitary" sewage pits, more than ten cemeteries, and the aqueduct tunnels, was now pressed into service to photograph work inside the caissons. Officially he was only a photographer until 1929, but perhaps no one else was willing to do the job. By this time he'd officially been promoted to inspector on the Ware River project, and, as a result, was working closer to home and his new bride, Bud Sawyer.

At around this time, the Commission hired another MIT alum, James Stalbird, as a sanitary engineer. Stalbird had graduated five years earlier than Spurr, in 1922; at MIT he had earned the unfortunate nickname "Chubby," despite being a team swimmer for the Engineers. Stalbird had spent some years doing railroad engineering in Boston, and then in Cuba. He began working as a sanitary engineer in 1932, performing tests on

Swift River water and living at the Swift River Hotel, which had just been reopened by the Commission for Commission business only.

Stalbird was encouraged to join the Enfield Grange by Homer Briggs and Russ Snow, who played in a four-piece, all-engineer orchestra some Saturday nights. For twenty-five cents for the evening, the Grange offered two hours of whist, dinner, and then two hours of dancing. Trudy Ward now spent Saturday nights at the Grange as well, after years taking care of her recently deceased invalid mother.

Jim was interested in Trudy. It was not reciprocal. "'He's a good catch!'" people would tell her, but she didn't think so. Yet Trudy, spirited and with a sharp sense of humor, was already starting to feel like an old maid at twenty-three. Trudy had only a ninth grade education, due more to her undiagnosed dyslexia and family obligations than any lack of motivation, and she didn't understand what an MIT-educated engineer would see in her.

Jim was, apparently, persistent. Jim and Trudy—both tall, big-boned, physically awkward redheads—were married in the Enfield Congregational Church in the fall of 1933. They were the last couple to be married there, although no one in Enfield had any idea at the time. It was the first marriage of the daughter of an old Enfield family to an engineer.

Jim mostly balanced his engineering job with his responsibilities to the town he'd married into. He became a senior member of the Grange and joined the local Masonic Lodge. Trudy often worked Sundays at the Howes' general store so her sister Ruth could take a break. "Jim used to come in Sundays and help me sometimes," she said. "Jim would be tending the ice cream counter, and you'd see this little hand barely reach the counter with a penny—it was Sophie Boyko! She wanted an 'I ceem cone.' So he put the other four pennies in, and then it was a nickel."[6] This apparently was not an isolated incident. On the other hand, Stalbird's first two years of his employment with the Commission were a little fraught; his personnel record notes that he was briefly laid off, and then returned to the job with a 10 percent pay cut.[7] While other engineers received promotions and raises, he never did.

The Diversion Tunnel

The caissons bore straight down. But the main dam could not be built with the Swift River in its natural position. To carry the river away from the construction area a curved tunnel was blasted through solid rock, a process already familiar to the workers.

By mid-1932 the drill carriages were in the diversion tunnel. Huge chunks of the hillside, visible from a distance, were loudly ripped away.

Generally, a work unit was made up of two engineers and five or six laborers. Outside the entrance to the diversion tunnel, huge wooden "experimental forms"—arches leading nowhere— were being erected to determine the best size for the tunnel. The aqueduct tunnels were ten feet by eleven feet, and the diversion tunnel would need to be about the same size. Once the forms were completed, the drill carriages were driven through them to ensure they would fit. By this stage, there were so many project components to photograph that engineer-botanist Russ Snow had to be dragged away from his seedlings to assist.

A Seditionist Gets His Own Highway

The state announced that the new highway around the Quabbin Reservoir, built to compensate for the roads lost and to increase traffic around the area, would be called the Daniel Shays Highway.

The Commission justified the naming as "commemorating a local event of national importance,"[8] "but it was "rare indeed that a state honors a rebel who led a losing cause against it," commented the *Christian Science Monitor*.[9] The *Boston Globe* noted that the section of the road going north from Belchertown to Athol, running outside the valley basin in parallel to the old Rabbit

Train, "follows the route taken by the rebels in their retreat before the forces of the State Government."[10] Was the naming a gesture of goodwill toward the people who were losing their land, a remembrance of their struggles 150 years earlier? Or was it patronizing, the equivalent of, after driving Native tribes off the land, giving the land its original Native appellation? In that case, "Quabbin" and "Daniel Shays" had something in common.

The town of Pelham was not against the name; it voted to erect a sign on town property designating it as the "Capt. Daniel Shays Highway." But a local professor was miffed; he wanted it just called the "Swift River Highway" in order to preserve the identity of the valley as a whole.[11]

A Community Christmas

The towns kept making budgets and nominating town officials. Children kept going to school. Babies were born. People went to work and tended their remaining farms. Iola Downing kept writing the *Ware River News* society pages, but now they included the doings of resident engineers and their families, including the new engineer babies. The engineers and their wives were joining the church and the civic groups. No one fought them, or prevented them from joining. It was the middle of the Depression, and survival was paramount. There was no time for fighting.

"The 1934 community Christmas tree seems to have been a great success," announced the *Ware River News*. Rather than cutting down a tree and upholding the tradition of bringing it to the lawn of the Swift River Hotel, the tree committee, made up of Ruth Junkins, wife of Commission chemist Walter Junkins; Anna Knight, wife of Commission Special Agent Charles Knight; and Inez Brown of Enfield, Nellie Brown's sister-in-law, chose the "large spruce tree growing in the rear of the cellar hole left when the Bartlett store burned nearly seven years ago"[12]—a huge tree from a previous Enfield century, and on one of the higher points in Enfield Center.

The committee's official rationale for using the Bartlett tree was that it was too dangerous and time-consuming for the men to find a new tree, cut it down, bring it into town, and anchor it; two years earlier the town Christmas tree had toppled over in the wind and broken most of the decorations. Given that a tree had fallen only once in living memory, and that the valley was bursting with trees that were going to have to be cut down anyway, their excuse seemed a little implausible, but no one questioned it publicly.

The volunteers bought three dozen bulbs for the Christmas lights, which cost so much that they had to ask for reimbursement. They cut and trimmed the spruce's large frowzy branches until they covered up the cellar hole. Then they asked the Central Massachusetts Electric Company to reconnect the power—just for the Christmas season. Enfielders William Granger and Frank Avery connected the power source to the bulbs. The lights came on—and they shone, for more than a week, for miles around.

The Rabbit's Last Run

The 50-mile Rabbit Train that ran through the valley had been a lifeline to the outside world. At a speed of about ten miles per hour, the train was another slow, intimate, and quaint feature of valley life. Enfielder Harvey Dickinson said that his mother went to high school in Athol, and "one time in the spring when the flowers were blooming along the track, the girls asked the conductor to stop the train so they could get off and pick some for their teacher. The conductor signaled the engineer, the train was stopped, and the girls got off, grabbed some blossoms, and got back on."[13]

"Everyone knew everyone on the train," said Norman Heidel. "It was part of the social fabric."[14]

"If someone was riding somewhere," said Bill Segur, "and the train came fairly close to their house—if you just let 'em know they'd stop and let you out, and you'd climb the fence, cross the briar-way, and go home. The train'd just get up and go right along."[15]

Like everything else in the valley, technology and automation had passed the Rabbit by. In early 1930s the trains began to decrease their size and frequency.

The Rabbit still had plenty of summer passengers as late as 1931, both for the summer camps and the mountain motorcycle races, and Greenwich's officially abandoned Dugmar Golf Course. But the passenger load, which for a typical run had diminished from 225 passengers to sometimes as few as 10,[16] wasn't enough to keep it running. The New York Central Railroad, which had bought the Rabbit Train from the Boston and Albany Railroad at the beginning of the century, knew that the railroad would be decommissioned before 1936, when work on the dam would start in earnest. A highway would be built on the other side of the reservoir, connecting the north and south endpoints of the route; everything else would be underwater.

How much was the Rabbit and its infrastructure actually worth? The Commission hired three different companies to evaluate, and, in 1934, settled on the sum of $575,000.[17]

Just a few months later, the so-called "Drunkard's Train" had its last run. The Saturday night train was given its nickname because on Saturday morning people rode the train south to Springfield, and that night returned, north, drunk. In the train's "obituary," the *Springfield Republican* described how the train ran late "supposedly to give the outlying districts an opportunity to visit the theaters but in reality used almost entirely as a chance to go on an old-time 'spree.' Often it had four or five cars full to overflowing." The conductor "was appointed railroad police with full authority and many were the fistic encounters which came to an untimely end through his interference. On one occasion a free-for-all fight was started [in Springfield] and when the train reached Indian Orchard the conductor-policeman had 27 fellows tied and bound with bell cords whom he handed over to one lone policeman . . . who locked them up." For its remaining year of service, the Rabbit Train would carry one freight car and one "smoking car," a combination freight and passenger car.[18]

The final "excursion" run of the Rabbit Train, also known as the "Soapstone Limited," took place on May 26, 1935. As with many of other "last" events in the valley, the number of locals was dwarfed by enthusiasts, curiosity seekers, and the press. The usually silent little stations were now filled with people waving at the train or hopping on board to be part of this last piece of valley history, while little boys in knee pants ran alongside it as it huffed to a stop. More train cars were added for the first time in years.

Donald Howe described how

> the scheduled twenty stops were made, despite the fact many stops were barren of either railroad stations or humans. Instead were hills and valleys, denuded of trees and vegetation. It was truly a ghost trip.
>
> In Enfield alone was there any life. There, the center of activity of the main dam and dike, a sizable crowd greeted the excursionists. The tracks ran almost directly through the center of the site of the dam, and every passenger left his seat to gaze on the huge piles of sand and rock which would be the foundation of the main structure. Practically every passenger had his camera busy taking the last pictures of what was left of the valley.

The railroad's dismantlement began July 3, 1935. Starting in Athol and moving south, workers methodically pulled up the rails and ties to be used for salvage. Cranes provided the initial heavy lifting, and workers followed along on foot, yanking the wood and metal from the ground. Gradually, a source of pride in the valley was replaced by nothing—just a miles-long path of stripped earth and dried grass, silent and tired in the hot July sun. The workers arrived at the dam site, the northern terminus of the Springfield route, at the end of the month.

Now the only way to get in and out of the valley was by vehicle, and soon, some said bleakly, by boat. The loss of the railroad and what it represented felt, to many, like a bitter emasculation of their independence. Even forty-five years later, Herman Hanson, formerly of North Dana, took it hard: "The thing that got me the most was when that damn wrecker came along, pickin' up the rails on the railroad track. That hit right to home. That was the end of our railroad, and the end of our village. Some of these things—" And the old man burst out sobbing. [19]

TEN

Social Organizations and Entertainment

I n the first half of the twentieth century, American civic and fraternal organizations were vibrant across the US, and a means to bring together rural folks who otherwise might have remained socially and culturally isolated. The residents of the Swift River Valley were no different: They had relied on collective activities for two centuries not only to feel less isolated but also to meet the people around them and build communities. How were young people otherwise supposed to meet and fall in love, or business partnerships to start? How would you know the people who'd come to your aid when a family member was ill or if your house caught on fire?

Barn dances, donut and sleigh parties, churchgoing, and town-hall meetings also served those functions, but as a rural middle class grew there was a greater emphasis on organizations that not only served the participants, but also gave charity to the "deserving poor," including in the organizations' own communities.

Enfield's Bethel Lodge Fraternal Order of Masons was founded in Enfield in 1825; its sister organization, the Order of the Eastern Star, was founded in 1909, during the US-wide surge in women's organizations.

The Masons prided themselves on the diversity of their members, but membership included a high enough financial barrier that effectively it was restricted to the upper ranks of valley society; member rolls throughout the Enfield Masons' history were filled with the names of those with the biggest houses and farms and the most social capital. The Order of the Eastern Star, for the wives, was not nearly as popular as the Masons, nor as diverse in membership as the Quabbin Club, although membership overlapped between the two groups. According to Ruth Ward Howe, Eastern Star meetings involved sewing and singing traditional tunes and hymns— "it doesn't sound like fun to an outsider, but we were so busy all the time it seemed like fun."[1] When Russ Snow joined the Masons, his wife, Grace, joined the Eastern Star, and Ruth became lifelong friends with her.

In her teens and early twenties, Ruth Ward Howe and her future husband, Ned, belonged to a young adult organization associated with the Congregational Church called Christian Endeavor. "We played games, and there was one minister who used to love to play Post Office—so he could kiss the girls! I didn't like him because his breath smelled."[2] (The Reverend John Curtis was the Enfield Congregational minister until the town was disincorporated. He was married and had a young daughter.)

In Dana, the Improved Order of Red Men, Neeseponsett Tribe, served a more rural, less sophisticated constituency, although some of its rituals—minus the ersatz Native language ("No person shall be entitled to adoption into the Order except a free white male of good moral character and standing, of the full age of twenty-one great suns, who believes in the existence of a Great Spirit, the Creator and Preserver of the Universe, and is possessed of some known reputable means of support")[3]—were directly taken from Freemasonry. The Massachusetts Red Men claimed to be descendants of the men who supplied the Boston Tea Party "Indians" with their equipment. "Grand Pow-wows" took place in "Native" costume.[4]

Each of the four Swift River towns had its own Patrons of Husbandry group, or Grange, with its own building. The Granges were a national fraternal organization built around the celebration and promotion of agriculture and, unlike most similar organizations, were not single sex or divided by gender. Women played important leadership and practical roles to such an extent that the Enfield Grange was predominantly women.

Granges required significant but not insurmountable dues. Some of the engineers who focused on soil or water technology rather than civil engineering joined the Enfield Grange, but, unlike the Masons, they were not a prominent presence. Sanitary Engineer James Stalbird may have joined because his new wife, Trudy Ward Stalbird of Enfield, was already a member, but he became a significant enough presence in the group that, by 1935, "Patron of Husbandry" Stalbird presented and signed off on Grange-sponsored academic awards to Enfield School students.[5]

William Fielding Sr. was another engineer whose family joined the Grange. "My mother got involved with the Grange because my father was inclined not to be all that sociable," Bill Fielding Jr. said. "But he went along too." Bill, his brother, and his mother found acceptance at the Grange by playing music there: "We had a trio—my mother played piano, my brother on trumpet, and myself on the violin." Other than music there were plenty of Grange activities where the family could meet people: "Right up until the very end they had functions every Friday and Saturday."[6] Engineer Ellis Barbier was a frequent attendee of Grange dances.[7]

Former valley residents had pleasant memories of their Grange experiences, and in June 1975 survivors met with valley historian Audrey Duckert to discuss their experiences. You could join the Grange as early as age fourteen, and you did not have to be a farmer or from a farm family. Local schoolteachers also had to join, because the Grange paid the teachers' salaries. The valley Granges were collectively called the Pomona Grange, but the Enfield Grange was called the "Garfield Grange" because it was founded the night after President Garfield was assassinated in 1886.[8]

Some Grange rituals were secret, but the meetings often focused on current social issues or were fundraisers, including "penny marches" (like musical chairs), fee-for-entry potlucks, and skit nights. Ray Lego, formerly of Greenwich, described it as "the first of your social affairs outside of the churches you belonged to. You had a uniform. It was nonsectarian, and you had a good time and got convinced to enjoy it."[9]

The Granges, the Masons, and the women's Quabbin Club all disbanded in 1938. According to Lego, who later sued the state for proceeds from his roadside fruit and vegetable stand and ultimately won $4,500, "I suppose there was a lot of speeches and things among the people, that they were sorry that the Grange was going to disband, but they had to because they had to give up the building. At that time, the active members had fled—they had scattered to find work here and there, to Athol and Orange and way stations and so forth—and different places. So it got down to just enough to have a meeting. But I don't remember any unusual thing."[10]

Even in the 1930s, the seeds of decline in social engagement had been planted, and not only because residents had begun to lose interest in group membership in a place that would no longer exist.

Dorothy Fitts was a former Grange and Quabbin Club member whose husband, Charles, worked for the Commission and was a Mason leader. They were invested in their community and in their local organizations. Forty years after the fact, Fitts still remembered "calling a rehearsal or something for one of the Grange degrees or the other . . . and I have a peculiar memory of this—one woman said, 'goodness me, couldn't you call this some other time? I'm going to miss *Amos 'n Andy* on the radio.' Of course there were people who would rather listen to *Amos 'n Andy* or whatever was on the radio than attend the Grange meeting. And of course it meant getting out of your warm chair and getting out into the cold wintertime, and so forth and so on, even if it was cars instead of horses to hitch up. It was easier to stay at home."[11]

There were, of course, other forms of entertainment if you wanted to stay in the valley and not go to Ware or Athol for the evening—or even Springfield for the day.

Music was popular: a number of engineers played instruments (horticul-turalist Russ Snow on saxophone with his wife, Grace, on piano; Commission draftsman Homer Briggs and his wife, Muriel, on trumpet) and sometimes they joined Nellie Brown's nephew, Lyman, on piano—Lyman had dropped out of the Eastman School of music to work for the Commission—and Bill Fielding and fellow high school student Sophie Boyko on violin. Nellie Brown's chauffeur also played piano.

There was always fishing, including ice fishing. At the west branch of the Swift River, there was a ski club in the winter, with a jump.

Sometimes there were talent shows, called "entertainments." These were largely put on by teenagers and young adults, but occasionally parents would join in; usually serious community members could be found putting on song-and-dance shows, or tap dancing.

After the Rabbit Train shut down in 1935 and the only way out of the valley was by car, movie theater owners from Ware would come into Enfield with a temporary projector and show movies in the town hall.

And, briefly, there was access to the Dugmar Golf Club, a nine-hole course and clubhouse that had been built as an enormous boondoggle by two entrepreneurs who were eager to buy cheap land in the valley and sell it to the state for a much higher price (the ruins of the golf course are still above the waterline and visible from the Quabbin Administration Building). After the owners abandoned the property, people played for free and no one told them to leave—there was no one left to enforce.

ELEVEN

All Hell Breaks Loose: 1936

T he *Christian Science Monitor* cheerfully announced in late March 1936
that the Quabbin project soon would wake from its winter lull and be
"humming again" in the following weeks.[1]

At that point, the Swift River Valley, unlike most local jurisdictions, was
in a rare position to get the Quabbin project—or any project—humming:
The valley had been spared the worst of a historic flood earlier that month
that had overwhelmed most of New England. Perhaps the residents and the
engineers felt lucky that they didn't need to be evacuated from their homes
like their neighbors in Ware and across the Connecticut Valley. What they
did not know was that 1936 would be a year of "fresh horrors," including a
devastating fire in Enfield and thousands of human "woodpeckers" bused
in from Boston for the summer to cut down the valley's native greenery by
day, and drink, carouse, and get into car accidents by night.

On the morning of March 19, Stuart Pike and his new assistant, Ellis
Barbier, drove around Enfield photographing the overflowing Swift River.
It had been raining in New England for eight straight days, and would rain
for another six. Barbier, in cap, dark sweater, and untucked white shirt—he
had just shown up at the Chandler House and, as a local, point-blank asked

LeRoy Hammond for a job[2]—posed in Enfield Center near the mill, where gawkers hung over the side of the bridge to watch the angry little river churn over the town dam. They drove the two miles to the foot of the immense, in-progress Quabbin Dam, with the Swift River running parallel to its base; telephone poles were immersed in the rushing water and small trees were almost completely submerged. Raw mist from the heavy winter snows that had never quite melted hung in the morning air. But the engineers were used to much worse with respect to physical discomfort, and they drove out to Packardville Road on the river's west branch and were happy to find it muddy and slick, but passable. People could still do their work. And so they wrote down the times and places they'd been, and came back to headquarters to tell the team that Enfield had dodged a bullet.[3] The river crested nearly sixteen feet over its banks at 6:00 P.M. that evening.[4]

Many places nearby hadn't dodged the bullet. During fourteen days of rain and snowmelt, almost all rivers in both New England and the Ohio Valley rose catastrophically. Towns on the banks of the Connecticut River were inundated. In the Connecticut Valley, the president of Massachusetts State College (now the University of Massachusetts at Amherst) called the president of Amherst College and asked him to help take in the Polish-speaking refugees from nearby flooded towns, using Polish-speaking students as interpreters. The families stayed in UMass and Amherst College gymnasiums for nine days.[5]

Ironically, the small size of the Swift River, which had prevented the valley from becoming even a midsize industrial player, saved it from destruction in 1936. No major construction equipment had been irrevocably damaged; after all, much of it was designed to work in wet conditions. Come April 1, the twenty-four-hour, three-shift, six-day weeks started up again, on time—and then the woodpeckers descended.

The Woodpeckers

Massachusetts governor James Michael Curley, a proud Irish Democrat, liked patronage and inside deals as much as he disliked Republicans. One of his missions, he had always believed, was to lift economically oppressed Bostonians from poverty and put them on the path to economic self-sustainment. The Quabbin project, with its multiple contracts and increasing need for workers, was fertile ground for the former, but to get the latter, Curley would have to work around the members of the Comission, who were old-time Republican Ivy-educated Yankees. Curley needed to flex his political muscles and perhaps pocket some cash before the 1936 election, where he would be upselling himself and running for US Senate.

Daniel H. Coakley was a state senator from the Irish, blue-collar Brighton section of Boston; he was also a member of Curley's Governor's Council and a similarly enthusiastic dispenser of local largesse. It was his job to deliver the thousands of workers needed for the summer's Quabbin clearing project. He was so successful that some people joked that MDWSC actually stood for "Men Desiring Work, See Coakley."

News that up to five thousand new jobs would be available working on the Quabbin project circulated quickly. At 7:30 A.M. on April 21, the day applications were first taken, a line of 150 mostly very young men snaked around the block outside the Boston MDWSC offices.[6] The lines became four men deep; nearly as many queued in front of the Chandler House, filling out forms handed to them one-by-one by N. LeRoy Hammond, who had been deputized as foreman of the project. Reports said that two thousand applicants had applied for the first one thousand jobs.[7] In fact, many of those jobs didn't exist except on paper; the Governor's Council had not approved the advertising for bids because they wanted to make sure their own people got the sweetheart deals.

According to a memo from Frank Winsor, the workers' job description was the following:

> Trees 12 inches or more in diameter at a foot above the ground shall be cut so as to leave stumps extending not more than 6 inches above the ground; and all other vegetation shall be cut close to the ground. Existing stumps not cut under this contract and standing more than 6 inches above the heights specified

shall be cut to these heights. All stumps decayed to the extent of approximately 50 per cent of the original cross section shall be broken off and entirely removed.[8]

Work began April 27. The Commission took over Nellie Brown's mansion on Enfield Common, which would now be dedicated to clearing-project work. Brown herself, not overtly sentimental about the fact that her ancestor, Civil War general Joseph Hooker, had lived in the house, pocketed the Commonwealth's money and bought herself and Miss Glass a flamboyantly ornate Queen Anne in Springfield.

The first crews headed out to clear the William Felton farm in Enfield, and a curious group of locals and journalists tagged along to view the action. The clearing project seemed like a high-energy, high-drama event to cover, and a fun way for local reporters to spend the summer.

Starting wages for the workers began at fifty cents per hour for "Ordinary Labor" and went up to eighty-five cents per hour for carpenters—shockingly high for Depression wages and for the work being performed. The project was originally projected to last two hundred days, or until the end of 1936.

Workers, including 120 men from neighboring Chicopee who were receiving aid from the Welfare Department, were quickly bused in. Representative Roland Sawyer was involved in promoting jobs for people in his jurisdiction, with no particular success despite having a "special registration" for those positions.

Employees working on the Greenwich projects were housed in Ware or Palmer, outside the watershed. But the Enfield workers had no place to live. Laborers and some Quabbin engineers had been sleeping in the engineer barracks in Enfield, but the barracks were designed to hold 150 at the most. Officially, Enfield had said that no provisions would be made for clearing crew room and board, but the residents, sensing financial opportunity and even a use for their empty houses, offered to rent rooms.

The *Ware River News*, which was closest to the work, was matter-of-fact about the project kickoff, reporting with as little smirking and eyebrow raising as possible:

> Each crew is around 25 men, with one local man as foreman. Most of the crew men arrived from Boston with cards from the Boston office authorizing a job. Most of them are obviously not regular laborers.
>
> The crew has a big tool box, filled with axes, brush choppers, cross-cut saws, shovels, scythes and a grind stone. A vast stock of such tools arrived last week and was stored in the old Haskell store.
>
> Each crew also has a movable Chic Sales retiring room.
>
> They started on a section of about an acre on a side hill, partly covered with brush and dead trees, etc. Everything is cut down, as close to the ground as possible. Then all the refuse is piled up, to be burned in due time.
>
> There was none of the hectic pushing which is expected on a contract job, where every man is on the jump every minute or somebody else is hired. On the contrary, it went much more like a WPA job. Men worked but didn't rush. The laborers who came from Boston couldn't stand up under a driving program, not now anyway.
>
> Nevertheless, it looks like a gigantic and never-ending task to clear off the tens of thousands of acres, in this manner. [9]

The engineers at the dam site were doing their best to ignore the clearing crews; they had bigger things to attend to—literally. They were constructing a "hog box" for the dam—a massive wooden contraption the size and shape of the downward slope of a wooden roller-coaster track meant for pouring materials for the dam directly onto it. According to Donald Howe, the hog box "had a flow of water pumped from the [nearby artificial lake], which flowed on [the stony riprap] as it was dumped by the trucks.

Then the materials were mixed and in turn flowed back to the edge of the pool at such places as were determined. The water was then pumped back to be used over again to bring more materials to the structure. So, the impounding of the Swift River by the use of its own water stands unique."[10] Trucks or trailers then carried the materials the last twenty feet to the dam.

It was more than a hundred feet down from the hog box to the valley floor. And for the engineers, that rarified position was just fine.

Curley's workers were city boys. Many looked like pale, overgrown street urchins. A large percentage had never left the City of Boston. Some had never worked, period. A few were pulled out of jail cells as a favor to "His Excellency" Governor Curley; they and their parents were loyal Democratic voters. Almost none had ever seen an axe up close. And it was immediately apparent that they were doing a terrible job—sloppy, slow, and inefficient.

At first the clearing workers were nicknamed "Curley's Thugs," and the project itself was sometimes known as "Curley's Summer Camp." But the people in the valley quickly gave them a snider epithet: "woodpeckers"—just as noisy as the little birds, and not nearly so effective. The woodpeckers themselves appropriated the term almost immediately as a perverse badge of honor—a Depression-era version of "deplorable."

Reports of price gauging on rent, transportation, and food were circulating by mid-May. Area cafés began taping signs to their front doors advertising their prices to show their honesty; some businesses began extending credit to workers who had not yet received paychecks. The *Worcester Gazette* reported that two Boston state representatives had accused local businesses of "profiteering," including "Ham, egg, or hamburg sandwich, 25 cents; coffee and one donut, 25 cents." The state representatives Curley sent to inspect the site accused the Commission of jacking up the price of a double room to $5.00–$6.00 per week (normally $1.50-$2.00) and raising the three-mile trip to the job site to $3.00–$5.00. Intrepid *Gazette* reporters were not so interested in scooping the prices of lodging or car rides; instead, the *Gazette* wrote, the food was much less expensive than the rumors stated, with a full box lunch of "three sandwiches, a bottle of milk, an apple or orange, and a piece of cake" selling for a quarter.[11]

Just as the engineers had filled up the towns a decade earlier, the woodpeckers, like unwanted summer tourists, were now crowding Enfield and the towns outside the watershed. But unlike the engineers, the wood-peckers were neither polite nor respectful, and often not educated, at least in the view of the country folk: "Few of the workers, and they include scores of college graduates, high school athletes of a few years back, profes-sional musicians and dozens of other artisans who have found the 'job of getting a job' too big for them, have never before labored in the country; most of them never spent a day on a farm, and while there is some question as to the authenticity of the tale that one young man termed a litter of pigs a herd of sheep, most of the newcomers are seeing how the ruralite lives for the first time." Nevertheless, "Ninety percent of the men have gained weight since starting their jobs two weeks ago; all have fine healthy color and brag of enormous appetites,"[12] a statement that certainly would have pleased the Curley-voting mothers of the West End or Southie.

Governor Curley continued to believe that the Commission and the locals were out to screw his "boys." After Coakley's visit to the project, Ralph W. Robart of the Massachusetts Division on the Necessities of Life toured the facilities, accompanied by Winsor, Commission Member Eugene Hultman, and Molt. Afterward, Curley expressed optimism that 2,000 workers could be fed and housed for ten dollars per week, and encour-aged setting up a cafeteria.[13]

The *Ware River News* described the project as "a roaring, sputtering, crunching maelstrom of tractors, power-shovels, trucks and dozens of sunburned and perspiring men."[14] Commission film footage shows just that: Shirtless workers hand-chopping old-growth trees while smoking cigarettes, and then half-heartedly dragging the branches to brush piles.

Away from the constant noise and chaos of the clearing project, seeds were quietly planted. The Commission had either purchased or partnered with a number of local farms and nurseries, some in the valley itself and others just outside the flood area. Here, botany-focused engineers, under the direction of Russ Snow, began to grow the seedlings of the trees that eventually would cover the Quabbin watershed. The trees grown in Enfield nurseries would be transplanted elsewhere once the valley started to flood.

Teams of engineers in long-sleeved white dress shirts crouched on their haunches in the summer sun and methodically seeded red pine, the first of many tree species.[15] The Commission's plan for the watershed was to have an environmentally sound and aesthetically harmonious canopy of native trees that grew at the same rate, and quickly. Many millions of trees would need to be planted in just four years.

By the end of May, there were more woodpeckers in the valley than residents and engineers combined. A temporary state police substation had to be set up in Enfield. The jobs were legally only open to Massachusetts residents, but men from all over the country were arriving and the valley was now worried about crime in an area where crime other than public drunkenness was seldom heard of.

The woodpeckers drank; they were loud; they played pool and packed local beaches and dance clubs; they got into car accidents; they flirted aggressively with whatever local girls remained in the area. Police as far away as Northampton were watching them, particularly as so many valley houses were already standing empty.

Around three hundred ultimately were "sent home." More than twenty were convicted of public drunkenness, with their sentences suspended "provided they go away and stay away." Anyone found to have a previous criminal record was also immediately dismissed from the project.[16]

The woodpeckers had their own weekly newspaper, *Quabbin News*, and a literary magazine of sorts called *Hello!, Timber!* A highlight of *Quabbin News* was a gossip column called "I Sawed U an' Axed U," which was heavy on the inside jokes and good-natured ribbing: "John P. Barry: How is it John that you go out with a girl once and then her mother keeps her in for six months?"; "Joe Kornickowski is not a cake eater by any means, but he goes heavy for 'cookies' after supper. Nice taste, Joe."

The newspaper also had bus schedules, advertisements for "Bob Garlo and His Broadcasting Band at the New Ain's Beach Club, featuring Free Bathing, Free Picnic Grove and Beer on Tap"; a list of movies playing in

Springfield and Palmer (*Charlie Chan at the Circus* and Humphrey Bogart in *Two Against the World*); and informational articles like "British Sailors' Slang Covers All Conditions" and "Auto Racing."[17]

The senior engineers tasked with administration found themselves doing fewer technical assignments and more administrative damage control. LeRoy Hammond found himself in an increasingly uncomfortable position: a division engineer turned director of a project that functioned somewhere between an overpopulated boys' summer camp and a group of sixty chain gangs. He was also in charge of the cemetery exhumation project, personally signing off on most coffins moved from native graveyards to Quabbin Park Cemetery. Even Winsor, who disliked stooping to such petty levels of management, found himself, at the request of the state's Division of Food and Drugs, asking Hammond to provide information about the price and safety of "ice cream, tonic, etc." and the business practices of the roadside vendors who were selling them to the clearing crews.[18]

Commission board member Karl Kennison was a point man for reporters from across the state who continued to find the clearing project a fun summertime diversion, and who sometimes adjusted the facts to make their subject more compelling. Kennison and *Boston Globe* reporter Max Grossman had a series of back-and-forth letters where Kennison gently chastised Grossman for inaccurate reporting on his draft of a *Globe* Sunday feature piece about the Quabbin ("the correct name of the Commission is on our letterhead, above"; "the Daniel Shays Highway is not Rte. 9.").[19]

Curley loathed Eugene Hultman—an MIT graduate who himself knew his way around city and state government—and did his best to smear his reputation. But zingers were hard to find. The best Curley could think up was that Hultman had taken manure from horses owned by the City of Boston and had it trucked to his country house to use as fertilizer. So Hultman was especially circumspect in giving the most positive spin on the clearing project for the *Boston Globe*'s "Beacon Hill Merry-Go-Round" column, most certainly read by Curley and his Governor's Council:

My men have done a great job getting going. Today we have 2200 working there . . . A splendid group of boys. I am delighted . . . Boys who really want a job . . . At a guess their average age is about 21 . . . Supervision is a problem. Many of them never swung an axe or a grub hoe before . . . Keep them well spread out or they'll chop each other's legs off . . . As soon as we can we are going to get some portable radios for the different groups . . . If a man cuts an artery or something we want to know about it without waiting two hours for them to be carried out of the woods . . . It's a fine thing to take young men off relief and give them a Summer working in the woods. [20]

The project was growing wildly, for the engineers as well as the clearing crews. Groups of new junior engineers, sometimes days after college graduation, were hired every week and unceremoniously dumped in the middle of the valley.

Senior Civil Engineer Laroy Harris, in charge of the sixty-plus clearing crews, probably had the most thankless job on the Commission that summer. Harris had to move from Ware to Enfield to supervise the clearing crew supervisors, and his memos reveal a man overwhelmed by the sheer number and ineptitude of his charges:

June 5: "TO ALL INSPECTORS: Please do not send the doctors into the field for 'old injuries.' The doctor's office has regular hours."

June 30: "TO ALL INSPECTORS: Will you please patrol your section at least one-half hour after quitting time each night for better control of fires."

July 7: "TO ALL INSPECTORS: Many workers have lost their badges. Any worker in the field who does not have his faces immediate termination."

July 16: "TO ALL INSPECTORS: Each Foreman and First Aid Man shall be instructed *not* to fly the Red Cross Flag except in case of an accident that requires the immediate attention of a Doctor. A Red Cross Flag must not be flown for minor cuts and scratches."

July 18: "TO ALL INSPECTORS: All poison ivy and dogwood treatment should be administered on site by the project medic, not a doctor."

July 24: "TO ALL INSPECTORS: There seems to have been an unusually large number of axe handles broken. Please investigate."

July 30: "TO ALL INSPECTORS: Workers *will* be laid off if they cannot provide ID in the field."

August 6: "TO ALL INSPECTORS: It has been brought to my attention that a large number of axes and brush hooks have been damaged to such an extent that they are of no further use. It appears that [tools] have been, and possibly are now being used as hammers, and/or wedges. Will you see that this practice is stopped."[21]

When a woodpecker was killed by a falling tree in mid-July, Harris was in charge of both collecting data on the accident and informing the family.

All of Hampshire County dreaded Wednesday paydays, "when the Ware bank kept open after hours to cash workers' checks, a weekly pay roll of 20 to 40 thousand dollars. Police were stationed along Main St. and inside the bank to handle the rush, and it was a common sight to see the bronze-tinted bare torsos leaping out of running automobiles, all anxious to get the first place in the lengthy line."[22]

The engineering teams, even the desk jockeys, were struggling through the hot and bothered summer as well. "One of the problems we had in Enfield," said Ellis Barbier, "was that up in the back of the Barlow House we had two rooms—a darkroom and a room for mounting pictures. Sometimes in the summer there was no water. You'd go to look at the pictures and there was supposed to be this big thing swirling around, and it was half full of sand with no water! Well, we'd just have to take them out and wait until the next day, until the pumps would pump some water in there, and we'd start in again and wash them.

"We made our own paste, too, for those thousands of pictures, with flour and water."[23]

Eighty-five years later, that paste is still attached to the linen pages of the Commission's photography books.

The Enfield Congregational Church Fire

What little joy remained to the old-timers was bound up with the Enfield Congregational Church, which was about to have its 150th anniversary. The church property had been sold to the Commission in 1934 for $40,000 and, unlike some of the other churches in the valley, was set to be destroyed rather than moved. But the physical church building with its grand spire, the visual symbol of Enfield, was still in fine condition, and a celebration was planned for the morning of Sunday, August 9. Reverend John S. Curtis planned to come out of retirement and give a heartening sermon. Invitations to present and past parishioners had been mailed out. The church choir practiced enthusiastically Friday evening, July 31.

At 4:20 A.M. on Saturday, August 1, church sexton and custodian Louis Jones was woken by a knock on his door. Three unidentified young men stood on his doorstep. "The Town Hall is on fire!" they shouted, then got into a car and sped away.[24]

The solid brick town hall was intact. The fire was on the other side of the town common: The wooden Congregational church, the chapel, the house next door, and the garage and barn behind it were all in flames. Jones could not get inside without help. He noticed another small fire burning in the Enfield Grange; Jones traced it to the Grange bathroom, where a fire had been set with rags soaked with gasoline stuffed into the toilet. Jones used a fire extinguisher to put it out. By that time, the Enfield Fire Department was on its way.

Residents of Enfield Center rushed outdoors in their nightclothes, the soft summer predawn obliterated by raging towers of fire and smoke. "I got up go to the bathroom, and I looked out the window, and my god, the sky was just red. And of course we all got dressed and went down," recollected Trudy Ward Stalbird Terry.[25] Enfielders still living in the grand homes closest to the church ran back and forth between the houses and Enfield Common with armfuls of valuables, flinging them onto the grass in the middle of the common in case their homes were ignited by the blaze.

The Enfield Fire Department's hoses were not up to the job; the water had to be pumped in from the Swift River and flow several hundred feet uphill to town. Fire crews rumbled in from Belchertown, Ware, Dana, Petersham, Barre, and New Salem. Engineers Paul Radasch and Norman Hall and clearing crew chief Robert Fryer dragged groups of sleeping woodpeckers from their bunks, jammed tanks of water on their backs, and ordered them to wet down hose lines near the fires. Local journalists began arriving, driving fast in the dark on country roads to make it to Enfield while the church was still aflame. Meanwhile, Dr. Segur took charge of the out-of-town fire departments, directing the fire chiefs and personally stamping out the many small blazes springing up from the flying embers.[26]

A crime, as well as an emergency, was in progress. Police stood sentry at either end of Enfield Center and police and civilian guards climbed on roofs so that no car or pedestrian could get in or out of the area without being approached and having its license plate numbers taken.

It was almost sunrise. The church steeple was consumed. Above the steeple was another steeple made of fire. The church roof had completely burned away. The arched windows glowed yellow, as if there were a party inside. The firemen had given up on trying to save the church, and instead focused on saving nearby homes and businesses.

At around 6:00 A.M., the church collapsed. The blackened wooden floorboards dropped into the cellar, taking down with them the mahogany pulpit, organ, pews, and choir balcony. The roof collapsed next, then the flaming steeple, weather vane, and the molten church bell, all crashing into the earthen pit. The church took down with it the few power lines that provided electricity to Enfield Center. They too sparked and had to be hosed down.

"Oh god, it was horrible. That lonely gap in the Enfield sky—that broke our hearts," said Ward Stalbird Terry.[27]

The fire was smoldering by 7:00 A.M. The weather vane, the life-size metal man that a young Francis Underwood imagined writhing in agony as the wind blew, lay in the ashes.

Police and rooftop guards stayed until afternoon. Enfielders helped one another collect their belongings from the Common and bring them back inside, but no one could imagine sleeping, or working. Arson was suspected immediately; the fire had started in the church's committee room, and then spread in the direction opposite the wind.

Three investigations were begun immediately: one by the Enfield board of selectmen, headed by Dr. Segur; one by the Commission, headed by LeRoy Hammond; and one by the state fire marshal. The town would not have power for several days. Damage was assessed at $75,000, or nearly $1.5 million in today's dollars.

One of the few items from the church that could be saved was the $2,500 organ and accompanying sheet music belonging to Anna Knight, wife of Charles S. Knight, recently appointed "special agent" to the Commission.

Enfield was close to panic. Someone reported that a group of wood-peckers in a car drove by him and said, "You haven't seen the half of it yet; wait until next week," before driving off again. Rumors floated that the "half of it" would be the conflagration of the Commission's Enfield offices. Or was the "fire bug" someone intent on wiping out the whole village, someone who would rather see it leveled than underwater? Some suspected that the criminal was an angry worker fired from the project, or the same person who had been accused of setting seven forest fires the previous summer. The Enfield office immediately started taking fingerprints. Gawkers arrived from across Western Massachusetts, staring at the smoldering wooden uprights until the police shooed them away.[28]

The task forces could not make a match with the arsonist's fingerprints.

The situation was too much, said the *Ware River News*, for the old-timers to handle: "The older residents, who have accepted even the loss of homes with gentle fortitude, find the loss of their beautiful old church . . . almost unbearable. Words cannot explain the tragedy of the way in which it had to come down from its hillside vantage, whence it has looked out upon the generations come and go, from ox carts to airplanes, pausing each in its turn for the time of prayer and the great ceremonials of life."[29] Behind the burnt-out church, the cemetery was full of empty graves and toppled headstones, because even that week, more remains had been removed from the churchyard and trucked to Quabbin Park Cemetery.

The Sunday morning church services of August 2 were held at the Masonic Lodge. New invitations to the 150th anniversary commemoration were mailed out, this time announcing that the ceremony would be held in the town hall.

The Enfield Congregational Church's parishioners were once so numerous that the Sunday school had three hundred pupils. About 225 people in total came to the August 9 commemoration, many of them recent refugees from the valley. Observers noted that it the service felt more like a reunion than a remembrance.

Reverend Curtis led the call to worship, reading from the 1913 *Congregational Church Book of Worship and Song*. The psalms added to the program and read responsively were all about loss and displacement:

> *By the rivers of Babylon, there we sat down, yea, we wept, when we remembered Zion.*
> *We hanged our harps upon the willows in the midst thereof.*
> *For there they that carried us away captive required of us a song;*

and they that wasted us required of us mirth, saying, Sing us one of
the songs of Zion.
    How shall we sing the Lord's song in a strange land?[30]

Parishioners were told to bring their own box lunches. Everyone ate in the town hall afterward.

No one was ever charged with setting the Enfield Congregational Church fire.

Some years later, the *Ware River News* reported that former Enfield resident and Congregational Church treasurer Fred Zappey was giving out dinner bells. According to the newspaper, "Little chrome-plated dinner bells of about four inches in height are finding their way into many Western Mass. Homes as tuneful reminders of the fate of the Enfield Congregational church . . . The church bell . . . fell into the cellar and later was melted to provide a smaller bell for the New Salem church. From the metal that was left over, the little dinner bells have been made and are being disposed of . . . Some of the former church members are having the dinner bells, which are of a suitably melodic tone, suitably inscribed."[31]

The Waning of the Year

By the end of the summer, nineteen Quabbin workers had died in accidents: Twelve on the Ware River project; two each on the Enfield–Greenwich tunnel and on the dike; and three at the main dam. Those were only the on-site deaths. They did not include the "indirect deaths," like the man, according to the *Ware River News*, "who was burned alive while sleeping in a labor camp on the tunnel job," or the several who died of pneumonia caused by working in the tunnels. One man fell down 240 feet between two caissons at the dam.[32]

Bob Ward drank himself to death while he worked on the Quabbin Park Cemetery project. Ward, the older brother of Ruth Ward Howe and Trudy Ward Stalbird Terry, was reputedly already an alcoholic and the cemetery job was difficult. Then his fiancée died in a freak accident in an elevator in New York City. Ward was thirty-five, and his death was one of the factors that led Trudy and Jim Stalbird to leave the valley that year.

Engineer Frank Fahlquist took a three-month leave of absence without pay from the project, then resigned at the end of October. LeRoy Hammond left that same month and found a much more satisfying position as a division engineer for the New York State Board of Water Supply, where he worked until near his death in 1963.[33]

In September, there were still two thousand workers on the clearing project, but everyone, resident and engineer, was too fatigued to be outraged anymore. The reporters had largely gotten bored. Those two thousand men got aboard forty chartered buses and were transported to Boston for the day to vote in the primaries. The Commission did not pay them for their missed work.

Red and Norway pines were added to the seedlings at Thurston Nursery, one of the many local nurseries the Commission had purchased for growing watershed trees.

Clearing work was 90 percent done by October. Curley wanted to keep his boys on the job for as long as possible, but on November 10, Hultman informed the governor that the project was going to be shut down in shifts through the end of the year. On that same day, the first ever Social Security Act registrations were mailed out to New England residents from the post office at Boston's South Station, less than a mile from Commission headquarters.[34]

As large numbers of woodpeckers began to leave the valley in November, four thousand tools also went missing. Dr. Segur commented that supervisors were still "finding axes and saws under brush piles, hidden away by thieves who never got around to retrieving them."[35] The *Ware River News* reported that "An entire crew of Quabbin workers was discharged . . . by officials investigating the destruction of tool boxes and disappearance of tools . . . Reservoir officials are wondering if some of the discharged workers are planning to cut down the trees in Boston Common."[36]

The workers sent a telegram to the incoming governor, Democrat Charles Hurley, who was visiting Washington, DC, at the time, warning,

"Mass meeting of 400 workers tonight requested unanimously to request you order continuance of clearing project until you get opportunity to investigate matter on your return to Boston. Eight hundred telegrams following to Acting Governor tomorrow. Please act before we lose our jobs."[37]

It is unclear whether those telegrams were ever received. By the beginning of 1937, only about two hundred woodpeckers remained. The annual Commission report for 1936, wrote one wag journalist, scrupulously did not discuss the quality of their work, nor did Frank Winsor's write-up of the project. The *Ware River News* published a goodbye cartoon of a male fashion model wearing outrageously baggy farmer overalls and carrying a hoe; the caption was "Good-Bye, Woodpeckers! You've given us a lot of thrills."[38]

A poem called "The Last of the Woodpeckers" from the January 26, 1937, and final, edition of the Quabbin project newspaper, ended like this:

The once verdant valley, Quabbin by name,
Is now so denuded it blushes in shame;
It calls for the waters to cover its head
And allow it to join with its ancestral dead.

But the "woodpecker" chirps, he is happy and gay,
Says the work in Old Quabbin was nothing but play;
Some wages he saved; the rest? hear him yell,
It's all over now. What's next? What the Hell.[39]

Governor Curley lost his 1936 Senate race to a moderate Republican, Henry Cabot Lodge Jr., by a sizable margin, which stood in contrast to the general election, in which Democratic President Franklin D. Roosevelt received 523 delegates, or 98.5 percent of the nation's electoral votes.

Curley's defeat was aided, presumably, by the 150 registered voters in Enfield—both native and engineer.

TWELVE

The Calm Before: 1937

James Michael Curley no longer ruled Beacon Hill, and in 1937 several state legislators suddenly became publicly concerned about the Quabbin project's price tag. A few even suggested that work on the project be slowed so that Metropolitan Boston's residential water taxes could be spread out more evenly over the next several years.

Realistically, it was too late for a slowdown; construction was about to move to 24/7/360+ schedule. Once work picked up for the spring, it would not stop—ever—until the valley was flooded. For those stationed at the Enfield job site, winter had stopped most everything but administrative work; labor was slated to restart in March or early April.

The perpetual work schedule affected everyone still living in the valley as well as Commission employees. "One day, a summer evening," said Bill Segur, "my father and I stood on the porch in Enfield—he had finished his day's work—and it was still, because it was a quiet little town. But you could hear the rumble of power shovels—steam shovels—not far away. They were excavating the earth for the Goodnough Dike. I was quite young, but I remember clear—he said, 'Bill, they're diggin' our life right out from under us.'"[1]

Most of the fresh crop of engineering graduates being hired were not going to be placed at the reservoir and other Swift River projects. Instead, the Commission needed young surveyors for the next phase of the construction—the so-called "pressure tunnels" that would move Quabbin water from the Wachusett to the Norumbega reservoir in Weston. LeRoy Hammond, who had held the Enfield office together, had left at the end of 1936.[2] The engineering force at the reservoir was aging—more engineers had wives and children to think about—and were getting burnt out by both the six- or seven-day work weeks and the grim living situation in the valley. The work did not stop, and the amount of energy and number of bodies necessary to do it seemed increasingly insufficient.

This depletion did not escape Frank Winsor, who recommended a 25 percent increase in personnel, and who announced in a memo to the Commission in March 1937 that the "work under way and in prospect is of such volume that no further reduction in the engineering force can be made at this time, and as the construction season begins it will be necessary to increase the force in the lower grades . . . It is of the utmost imprint that the faithful service of our employees be given recognition by promotions and increases as therein recommended. Thirty-four resignations during the past eighteen months indicated that men have received and are receiving better offers, and with the opening of the construction season further resignations of men who should not be spared may be looked for with practical certainty unless salaries are increased. In order to preserve the esprit de corps of the organization and to hold a proper organization together, it is essential that faithful service be given recognition."[3]

Engineer diaries from 1937 depict the monotony, complexity, and relentlessness of the work that year. In March there were at least nine active contracts, including the core wall at the main dam, the embankment at the dike, construction of buildings over the shafts, and new roads. Three of the projects were either in litigation or lawsuits were imminent. The incipient construction of the Administration Building next to the dam would require at least one contract. Inspecting Engineer Millard Aubrey was assigned to the main dam site. Entries for May 1937 include:

Wednesday, May 19, 1937
 First sluicing today—
 Started system at 1:00PM worked intermittently until 4:30PM. LeTourneau supply dry box from adjacent area. Material sluiced to NW corner of beach.
 Road scraper harrowing surface of impervious.
 Hydraulic plant—Crew working on terminals and small changes developed by sluicing. Crew at dry box cleaning up and cutting roadway into stone pit. Crew working on sluice lines. Electricians working on pole lines for light towers. Repairing leaks in clear water lines.
 New shovel arrived. Today (Marion)

Saturday, May 22, 1937
 Hydraulic plant ran 5 hrs. 6 min. Placed 3181 yds on south side at west end. Shovel #20 leading wagons also 5 scrapers.
 Carpenters building sections of movable conveyor.
 Preparing for concrete at water supply tank.
 Electricians working on flood light towers.
 Cleaning off ledge at west end. Setting forms for concrete.

Sunday, May 23, 1937
 Misc. work on hydraulic plant. [4]

Division Engineer William Peabody's work also included unwanted legal headaches:

Friday, June 25, 1937
 Weather: Fair
 Attended Snow Co. hearing in Boston. LaRoy Harris telephoned in morning that contractor had done nothing about repairs to washout on Contract 55. Also stated that State Highway Department has requested that warning signs be placed on Contracts 55

and 57. Told Harris to see that this was taken care of in a satisfactory manner.

Saturday, June 26, 1937
  Weather: Fair
  Visited Shaft 8 office and Enfield office. Looked over correspondence and visited dam and dike. Saw Mr. Gow and discussed work on Contract 52.

Monday, June 28 – Tuesday, June 29, 1937
  Weather: Rain
  Attended Snow Co. hearing in Boston. [5]

The photographers also kept diaries. Stuart Pike's January 4 entry included a record of photographing the "John A. Dennison prop., showing property line," followed by "Developed, titled, printed, and mounted the above and also photos of the Addison Moore ice house."[6]

Despite the Quabbin project's staggering budget, all the engineers taking photographs were still sharing the same single camera that had been purchased for them a decade earlier. Finally, in 1937, they received a new one: an Agfa with a five-inch-by-seven-inch lens so that the new photographs would match the old ones (all photographs were put into photo books labeled by contract or, in the case of the cemetery and real estate, by subject).[7]

Stuart Pike and Ellis Barbier were still photo buddies. "We took progress and record pictures of every single thing that was done in this area," said Barbier in 1993. "They made special elevated platforms for us to stand on when we photographed the dam. We took pictures every week. And we photographed every gravestone, and every house and barn."[8]

They also went outside the valley to the towns of Rutland and Holden and photographed there, because the infrastructure was going to be part of the ware river watershed.

Pike was the outdoorsman, Barbier the tech guy. "[Pike] was out all the time, takin' pictures. I did the inside work: developing, printing, mounting pictures on photo mount cloth, puttin' them into albums, and typing the pertinent information to go with the photographs. I tried to keep it in alphabetical order on the real estate deals, different contracts—I don't even know how many contracts—it was close to 100—even the contracts of the little things." [9]

In March, Bun Doubleday had had enough—both of living in his deteriorating community and working for the Commission. With a college engineering degree, a fair amount of personal wealth, and a lot of social capital from his old and comparatively affluent family, Doubleday was one of the few valley natives who could move easily between the two worlds.

It was difficult for him, though, to watch his family's history be destroyed. When he was asked by an interviewer in 1980 what it was like to work on the project, "in effect participating in the destruction" of his own home, he said, "I just didn't stop to think about it. It was a job, and it was a good job, and my wife and I had a comfortable living, and that was really about all we considered about it. Once in a while, when the subject came up, we said 'oh, it's too bad that the work has to be this, but at least it's work anyway, and we were getting paid for it.' I had to accept it from a practical standpoint. We were in a bad depression, and I was delighted to have a job that enabled me to get married and start having a family, and I was more fortunate than many, because a great many couldn't find a job anywhere." [10]

Doubleday left the valley for Keene, NH, to start "Farrar and Doubleday, an electric motor repair business." [11] At this point every new crack in the carefully balanced valley society was noticeable and painful, particularly among the women. Luckily the Quabbin Club would not let Mrs. Doubleday go quietly. *Ware River News* society page reporter Iola Downing wrote:

> Mrs. Doubleday was tendered a complete surprise, going-away party by several of her friends at the home of Mrs. Jerome L.

Spurr, with Mrs. Norman D. Hall and Mrs. Edward N. Sheffield in attendance.

During the evening three tables of bridge were enjoyed with prize winners as follows: First, Mrs. Clifton Wells; second, Mrs. Russell Thornquist; and consolation, Mrs. John Toelkin.

Mrs. Edward N. Sheffield with pleasing and appropriate words presented Mrs. Doubleday, guest of honor, a walnut Priscilla sewing cabinet, from her many friends. The evening's pleasure was brought to a close with the serving of delicious refreshments by the three hostesses. [12]

In fact, Russell and Barbara Thornquist and their family were going to move immediately into the Doubleday home once the Doubledays left; the house had just been purchased by the Commission, [13] and engineers frequently moved from house to house, either out of choice or because the property was next in the schedule to be demolished.

New Homes for Buildings

Most buildings in the valley were just razed. But the surrounding area now was being dotted by transplanted buildings as well as transplanted people. Some were moved in their entirety on truck beds, usually short distances away. One house was purchased by Amherst College; a schoolhouse found its way onto the Mount Holyoke College campus. A church was moved to Pelham; another church, from Prescott, became one of the two buildings of the Swift River Valley Historical Society in New Salem. One house was transported as far as Staten Island. In 1937, at least seventeen valley buildings were hauled north to Dorset, VT, by a former tour guide turned antique home builder.

Charles Wade used to drive summer residents around Dorset in a horse and buggy, where people talked to him about all the old homes they had seen in other vacation spots. The automobile put him out of business, but he was inspired to change careers after a discussion with a woman who told him she wished she could bring a colonial-era house from Massachusetts to Vermont.

So Wade became, in modern terminology, a "house flipper." He bought cheap from the Commission or from individuals—he tried to offer families more money than the Commission—then dismantled the buildings, shipped them up by truck, rebuilt and refurbished them, and sold them to wealthier people at a large markup. He was a skilled marketer, playing on the 1930s fads for antiques and "authentic" Yankee culture.

Wade's grand prize was the Robert Field house, which had been built by the founder of Enfield in 1777 and had been lived in continually ever since. The Ward children—Trudy, Ruth, and Bob—had been born in it in the first decade of the twentieth century. A reporter from the *Christian Science Monitor* gushed over its three upper-story rooms that could be made into one by "swinging up hanging partitions and hooking them to the ceiling." The upstairs also had a bench and a "fiddler's throne," two-foot-wide chestnut paneling, and "paneled doors and closets and cupboards to delight the heart of an antiquarian."[14] (The Field house still stands in Dorset and can be visited as part of a larger annual tour of Quabbin houses.)

Susan Lord of Chicago, a Dorset summer resident, decided that her grandchildren should have a play house on her property. She turned to Wade, who presented her with the Prescott District School. "With very little remodeling," said the article, "this sturdy building was reconstructed at Mrs. Lord's home, where it rings again with the merry sounds of frolicking youngsters."[15] Presumably the children of Prescott who attended that school never found out how it had been repurposed.

For valley kids and teens, the empty cellar holes were less mournful and more a source of adventure. Norman Heidel and Bill Fielding climbed to the top of Quabbin Mountain where the Woods house had stood. It had been destroyed, but the lumber remained. In the middle of the violet fields, they built a fort with the remnants, and camped out in it.[16]

The *Times* Likes What It Sees

The *New York Times* finally decided in 1937 that the Quabbin project was worth covering. A reporter from the "Newspaper of Record" was now at the actual dam construction site. In a May 23 article, the reporter conveyed how impressed, like everyone else, he was at the scale of the construction:

> The first loads of the 500,000 tons of earth and rock which will constitute the big Quabbin Dam on the Swift River to provide an additional reservoir for the metropolitan supply of Boston were dumped this week.
>
> A large part of the earth for use in constructing the dam, which will be 150 feet high, will come from near-by areas and will be shot down to the dam site from a hilltop through twenty-inch rubber lined pipes. These pipes will have a capacity of 800 cubic yards per hour.
>
> The earth will be dropped into a huge hopper at the top of the hill, mixed with thousands of gallons of water and then shot to the dam location, while four pumps of great power, placed on a barge floating on an artificial lake, will force water to the hilltop to form a continuous operation of the work. [17]

While this was a neat summary of the work being done, the *Times* also had praise for the related project at the dam site: "High lookout towers have been built for setting up large searchlights to make night operations as practical as work during the daytime. Loud-speakers will be put on these towers to enable officials to transfer orders from point to point over the field of work." [18]

To anyone living within ear- or eyeshot of the dam site, construction noise and light would never stop, including in the middle of the night and on Sundays. To a modern reader it is eerily reminiscent of the descriptions of prison camps.

Articles on the front page of the *Times* that day included "Kennedy Pledges Merchant Marine to Equal Any Rival"; "Eckener Lays Airship Fire to Static and Leaking Gas"; "WPA Offices here Picketed by 6,000 Scoring Fund Cut"; and "18 Catholic Printing Shops Reported Seized by Nazis."[19]

By June, all the shrubbery nominally felled by the woodpeckers had grown in. A good chunk of their pecking had been rendered useless. Photos show engineers standing, bemused, in front of seven-foot-tall flowering bushes that weren't supposed to be there at all. Another clearing crew would have to come in to finish the job in 1938.

The Greenwich baffle dam, designed to circulate water from the less-clean Ware River through Swift River water until it was so diluted the impurities were undetectable, was nearly finished. To build it, the Commission had torn down Walker's Mill, where most of Greenwich storekeeper and town council member Stanwood King's family had worked; Commission agent Roy Kimball had moved into the nearby Walker home itself, and became the de facto Commission head for Greenwich.

Walter King (no immediate relation to Stanwood King) worked as a "sand hog" on the baffle dam contract, which was a comparatively quick job. "The first thing they did there was tear down the houses, the school house . . . this was in Greenwich Village. They dug a little canal for the water to go one way, and just to the west of it they dug a big ditch there, and after they got that they plugged up the canal. Actually speaking, there were two baffle dams out there, the main baffle dam and what they called the 'south' baffle dam.

"I was running a lot of sand. I was keeping the vehicles loaded and making sure they were being taken up to the hopper. They needed to make concrete." Luckily, Greenwich was at one time the shore of a glacial lake: "We didn't have to look very far for clay soil because there were some damn good clay banks near there. And some damn good sand banks too."[20]

Stanwood King owned a store almost literally on top of where the dam was to be built. "Well, [the construction crews] came in there," said King in 1975, laughing, "and they started tearing things to pieces. They tore the bridge off—the bridge that went across by the mill—and then they tore the dam out—there were big turtles under that bridge. Supposedly there's a turtle that came back to the dam every year."

"When they started dumpin' the stones [for the dam] it forced the turtles out and they started coming out behind the store!" King's store manager, Dorothy Moult, added.[21]

In 1936, woodpeckers had been most of Stanwood King's customers. In 1937, the customers were a combination of engineers working on the baffle dam and remaining locals—nearly all of whom were renting back their houses from the Commission and who didn't want to make the effort even to travel to Enfield for provisions.

King, who was also a Greenwich selectman and the police chief, took advantage. "They called me 'High,' because Clorox was 20 cents to the gallon! They used to come into the store and say, 'How's High today?'" Then it occurred to him that he might be able to make some extra money by collecting leftover memorabilia, however scrappy, from Greenwich—and, if no one wanted it, then he could keep it for himself. "I've got the mailbox from Greenwich, a piece of clapboard from the school and also a big school bell from the school. They were going to destroy the school, and I took the bell—my father and grandfather had also gone to that school and were summoned by that bell."[22]

Where the foliage was still unravaged, summer was as beautiful as ever. Flower beds grew around empty cellar holes. Abandoned gardens were lush. But the buildings left standing were sagging, unpainted, and a good deal of them were uninhabited, and uninhabitable. A Commission photo shows an empty Enfield Common, its Civil War honor roll and cannon still intact for now. But behind the common, where the Congregational church stood, there's nothing—just a pile of blackened bricks and half a burnt iron gate, which used to open up into the terraced cemetery. Now there was very little cemetery left; most of the graves had been moved to Quabbin Park Cemetery, which was nearing completion.[23]

Congregational church services were being held at the town hall. This confused the Congregational Home Missionary Society, which had sent representatives to Enfield after the Enfield church burned down, asking the church deacons for the leftover money from the congregation. Congregational church headquarters in Boston was unaware that the congregation still existed and was still collecting money from its parishioners.[24]

Fewer people—and no more woodpeckers—in the Quabbin equaled less crime. As Enfield deputy sheriff, Commission Special Agent Charles Knight's prime crime involvement in 1937 was transporting a drunk ice-truck driver to Ware police headquarters, after driving to the nearby Spurr home and taking a deposition of the man whose truck had nearly been front-ended. (The driver spent a month in the Hampshire County Jail in Northampton.)[25]

Apprehending minor criminals was a comparatively easy aspect of Knight's job. He was also the rent collector for Commission-owned properties, and people usually paid him in cash—unless they were hard up and then asked for barter. Knight traveled in his state car with two German shepherds; perhaps this was both a form of intimidation and self-protection when he carried that much cash. "He went into a lot of empty houses," said Norman Heidel. "He had the dogs with him because it was a spooky job. A lot of back roads and dead-end roads."

Because the empty houses were Commission-owned, the Commonwealth had rights to whatever was left behind, and sometimes, according to Heidel, Knight took advantage of that. "The rumor was he went into old houses and took stuff he thought would become valuable. He took an old weather vane from a mill, and somehow, after his death, the weather vane sold for more than $80,000."[26]

Construction had also begun on the Quabbin Administration Building and associated structures. The Administration Building would be the permanent nerve center for the Quabbin project after the flood. Uphill of the dam's south edge, and, before the flood, on the Enfield-Belchertown Road near Route 9, it was to be an impressive solid-brick Georgian Colonial with three stories, two outbuildings, a hangar for a water plane, and spectacular views right down the center of the reservoir. It would house offices, labs, storage, equipment, vehicles, and even engineer dormitories. And it would forever watch over the dam, the park, and the nearby shafts.

Very few state engineers worked on the construction of their new headquarters; it was purely a construction job, and the engineers themselves were consumed by the day-to-day exigencies of the dam and dike.

In October, the Quabbin Club began its fortieth and final year. The *Springfield Union* printed a photo of the group standing under a large oak tree near the Enfield School, with the headline "Quabbin Club Opens Season, Perhaps Last—Group Feels Work on Reservoir Likely to Be Interruption Next Year."[27] Anna Chase Spurr was nominated president of the club for the 1937–1938 season. The first meeting, held at the still very intact Downing home, was a lecture by Newton, MA, author Sarah Pomeroy Rugg on "London During Two Coronations." Members talked about their "highlights of the summer," and agreed to the topics of the monthly Tuesday meetings, including an illustrated lecture by a Springfield professor called "Three Thousand Miles in the British Isles." All committees, headed by one local and one engineer wife, were still engaged. The club's flower remained blue gentian; members were encouraged to wear gentian blue to meetings.[28] No minutes of these 1937 meetings still exist; perhaps the Quabbin Club members discussed what they'd be doing after the flood, or perhaps they chose not to discuss it at all.

At this point it was unclear when, exactly, everyone would have to vacate the valley. Molt had been threatening January 1, 1938, although mail service, electricity, and telephone would continue beyond that; people had also heard April and even July. It was no longer pleasant to live in the valley, even for the die-hards who refused to go or the engineers who were so embedded in the work they didn't have time to commute. The landscape wasn't entirely bare, not yet. But the projects—dam, dike, baffle dam, aqueduct, and now Administration Building—were the focus of people's physical and psychological attention.

Fewer than twenty students were left at the Enfield Center school at the end of 1937, and, regardless of the official vacating day in 1938, the 1937–1938 school year would be the last in the valley. Nevertheless, the school, which—like the valley itself—felt strongly about tradition, decided to give its pupils one last year of annual Christmas exercises. On the evening of December 21, Enfielders—adult and child, native and engineer—congregated at the town hall for one final year of caroling, speeches, and a community presentation of *A Christmas Carol*.

After the little children came into the auditorium singing "Hark the Herald Angels Sing," young David Dyer greeted the audience. Other first- and second-graders gave short speeches; Marion Tryon read aloud from her essay "A Christmas Vow," while William Dickinson explained the nuances of "Writing to Santa Claus." Everyone sang "The First Noel" and "Joy to the World." The second act was a fairly elaborate presentation of the play with engineers Paul Radasch and Homer Briggs in the supporting roles. Everyone sang more carols with the cast as the curtain came down.[29]

THIRTEEN

Quabbin Park Cemetery

F inding new burial spots for more than seven thousand bodies and their headstones was supposed to be the Commission's way of giving back to the living, whose ancestors were scattered across multiple churchyards, town cemeteries, and private properties. Regardless, the reservoir water had to be pristine, with every impurity removed from both the flood area and the watershed around it.

The Commission had promised the Swift River Valley a cemetery location "in one of the most delightful spots in New England, far enough from the main highway to assure peace and quietude yet only a few minutes from the Berkshire Trail artery . . . A virgin woodland was selected and the work of removing trees, brush wood and rocks has begun. Enough trees will be left standing to preserve the natural beauty of the spot. Hills and valleys are abundant enough to provide a pleasing contour."[1]

Valley residents were to be involved as much as practicable. At an Enfield town meeting in February 1928, the town voted to "give deeds to people who own unoccupied lots in the cemeteries in the town of Enfield."[2] In a November 1928 to memo to Frank Winsor, Division Engineer

LeRoy Hammond, who was in charge of the cemeteries, said, "Mr. Charles Felton, Selectman of the town, has made inquiries of me as to what might be the method adopted by the Commission relative to their acquisition of unoccupied cemetery lots owned by individuals. It appears that the object of the passage of the foregoing vote was to give lot owners a title in their lots whereby they would be able to release their rights to the Commission probably for financial consideration.

"I advised Mr. Felton," Hammond continued, "that it was my opinion that the Commission would provide a lot in the new cemetery equivalent to an owner's holding in the existing cemetery. He expressed the opinion that many owners would prefer to dispose of their lots for a financial consideration and purchase lots in a cemetery nearer to whatever location they themselves might move. I expressed to him the idea that the elements of financial gain should be eliminated from all matters to do with the cemeteries and that each case might be governed by its actual facts."[3]

In August 1932, at its monthly Boston meeting, the Commission held "that the cemeteries located within the Swift River area to be submerged and to be taken for reservoir purposes . . . the bodies therein shall be removed, and that the Secretary be authorized to notify the authorities having charge of these cemeteries that a suitable burial ground has been provided by the Commission and requesting that no further interments be made in those cemeteries."[4]

The Commission's logistical care of the dead involved, to start, many, many photographs. More than two thousand photos—one of each family plot or individual marker in all the valley's existing cemeteries, plus progress photos of Quabbin Park Cemetery's construction—were taken between 1928–1938, more photos of any individual work project other than real estate. Like most of the real estate photos, the early cemetery documentation fell to Chet Chetwynd.

Chetwynd drove to, then trudged through, plot after plot, cemetery after cemetery, setting up his camera each time, writing up meticulous notes on who was buried where, and taking serviceable photos to go with the notes. Then he drove back to the Enfield photo lab to mark and develop each photo. Chetwynd spent all of September 28, 1928, for example, at the Pine Grove Cemetery in North Dana. The grass around the graves—some eighty years old, some eight—was unevenly mowed, as if individual families carefully cut the grass around specific groups of headstones while other headstones were ignored and obscured by tall grass. The weather was volatile; sometimes hot and sunny, with puffy clouds, then, abruptly, rain was imminent. It was tiring work, like nearly everything related to the Quabbin, and Chetwynd's photos turned a little careless at the end of the day.[5] The graves probably were abstracts to him; maybe it was a depressing process, or he just thought about it as work. But every photo he took mattered deeply to a local family.

Later, Carl Remington and Russ Snow, coach of the Enfield Engineers baseball team, took up the cemetery burden for Chetwynd, and, starting in 1932, Stuart Pike was the photographer for the acreage that gradually became the cemetery. Photography continued up through the end of World War II, increasingly on the development of the cemetery itself as the small graveyards were emptied. One of the last photos of the cemetery, taken in 1946, includes the first image of a non-white person in the Commission's catalogue: a gardener or groundskeeper standing in front of the cemetery's tool shed.

In some cases, residents were more upset about the idea of graves being dug up than of the living being forcibly turned out of their homes. "That cemetery part is the most heartbreaking," said one anonymous letter to the editor of the *Springfield Union*, "that our dear ones should be shoveled up and dumped into a box."[6] But the Commission wanted to reassure the worried descendants that the dis- and re-interment of the bodies was meticulous and professional, as carefully monitored and documented as every other aspect of the Quabbin project: "In the cemetery project each of the graves was surveyed; the tombstones photographed, every inscription was recorded and every deed copied. This tremendous task took many months to complete. The information was then assembled at headquarters in Enfield and a comprehensive filing system inaugurated, the latter so cross-indexed that data can be found immediately if the seeker has any information whatever regarding a burial."[7]

The Commission filled out three-inch-by-five-inch index cards for every re-interment. Data included the name of the deceased; information on the original burial (cemetery, year of birth and age at death, and the "lot representative"); re-interment (where in Quabbin Park, date, "box size," and the initials of the undertaker—usually Hammond); and "Other Bodies in Common Interest." Based on the dates on the cemetery cards, the graves were disinterred roughly in the order that the towns were destroyed: Prescott, Greenwich, Enfield, then Dana. These cards were moved to the Administration Building once it was built, and remain there today.

Every set of remains was carried to the cemetery in a hearse, as were remains re-interred in cemeteries other than Quabbin Park. Burial in Quabbin Park was free. If families wanted to bury elsewhere, the Commission would pay for the transport, but families had to buy the plot themselves. They also had to appear at the cemetery at a predetermined date and time; if they were not present, then the hearse would turn around, drive back to Quabbin Park Cemetery, and re-inter the body there.

If families chose Quabbin Park Cemetery, the Commission claimed it would try to arrange family plots in the same configuration they had lain at local cemeteries. This was true, up to a point. Despite the Commission's reputation for meticulousness, in the last rush to remove bodies from valley cemeteries before the flood, remains were buried in approximate, rather than exact, locations. People in the intervening years have complained of trouble finding their complete families. But it wasn't until 1998, during the first recorded dive into the Quabbin, that researchers realized how slipshod the cleanup process had become.

Out of more than 7,600 preconstruction graves, around 6,600 were ultimately buried at Quabbin Park. Records prior to 1985 indicate that people who chose to be buried there never left the immediate geographical area, although perhaps this was a self-selecting group. One woman who died in Connecticut in 1944 had the farthest to travel.

When the cemetery engineers didn't have enough information on the dead to determine where to put them, they turned to the Commission's list of old-timers in each town who might be able to provide more data.

The Commission had a sheet of "Sources of Information" for Enfield: "H. Clifton Moore: Undertaker and cemetery commissioner for some years. His father also was undertaker and commissioner before him. Records consisted of notes of funerals he had conducted. Living relatives and addressed were secured from him only through his memory." "Albert E. Randall: Caretaker of cemetery—about 85 years of age and has good memory—no written records—information obtained from him concerning relationship of bodies buried in the various lots." "Elizabeth K. Ritchie: Town Clerk for about 25 years; some information concerning old inhabitants. Copies of death certificate records in Town Records." "Several other old inhabitants were also interviewed as to the whereabouts of different parties."[8]

Being a gravedigger was considered by outsiders to be dangerous work. "Many weird tales have been circulated," said the *Springfield Republican*. "The rumors included that the men must submit to a rigid examination by physicians, then go into quarantine for two or three years to avoid the spread of disease . . . Other stories have spread that sealed caskets would be needed for the transfers, and that looting would have to be prevented."[9]

LeRoy Hammond laughed off these ideas and told reporters that grave moving and grave digging "was just an everyday job to the ordinary laborer." Hammond had "personally supervised each exhumation and his physique is ample contradiction of the rumor of unhealthy results."[10]

"A lot of people came here to take the cemetery job," said Ken Cross and Walter King in 1989. Adding another job title to their Quabbin work, they said had been gravediggers as well as sand hogs. According to Cross and King, cemetery workers came from all over. "They thought they were going to be paid $5 an hour. But they got $.65. If you worked the cemetery job—digging up graves—you got paid $3.60 a day. Period.

"You had people saying, 'oh my father come up here and got 50 bucks a day—he was in quarantine—he got a lot of shots'—there were a lot of wild stories—that they'd disinfect you and all this stuff," said Ken Cross. "A man come in to work digging graves, and he went to work and went home. The only shots he got was if he got a rusty nail.

"The undertaker got $50 a day. And he was there for every box. And a lot of 'em was just dust."

Walter King added: "They used a pine box. It was about 12 or 14 inches wide and about 4 feet long. That was for someone whose remains had been there so long they could do that. Now, for someone who hadn't been buried too long, they'd take out the coffin and put it in the new cemetery. If they dug up someone who had been there 20 or 30 years, they were in for a hard day's work, because the body would be in a certain amount of decomposition and a lot of odor, and the box would break up when you got it, so they used to bring concrete vaults in—I guess this was the first place that concrete vaults were ever used around this area."[11]

The official public opening of the cemetery was slated for Memorial Day 1938. The state purchased seven hundred wreaths to decorate the graves of every war veteran in the valley, and "four huge wreaths" to be placed on the town commons of each of the four towns.[12] But, said the *Springfield Republican*, "Work on completing the new gateway to Quabbin Park Cemetery has been hindered by a scarcity of old fieldstone used in construction of the entrance wall. Two granite tablets, to be set in the two corner posts of the wall, have arrived but will not be in place until next week due to the delay in obtaining stone. The tablets contain the name of the new cemetery, the state seal, names of the towns whose dead are buried in the cemetery and the names of the cemeteries from which the bodies were removed."[13] One of the tablets also contained the list of the commissioners, the assistant commissioners, and the chief engineer, some of whom would ultimately be buried at the cemetery themselves.

FOURTEEN

The End of Everything: 1938

Part I: Before the Dance

1938 was a year of "lasts" in the valley: last town meetings; last school year; last meetings of the fraternal and social clubs; last public events in Enfield, Dana, and Greenwich. The last opportunity to see your hometown as dry land. And the last to say you were from one of the four towns in the Swift River Valley, before they were removed from maps forever and replaced with water.

Olive Molt's oil paintings and pastels of the valley, mostly churches, old homes, quaint bridges, and rivers, were beginning to be exhibited in Boston and in the suburbs. Not terribly artful, they nevertheless conveyed a certain rustic pathos that dovetailed neatly with stories in the papers. Closer to the truth were the photographic shots she used for studies—bleak, simple views of half-destroyed forests with hewn tree trunks falling into ponds, or the post office and gas station at Greenwich Village, dwarfed and already made obsolete by a sixty-foot-high pile of stones that made up the baffle dam.

In the cold and muddy early spring, surrounded by bare trees and previous fall's decomposing leaves, a wrought-iron gate, attached to nothing, flapped open toward the empty graves up the hill from the burnt-out stones of the Enfield Congregational Church. The Quabbin Park Cemetery was almost ready for opening day; the valley cemeteries were largely abandoned. Flanked by wide pillars, the drive for the hearses to carry the bodies up the hill was torn up with muddy tire tracks—for taking the bodies back downhill. The remaining headstones looked like chipped, broken teeth.[1]

Commission photographers preferred to take real estate photos without any people in them. But without humans going about their daily lives, Enfield Center in its last days as a town looked puny and wistful. No one had raked the leaves from the previous fall, which had settled around the carefully planted trees from the previous century. The road around the common was rough. The sidewalks were packed earth, and breaking off in pieces. Just as people had stopped bothering to maintain their homes, the entire town had suffered from lack of maintenance, except what the Commission kept up for its own purposes.

The Commission had its own gas station now, so Coolbeth's Mobil, the last privately owned station in the valley, shut down. A Springfield paper was present to witness and photograph the last "gassing up."[2] The Swift River Hotel at the edge of the common, after being purchased by the Commission in 1931, was finally being torn down: By the end of January, the top two floors had been removed and only the portico and the lower halves of the front pillars remained intact.[3] There would be no more overnight visitors in Enfield.

In a family photograph, a man with his wife and adult daughter linger in front what is left of an Enfield Center storefront with their home on the second floor. Just a few years earlier, this same building was clean and well-kept, with white laundry flapping on the upstairs porch. Now it appears gutted, and one of the upstairs windows is broken. The store's plate-glass window and the neon signage remain intact, but a dismantled soda fountain or beer tap has been dragged out to the sidewalk in front of the building. The man looks at the camera angrily; the mother and daughter look grim and resigned.[4]

Aboveground was destruction; belowground construction continued. Inside the massive diversion tunnel, an inspection team slowly paddled through knee-deep water in a canoe. Engineer Gerry Albertine had been working on the diversion tunnel since dynamite blew open the first rock ledge in 1932, and he had a certain equanimity about spending days in the sloshing, echoing underground tunnel. Nor, as the head of the team, did he ever forget to wear his tie and fedora.

His work group of three engineers and a laborer seemed to have gotten the rhythm of the tunnel as well. Standing in the water next to the canoe in rubber hip waders, clearly cold and damp, they are also—amazingly— eating their lunches, nonchalantly pulling their sandwiches from brown paper bags while they hold their flashlights with their free hands.[5]

In February, Enfield held an election for town officials.

Elizabeth Ritchie was reelected town clerk with twenty-three votes, but Edward Sheffield, an engineer, got a write-in for three votes. Ritchie also was reelected for treasurer, again with twenty-three votes.

Three selectmen—Elliot Harwood, Donald Rowe, and Dr. Willard Segur—ran unopposed. All of the positions held one-year terms, but the assessor positions, won by Ed Dickinson and Fred Zappey, were three-year terms.[6]

Two months later, the towns held their final town meetings. On the night of April 8, twenty-six current and former Enfielders, all of them no longer property owners and thus technically ineligible to vote, gathered in the town hall during a historically late sleet storm to "witness the death" of Enfield town government. So did at least two reporters, one from the *Republican* and one from the *Ware River News.*

Traditionally the town meetings had been held upstairs in the main hall, but Dr. Segur decided it was too cold and damp, and moved the meeting to the first floor, where there was a wood stove. The room was dark-paneled and gloomy, and people were reluctant to remove their coats.

Town clerk Elizabeth Ritchie read "with a wavering voice" the six articles of closure.[7] Edwin Howe, as the only remaining business owner, was selected as moderator. The group appropriated $1,800 for the purchase and erection of a monument to World War veterans. Dr. Segur explained that the Civil War statue on the common would now be moved to Quabbin Park Cemetery, and the World War plaque could be placed on one side of the statue. On the other side would be another plaque, "to contain a tribute to the townspeople themselves." If they felt uncomfortable with the attention, Dr. Segur added, generations to come would visit the cemetery and the statue, and remember the town as well.

The meeting was adjourned. Few people left. Instead they stayed in the building for hours afterward, talking and huddling around the stove, waiting for the unseasonably late storm to pass.[8]

"Letters from Quabbin"

In the first half of the year, the Letters to the Editor sections of local papers filled with the angry, grieving screeds of deracinated Quabbinites.

One anonymous, disgruntled resident, now displaced to Belchertown, wrote to the editor of the *Springfield Union*, complaining:

> *Some 25 years ago or more there appeared in this vicinity some engineers supposedly sent by the state authorities to test the water and various other things. The residents did not realize at that time what it was all about but as time went by the seeds that were sown took root and began to sprout and have steadily grown into one of the greatest rackets that was ever perpetuated on the residents of any state.*

Until now the Metropolitan Water Commission under the guise of the State has acquired about a hundred square miles of territory for the purpose, they say, of a reservoir to supply the city of Boston with water . . . and when hard times began to set in they were quick to take advantage and went on a buying spree knowing that most people were hard pressed and, in most instances, would be glad to sell out their holdings. So they have acquired and taken away hundreds of homes from the people . . . There is one thing these hundreds of homeowners have come to realize—that no longer can they boast that their home is their castle, that it is invulnerable or that it is sacred. The Constitution at this point appears but a scrap of paper to them.

This territory should no longer be known as the Swift River Valley but should go down in history as the valley which was full of bones, for there have been thousands of the remains of dead people removed from the various cemeteries . . . and the bones put into small boxes to be carried to the Quabbin Cemetery in Ware, there to be opened and filled with gravel and dirt and put into another hole in the ground. If this is not desecration of the dead, then what is it? If these corpses could only come to life it strikes me that there would be war until they had avenged themselves upon their enemies. They would fight for their brethren, for their sons and daughters and for their homes. The Governor and legislators with the commissioners who have been instrumental in bringing these things to pass have nothing in the way of justice to their credit.[9]

A week later, another letter, a response to the first:

There is no doubt that there has been many a heartache caused through the rightly named racket and there is no doubt that there will be from now on many a headache among the people in the metropolitan city of Boston. I would suggest that the druggists of that city stock up to the brim with aspirin tablets.[10]

And, a week after that, a third:

Yes, it is the people's money that pays for this extravagance. Look what it cost when the "woodpeckers" were here. One day I watched a group because they had a fire in one of my buildings and 11 men just stood around and did nothing all day, but they drew their pay just the same as the few who did work . . . Yes, we have been driven from our homes by the Metropolitan Water Company and it looks as though we would be driven out of our new homes by taxes. [11]

The *Union* had prepared a response. Greenwich residents Mabel Jones and Amy Spink, wife of engineer Herb Spink, were tired of the smarmy, condescending articles typically written about the valley. With the intent of, in modern terminology, "changing the narrative," they had pitched the *Union* with a series of twenty-seven twice-weekly five-hundred-word articles, with accompanying photographs, written about the valley. These were promoted by the newspaper as "Letters from Quabbin" and ran from April through July 1938. The effort was intended to be warm-hearted but unsentimental, focusing on aspects of valley life and history typically ignored by the press.

Both women had unusual perspectives. Jones was born in Quebec and did not become a US citizen until she was twenty-one. She married a valley native but lived outside the watershed until 1931, when they moved full-time to their summer home in Greenwich. Spink had studied at what is now the University of Rhode Island. After meeting Herb Spink when he was working on Rhode Island's Scituate Reservoir, they married and moved to Massachusetts, where he worked on the Wachusett Reservoir and then on the Quabbin. The Spinks lived near the Joneses on a farm rented from the Commission. Both families had children who attended the Greenwich school, and both women were members of the Quabbin Club.

Jones and Spink both also had been schoolteachers, and Spink wrote essays and opinion pieces on the side, although none were ever published.

They decided that Jones would do the research and Spink would write the text.[12]

"Letters from Quabbin" was more akin to a modern blog than a traditional newspaper column. Spink and Jones wrote about events that had just happened from the perspective of people who had just lived, rather than witnessed, them. The articles provide a rich source of historical information about the valley's last days that otherwise would have been ignored by a newspaper more intent on sensationalizing than humanizing.

"Letters from Quabbin" typically alternated between topical overview and a recap of current events. The articles fell into a number of broad categories, including the actual business of reservoir building ("The Great Dam," "Quabbin Park Cemetery"); history of the area ("Dana, 'Forgotten' Town"; "The Old Families"); the dissolution of the communities ("The Exodus," "The Last Graduation"); notable people ("Distinguished People," "The Doctor"); and nature ("The Fishing," "The Wild Flowers").

Jones and Spink knew who to talk to, and how to balance the interviews. "One man, 80 years old," they wrote, "replied, when asked when he was going to move, 'Not 'til the water come up to my steps; that will be time enough.'"[13] At the same time, they discussed a "woman who lived back from the main road in the place owned for generations by her family, and worked hard to care for her parents. The house was in need of repairs, and the farm generally worn down. Muddy roads in spring and snow in the winter made travel difficult, and there was no money to move to better surroundings." Now, after being bought out by the Commission, "one can find her on a much-traveled road, owning her own home, and desirious only of enough time to sit on her front porch for one whole day and enjoy the grand view."[14]

"Letters from Quabbin" even included a guest column by their friend Robert Johnston that revels in the magnificent fishing opportunities in the valley: "From the time we were able to distinguish the fish in the Swift waters in the spring, every boy with this apparently inherited love for the woods and streams was anxious to be able to be the first to spread the word that 'The trout were running' and 'laying in under the dam and bridge.' Books could be written about fishing and the many stories handed down from father to son of the catches yielded by this or that stream."[15]

The May 31 installment, "The Engineers," was the first time the engineers' ten-plus-year work on the project had been summarized. As in nearly every other article in which "the engineers" were mentioned, Jones and Spink used no names. But even in their limited word count they did tell the engineers' story, defended and humanized them.

> Skillful, Hard Working Men Who Are Building the Reservoir Once Were Hated, But Have Won Place in Hearts of the People . . . We have seen them perspiring in the heat of summer, drenched by the autumn rains and pushing through the snows of winter. We have seen him descend 600 feet under ground in the dark tunnels, and carry his flag to the highest point on the hills . . . Given the opportunity, the engineer has proved himself a good organizer, a loyal member of a group and has been given the highest offices in every organized group in the towns where he lives. He can talk interestingly on other jobs nearby or in distant places, he can enthuse about his hobbies when this project is completed he too must seek a home and employment elsewhere.[16]

The End of the Quabbin Club

Throughout the 1930s, the Quabbin Club had been a haven for young and middle-aged engineer wives who had found themselves dragged from the city and deposited into a dying town where they needed a car to go anywhere, and whose husbands probably took the car to work in the morning unless they lived right in the middle of Enfield. For those women who dreaded the loneliness and alienation of being surrounded by Puritan "farm wives" already predisposed to resenting them because of their husbands' jobs, the Quabbin Club must have been an oasis of culture and kindness.

By the time the Quabbin Club held its last meeting in April 1938, the membership, capped each year at thirty with a waiting list, had become nearly half-comprised of women whose husbands worked for the Commission.

On April 12, the thirty dues-paying Quabbin Club members and twenty-five guests—mostly former members—gathered at the Homestead Inn in Ludlow, MA, for the last annual meeting.

The meeting was one, said the *Springfield Republican*, "at which no officers were elected and at which no program of community service and self-improvement was planned for the coming year."[17] There were, however, many posed group photographs for all the local papers: President Anna Spurr, in an off-white satin dress with matching beret and shoes, tightly holding the hand of shrunken Annie Howe, one of the remaining founding members of 1897, when the Quabbin Club was created as a local study group. Another photo shows Spurr sitting modestly at a long table with the prior club presidents. In still another, published across the state, the active club members stand as a group outside the inn: most women wear flowered dresses with small tilted hats, looking a little chilly without coats; the older ones wear black wool suits.

The Homestead Inn provided a "ladies' luncheon" before the official meeting. Each current member received a souvenir folder with a reproduction of the illustration used in the first Quabbin Club yearbook, and inside, a copy of a poem called "Quabbin Elegy," written by a member who had asked to remain anonymous.

The closing ritual began with the gaveling-in. Anna Spurr handed the gavel to Annie Howe, who handed it to Marian Zappey, whose late mother had purchased the gavel for the club when she was president. Zappey would give the gavel to the Somers, CT, Women's Club, a "daughter" of the Quabbin Club. Nellie Brown agreed to take the club records; they would go, she said self-deprecatingly, in the "third floor museum" at her new home in Springfield until they would be presented to the Belchertown Historical Association[18] at some later point.

Club secretary Bertha Marsh, wife of former Enfield Congregational minister Burton Marsh, summarized the programs of the final year. Treasurer Anna Knight, wife of Commission Special Agent Charles Knight, appropriated the remaining club funds to the Olivet Community House in Springfield. The Enfield Christmas tree lights would be given to Mary Lane Hospital in Ware.

Members read their poems, including "Leaving the Old and Greeting the New," by Geneva Heidel, Norman Heidel's mother. Tears were shed. Mabel Jones and Amy Spink, the authors of "Letters from Quabbin," took copious notes.

The author of "Quabbin Elegy" was urged to come forward. Mary Cushman Hardy, wife of engineer Charles Hardy, who had just joined the previous year, acknowledged her authorship, admitting she had received her inspiration as she "walked the quiet woods of the Swift River Valley."[19]

The climax of the event was a "short playlet" called "The Collect Speaks," directed by Grace Sheffield, wife of engineer Ed Sheffield. The three characters were "Madge, a non-club woman" (Grace Walker, wife of engineer Charles Walker); "Jessie, an ardent club woman" (Wilma Hall, wife of engineer Norman Hall and half of the "most popular couple in the valley"); and "The Collect Which Speaks," played by Spurr.

According to Jones and Spink, "At the conclusion of the playlet, Mrs. Spurr, clad in shimmering white satin, personifying all the virtues of the clubwoman, stood on a raised platform, and as the last words of the spiritual playlet were said, she raised her arms for all to rise and join with her in these last rites of the club, and the beautiful words of the Collect, 'Oh lord God, let us not forget to be kind,' were heard by voices husky with emotion and fell as a sweet benediction on the end of the Quabbin Club."[20]

FIFTEEN

Two Dances, an Auction, and a Hurricane

1938: Part II

The first "farewell ball" at the Enfield town hall was sponsored by the Order of the Eastern Star on Saturday, March 26. It was a pretty big deal at the time. Three hundred people, including some Eastern Star and Masons members from outside the valley, donned their tuxedos and evening dresses and, according to the *Boston Post*, "swung their partners with somewhat preoccupied gayety" through an evening of step calling, including the "rollicking" fiddler contradance tunes "'Money Musk,' 'Hull's Victory,' and 'Pop! Goes the Weasel.'"[1]

A reporter from the *Christian Science Monitor* attended and, as was often the case for Boston journalists, got some facts wrong. The dance was not, as the reporter claimed, "the last event ever to be held" in the town hall. The reporter also claimed to see "the lights go out one by one and the locks snapped on the doors for the last time before demolition of the building commences." This was patently not true—children would be arriving for school in the town hall that Monday, and the last Enfield town meeting was yet to be held. Nor was everyone being forced out of the valley by April 1, as the article claimed. The building wouldn't be demolished for another year—it had yet to be sold to someone willing to do the dirty work. The author even claimed that the "Northern Lights showed coldly brilliant" above the dancers—not impossible, but improbable—another embellished detail to heighten the small-town drama.[2]

Probably few people in the valley even noticed the press coverage. Too much else was happening. The Swift River Hotel and gas stations had been demolished. So had the mills in Smith's Village. Construction was being completed on the Administration Building at the dam site, which was now the fanciest property in the valley—or, technically, right above it. Reporters were nearly as unavoidable as demolition equipment.

So why, then, would members of the Enfield Volunteer Fire Department (and some of their wives) decide to use the rest of the department's $400 holdings to sponsor another "final ball"?

The handwritten minutes from the "Special Meeting Called April 11, 1938," are vague: "The meeting was called to order by Chief W.B. Segur. After much discussion a motion was made and seconded to hold a Farewell Ball. A committee was appointed, headed by W.B. Segur, Chairman, Edwin C. Howe, D.G. Rowe, A.J. Stock, and W.H. Young. The committee was instructed to appoint all other committees necessary for the occasion."[3]

Congratulations to whoever designed the cleverly evocative invitation and dance card for the ball. Both were on white cardstock with an embossed black border, as if for a funeral. The cover of the dance card read, in various Art Deco fonts:

FAREWELL BALL
Enfield Fire Department
Wed., Apr. 27, 1938

Town Hall
8 till 2
A Last Good Time for All[4]

For the price of $400, the Farewell Ball was not just a dance—it was a full living-memorial extravaganza.

The fire department's original intention was to hold a combination parade/funereal procession down Main Street to the town hall, but there weren't enough firemen available. So as a compromise, "black draped horses" led the town's old fire engine to the town hall doors, where, by dusk, hundreds, then over a thousand, people were already lined up—some with connections to the valley, some who wanted to visit at the town's jazzed-up deathbed—and, of course, many reporters in fedoras, gathered in groups or discreetly trying to sneak inside.[5]

There was a sense of unease, even franticness, at the door. Cars and trucks constantly pulled up, discharged passengers, and then drove away to look for ever more remote parking. Over at the Grange Hall a volunteer staff of twelve served sandwiches, ice cream, and coffee.[6]

According to Quabbin historian J. R. Greene, "the crowd at the door became so large that ticket seller Harry Ryther was told to sell no more tickets at the door." A thousand people were let in; twice that number waited outside. When they finally made their way in, the planning committee realized that someone would have to remove the bolted-in seats, but people already inside the building refused to leave, fearing that they would not be re-admitted, and the workers had to maneuver around the agitated revelers.[7]

The *Springfield Union* described the overall décor and ambience as "profusely decorated, the motif being soberness. The hall, however, is generously supplied with colored floodlights, most of which are pointed at the center ceiling decoration. Lights with deep-blue bulbs are strung across the street in front of the hall. To add to the gloomy atmosphere is the scene of workmen ripping apart a large tomb of the cemetery behind the Common, directly opposite the Town Hall."[8]

Springfield-based McEnelly's Orchestra, known up and down the East Coast, played a concert between 8:00 and 8:30, then stuck around to play for the ball proper. Billy Syner's Floor Show, made up of students from Billy Syner's School of Dance in Springfield, performed between 8:30 to 9:00. The younger children were greeted with amusement, but a high school girl, dressed in white tights with white feathers in her hair, performed some very high kicks at very close range to the audience, to many adults' great embarrassment.

Dr. and Mrs. Segur led the first Grand March; Engineer Norman Hall and Muriel Briggs, engineer Homer Briggs's wife and a Farewell Ball committee member, led another. The orchestra played a mix of current swing dances and old country barn dances: waltzes, quadrilles, fox trots, Virginia reels, and two Paul Jones two-steps.[9] Lewis Johnston of Greenwich was the local step-caller, as he usually was for similar events. The seamless transition between swing and barn dance was very Enfield.

R. Nelson Molt himself was in attendance, but without his wife, Olive. It is unclear if he participated in the dances. Trudy Ward Stalbird, pregnant with her second child, took a series of buses from her new home in Saranac Lake, NY, in order to get to the ball on time and wore, as her formal, the wedding dress she'd worn less than five years earlier in the Enfield Congregational Church.[10]

The packed town hall was hot and growing oppressive as the night wore on. Dancers were sweaty in their constricting formalwear. There was little room to maneuver. The building felt unsound with so many people in it, but leaving to go out into the cool night for a breather risked being denied reentrance. It was loud, with a cacophony of voices and instruments in a tight space. Everyone was giddy and anxious, and, as the night went on, a sense of dread was building.

As the clock hands trembled on the edge of midnight, the atmosphere, the *Springfield Union* wrote,

> as dramatic as any in fiction or in a movie epic . . . A hush fell
> over the Town Hall, jammed far beyond ordinary capacity, as

the first note of the clock sounded; a nervous tension, growing throughout the evening, had been felt by both present and former residents and casual onlookers.

The orchestra, which had been playing throughout the evening, faintly sounded the strain of "Old Lang Syne" when the stroke of the clock was heard in the hall, previously silenced by the chairman of the ball, Dr. Willard B. Segur.

Muffled sounds of sobbing were heard, hardened men were not ashamed to take out their handkerchiefs, and children, attending the ball with their parents, broke into tears, not because they knew what their mothers and fathers were weeping for, but merely because they were weeping.

The last note of the clock's bell hand changed a town into a nameless waste, a name into nothing.

The ball went on for another two hours. The *Republican* noted that the attendees now danced in a building that was no longer a town hall and no longer in Enfield.[11]

Finally, sometime around 2 A.M., the party broke up. Those who stayed until the bitter end left slowly and stood outside in groups talking quietly as if after a funeral. The *Springfield Union*, too, stayed to watch: "One by one the lights were extinguished. The janitor snapped on the padlocks. They probably will not be removed again until the hall has been torn down. Outside in the street the hills rose steeply over the little valley and the new dike and dam, still unfinished, brooded like twin executioners."[12]

Forgive this good reporter his or her poetic license. This "final padlocking" had not been true in March—nor was it any truer in April. As for the looming dike and dam, anyone standing in Enfield Center perhaps would have an unimpeded view of the dam two miles away, but the dike was up on Quabbin Hill and completely out of sight.

The next morning, right at 9 A.M., R. Nelson Molt arrived at the town hall with representatives of the state auditor's and state secretary's offices to officially take over the former communities.

A Valley for Sale

R. Nelson Molt had posted another ominous notice in the Boston papers:

PUBLIC AUCTION

The Metropolitan District Water Supply Commission will, on September 10, 1938, at 11:00 A.M. Daylight Saving Time, sell at public auction property of the former towns of Dana, Enfield, Greenwich and Prescott at the Town Hall in the center of the former village of Enfield, as follows:

School equipment and supplies comprising students' and teachers' desks, book cases, text books, maps, etc. Also some playground supplies and equipment.

Office furniture, viz.: desk, chairs, book cases, cabinets and files, railroad and barrel stoves, settees, counters, weights and measures, scales, office safes, etc.

Town buildings including town hall, schools, hearse house, and fire station.

Fire equipment including steam fire engine, hose, ladders, belts, etc. and other articles too numerous to mention. The Commission reserves the right to reject any and all bids.

TERMS: Cash on day of sale.

R. Nelson Molt, Secretary[13]

The flood was hastening, and the Commission began its rush to sell town-owned objects and remove them from the area. Molt had deputized Commission agents Roy Kimball and Charles Walker to represent the towns in liquidating their inventory. Ellis Thayer, whose house, moved out of Greenwich on a flatbed truck the following winter, would become a visual symbol of the valley's last days, was hired as auctioneer.

The auctions were another tourist and press draw. The valley's dissolution never got old. "Dana and Enfield End Their Careers on Auction

Block—Last Possessions of Two Towns Disposed Of—Items Range from Pencils to Fire Engine," announced the Springfield *Sunday Union and Republican*.[14]

Worcester-area socialite turned Quabbin chronicler Evelina Gustafson attended the auction "so that I might purchase a bit here and there as a remembrance of that little part of old Massachusetts that held such a fascination for me." Gustafson, like many present that day, was both saddened and excited by the proceedings: "There was a very large crowd due to the fact that it was held by the Commission and consisted of the articles left in the houses they had purchased and the several buildings that were to be sold. It was a beautiful day and the street outside the Town Hall was thronged with cars.

"It was like visiting a museum," she said, "to walk through the lower floor of the Town Hall that day. There were spinning wheels, cheese presses, large looms and small hand looms, ox yokes and old torches which the men carried when fishing at night."[15]

Gustafson watched two men looking at the ox yokes. "'I like the adjustable one best,' remarked one of the old-timers. 'How about you?'

"'No siree—', grunted the other. 'I always used this other 'un. I think it is downright cruelty to put those heavy things on those poor critters.'

"'They may be heavier'—answered his companion. "'But as for cruelty—these are adjustable. In that other 'un the poor animal was wedged in tight and had no freedom to turn.'"[16]

Little merchandise—the *Republican* mentions some school bells, school books, and two hot-water boilers—sold that morning. At 12:30, everyone was told to take a half-hour lunch break. At 1:00, the Commission began selling real estate and large items, like fire equipment, that would be difficult to bring indoors. Then bidding exploded. "Within an hour," said the *Republican*, "five buildings, three fire bells from Dana, Enfield [and other fire equipment] were sold." So was a large antique bronze ram, formerly a weather vane, now sold to the Deitner family of Belchertown for their daughter Marguerite to use as a hobby horse. A photo shows Marguerite, probably four or five years old, in a navy sweater, white Mary Janes with ankle socks, and a big white hair bow, sitting astride the ram and looking knowingly at the camera.[17]

Real estate included the North Dana firehouse ($35), the Dana school ($110), the Dana town hall ($90), the Enfield schoolhouse ($165), and, finally, the Enfield town hall itself, purchased by the City Wrecking Company of Springfield for $550. According to the terms of the sale, all buildings had to be wrecked and material removed within thirty days. The terms were not enforced, though; the town hall remained intact until the following year, the very last building standing in Enfield Center.

The most dramatic bidding was for the town of Dana's steamer fire engine. Climbing on it beforehand was not forbidden; children Ian and Sandra Hanson of Wilbraham used it as "grandstand seating" during most of the auction. At last, as Ellis Thayer "mounted the driver's seat of the steamer to call for bids, buying interest was shown only by three persons, a farmer, a metal dealer and a museum representative. A crowd of more than 300 gathered to watch the disposal of the relic, to cheer on the bidders and to heckle the auctioneer. Starting at a $10 bid, Mr. Thayer got the price up to $25 quickly in $5 increases. Here the farmer dropped out. It had been his intention to the use the pump for farming irrigation." Finally Albert Garganigo, representative of the Princeton, MA, Museum of Antique Automobiles,[18] won with a $67.50 bid and "announced that a trailer truck would come to Enfield Monday to transport the steamer to a final resting place in the Princeton building." He handed his check to Roy Kimball, and the photo bulbs went off. (The fire engine is now in the collection of the Swift River Valley Historical Society.)

On her way out, Gustafson asked one old local if he was interested in buying anything, or was just looking. No, he said: "Even before my farm was bought by the Metropolitan there were people stopping to ask if I had any old furniture I wanted to get rid of. My children weren't interested in keeping the old things so I sold most of it. I even sold an old bed which had been in my family for years. It had ropes stretching cross-wise in the bedstead, we had straw on top of that and then a featherbed topmost. Say

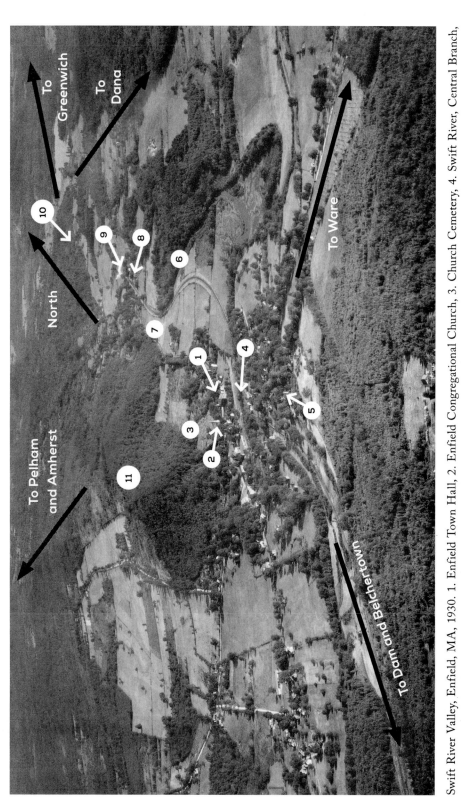

Swift River Valley, Enfield, MA, 1930. 1. Enfield Town Hall, 2. Enfield Congregational Church, 3. Church Cemetery, 4. Swift River, Central Branch, 5. Chandler Mansion, 6. Rabbit Train railroad tracks, 7. Linda Vista, 8. Smith's Village, 9. Rabbit Train, 10. Greenwich, 11. Prescott. *Courtesy: Friends of Quabbin.*

ABOVE: Enfield Engineer's Club, 1928. *Courtesy: Swift River Valley Historical Society.* BELOW: Chandler House, Commission's valley headquarters. *Courtesy: Mass. DCR.*

Engineers "holing through" aqueduct Shafts #6 and #7, 1929. These are the subjects of the *Worcester Telegram* "Human Moles" story. *Courtesy: Mass. DCR.*

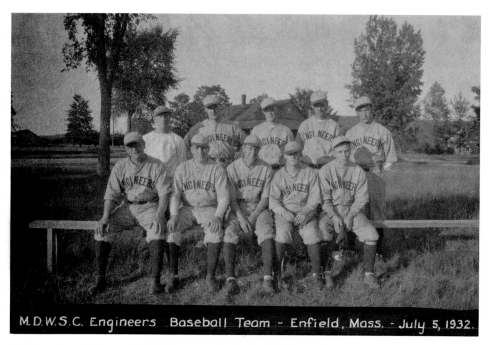

M.D.W.S.C. Engineers Baseball Team - Enfield, Mass. - July 5, 1932.

Engineers baseball team, 1932. Front row (L-R): Dick Jackson, Homer Briggs, Chet Chetwynd, Stuart Beach, Bill Potter. Back row (L-R): Russ Snow, Preston Putnam, Carl Crawford, Joe Bruce, Harold McLeod. *Courtesy: Mass. DCR.*

ABOVE: Stripping land at dam site, prob. 1938. *Courtesy: Mass. DCR.* BELOW: Enfield Congregational Church fire, August 1, 1936.

Quabbin Club Final Group Photo, April 1938. Front row (L-R): Annie Howe, Anna Chase Spurr, Ruby Dickinson, Anna Rice Knight, Unknown, Wilma Hall, Marian Zappey, Unknown. Second row: Center Geneva Heidel (in fur stole); second from right, Grace Harris; far right, Iola Downing. Third Row: Barbara Sheffield (in white dress), Ruth Ward Howe.

ABOVE: Flyer for the 1938 Farewell Ball. *Courtesy: Belchertown Historical Association/Stone House Museum.* BELOW: Grand March at the Farewell Ball. Front row: Muriel Feindel Briggs, Norman Hall, Wilma Hall, Homer Briggs. Second row (left): Anna Chase Spurr, Jerome Spurr (in glasses and bow tie).

ABOVE: Enfield Town Hall, March 1939. *Courtesy Mass. DCR.* BELOW: Enfield Congregational Church Cemetery Crypt below the Quabbin Reservoir, 1998. *Courtesy: Ed Klekowski.*

what you will, these new-fangled beds and mattresses aren't as warm and comf'tible as those old feather beds were on a winter's night."

"I remember my feelings as I drove homeward from the auction that day knowing that the death knell of this lovely, little countryside had now rung," Gustafson wrote. "The beauty of those proud hills and rolling fields broke on me anew. The houses we passed, which were being demolished, were many of them several hundreds of years old. It seemed a sacrilege to destroy such perfect examples of early American architecture."[19]

Like so many others who attended the auction and snapped up everything from wooden pegs to school books, Gustafson, wearing her fur stole, the trunk of her "little roadster" filled with antiques, was truly sorry for the valley's passing—sorry enough to self-publish a book about it in 1940. But like other outside observers, her sadness was steeped in an outsider's sense of history. It was not her home that was being destroyed or sold under her—a feeling someone on the outside could not truly understand.

The Hurricane with No Name

It had rained for most of September, and the Connecticut River Valley and the Swift River Valley had flooded. On September 21, the largest hurricane to strike New England since the seventeenth century tore through Long Island, Rhode Island, and Connecticut before ravaging central Massachusetts—another weather-related cataclysm that stalled Great Depression recovery across the US.

Weather reports didn't anticipate that the storm would bear so far west. But the eye of the storm followed the Connecticut River north into Massachusetts. Hartford, CT, and Ware, MA, were underwater for the second time in two and a half years. Winds and flooding killed at least one hundred people. That afternoon, nearly six more inches of rain fell on the western half of the state. The Connecticut, Chicopee, and Swift Rivers all flooded; a bridge in Chicopee fell into the water. When it was over, Smith College students deputized as nurses came down the hill from campus into Northampton, where the water on Main Street was waist-high and the sewers were no longer working. The people of Ware had to be air-dropped food and medicine.

Residents of the Swift River Valley did not need the aid—so few of them still lived there, and the Commission went out of its way to ensure they were safe and provisioned.[20]

The Commission's own structures were undamaged but roads not already cut off by the flooding were made impassable by felled trees and wires. As soon as the storm roared through the valley and north to Vermont and Maine, and in the following forty-eight hours afterward, every member of the Commission workforce cleared roads, repaired means of communication, and, inasmuch as was possible, checked on people still living in the valley.

According to the Commission, the hurricane "felled about 20,000,000 feet of merchantable pine timber and an unestimated amount of other smaller timber on the Quabbin watershed and 3,000,000 feet of merchantable pine timber on the Ware River watershed." That timber was going to be turned into funds to help the state pay for the remainder of the Quabbin project. "While the Commission immediately engaged in salvage operations and is negotiating with the Federal Government for the sale thereof, the hazard of fires and the preparation of the area for reforestation present a greatly enlarged task on both watersheds," the Commission said.[21]

At Quabbin Park Cemetery, the hurricane uprooted or bore off practically all the large pine trees, damaged several hardwood trees, and knocked down or dented approximately one hundred headstones. Three headstones were damaged beyond repair; the remainder were straightened and reset.

Photographs show a row of pine trees draped over the tombstones and across the car paths.

At the time of the hurricane, Jerome and Anna Spurr and their four-year-old son, Robert, were living in their Colonial-era "dream house" in Enfield, which Spurr had been restoring since the early 1930s. The property belonged to the Commission, but the Spurrs had seriously considered purchasing it and moving it out of the valley by truck in the subsequent months, if only to Belchertown: "There were a number of problems involved," Spurr said in 1987. "I used to say jokingly that it was 25 percent chimney, at least—it had a big central chimney with three fireplaces on the first floor and one on the second floor."[22]

On the day of the hurricane, Spurr was not aware of either the severity or the trajectory of the storm. "I was on my way to Springfield with Anne, my wife, to teach at Northeastern University [where the university had a commuter annex]—and finally I decided it was best to turn back before we were trapped by the storm. I had to take my ax out and clear a path through fallen trees. We finally made it back to Enfield, quite a bit concerned because of the two trees in front of the house, and the girl who was serving as a maid and the youngster could easily have been injured. So with some trepidation we finally made our way to the house, and the trees had blown across the road instead of on top of the house.

"With the hurricane, we lost electric power and telephone, and we were dependent on the electricity for lighting and pumping water. It was either a question of trying to stay on for a little while, or pulling out." They left for a rental in Belchertown by the end of the month.

"About that time," Spurr added, "it was rumored that an artist who lived on the Cape had his eye on the house, and the state was offering to move houses for a very small fee—the rumor was that the artist had offered $500—and I was kind of hesitant with all the other expenses of moving it, but the hurricane forced me out. A contractor moved in and not too long a time passed before it burned down. The understanding was that he'd gone off to Ware and left a good fire in the fireplace. So it ended up with nobody having it."

Greenwich shopkeeper Stanwood King "didn't get the message" about the hurricane, either. "I kept working in the store . . . I was delivering groceries, you know, and it blew the devil out of the house and the barn and everything else, and after that I couldn't get through the valley to get home. I had to go up and around and through other people's properties, and the bricks had been blown right out of the chimney in the house. The fireplace—my god, it was black all over the place."[23]

George Boynton had moved his farm to Ware, but it was destroyed anyway. The hurricane "blew down just about everything that could be blewed down. I had water all the way up into my barn, and it flooded an area of about 100 acres . . . the wind blew, and I had a henhouse 100 feet long, and I had Rhode Island Red chickens that were just starting to lay, and the whole thing collapsed and blew onto the railroad tracks, and the chickens went up into the air and landed in the flood waters. I lost everything. The roof from my house was completely wiped off, and I had to get shingles somehow, which I did, and shingle it . . . I had about 3,000 lbs. of lumber, all planed and ready to use, and the silt just ruined the whole works." Like many, Boynton had no insurance.[24]

No trees had crashed the roofs or porches of either the Chandler or Barlow houses, but their roads were impassable except on foot. Engineers whose scientific and administrative work resided only at those two buildings arrived on-site the morning of September 22 to evaluate the damage. Nothing was lost, but the engineering team quickly set up a large portable generator at the Chandler House, where it remained until the building's destruction.

The valley was already becoming nearly unrecognizable—"strange and unreal"—with familiar roads, buildings, and other land markers gone. Donald Howe describes the hurricane as leaving the valley "a shambles of twisted and uprooted trees and brush. The Swift River in one last mighty effort tried its strength against the partially completed structure of the Commission, but spent its power against the rock walls of the diversion tunnel and left the works unharmed."[25]

After that, the state hired even more laborers to finish the woodpeckers' sloppy cutting, compounded by the downed trees: "[T]he axes of the clearing crews and of the contractors' forces rang through the valley, and the tree dozers whose sharp prow could cut through a one-foot tree cleared the valley floor. By night the light of hundreds of brush fires reddened the clouds, and the reservoir was ready to receive the waters to be impounded."

A reporter for the Fitchburg, MA, *Sentinel* described the valley in early October as a "scene of increasing desolation, heightened by the results of the recent hurricane.

"One finds whole families in some places busy at the job of tearing down their former home, removing nails from salvaged boards and otherwise preparing to take as much as possible away in the form of lumber, hardware, doors, etc.

"The scene is not wholly unlike a large valley that has been visited by war, largely depopulated, and stripped of trees and buildings."[26]

Bill Segur was working for the Commission as a laborer in late 1938, a member of the field party "cutting lines" for the surveyors. The Chandler House was a short distance from the Segur house. One morning, he said, "my mother said, 'Bill, when you get home, get a ride to Ware because we just bought a house in Ware and we're going to move there.'

"When I got back from work, in front of me was the place I had been born, and it was just a cellar hole. It was still burning. They'd burned it all day long. Those houses were old and dry, and they could burn in a day.

"That hit me pretty hard that day. I knew we were going to have to move, but I really enjoyed a childhood in that town. I wanted the hills, the fish, the streams . . . it was really nice."[27]

SIXTEEN

"Valley of a Thousand Smokes": 1939

E arly in 1939, the valley was still, barely, habitable: a few homes, some trees, a post office, a telephone exchange, passable roads, and at least one store. By the end of the year, the Chandler mansion was the only structure left standing outside the dam site, a dilapidated Victorian memory on a vast treeless, plantless, grassless plain. Two prominent figures in the valley were dead. The world was going to war, again. And everything in the valley was, literally, aflame— "the valley of 1000 smokes."[1]

The Last Mail Run

Enfield Postmaster Edwin Howe usually vacationed in Florida after Christmas. This January he was in limbo, waiting for the notification that the Enfield Post Office was to be shut down for good. Finally, the Postal Service obliged: *"An order having been issued discontinuing the post office at Enfield, Massachusetts, effective January 14, 1939, all mail addressed to that office will be sent to the post office at Ware, Massachusetts, after that date."*[2]

The weather on January 14 was miserable, with heavy swirling snow-flakes that intimated a coming storm. R. Nelson Molt's wife, Olive, used her Brownie camera to photograph the cold, mostly unhappy group standing outside the post office. Ed Howe was smiling broadly, almost in relief, about to hand a big burlap sack of mail to the postal worker leaning next to the cage of the postal truck. Howe's wife, Ruth, and the other telephone operator stood behind him, eager to get back inside where it was warm. Howe's small dog, Laddie, crouched loyally next to him. A line of men stood on the sidewalk in front of the store including Edwin Howe Sr., looking grim and frail, and Molt, looking a little peeved.[3]

Laddie and his St. Bernard companion, Happy, had already been photographed for the *Springfield Republican* that day—Laddie curled on the post office counter; Happy standing on his hind legs, paws on the counter like an impatient customer, while Howe searched for their mail. According to the caption from the *Republican*, they were, in fact, expecting mail: "Happy, with back to the camera, and Laddie, on the counter, called for their mail just before the Enfield post office closed its doors yesterday. It being a very special occasion, both found letters addressed to them with 'last day' postmarks." It was a moment of half-contrived, half-genuine charm, and probably the last *Saturday Evening Post*-ish scene the valley would ever see.[4]

'Crossing the Bar'

Some valley residents had sued, or were settling with, the Commission for lost income and property, with varying degrees of success. Country doctor Willard Segur's financial loss, at age seventy-three, included both his home and his decades-long medical practice. Segur loved his adopted community as his own and had served it as a selectman, health officer, member of most town boards, head of the fire and police departments, staff doctor of the Mary Lane Hospital in Ware, and, later, as the Quab-bin's medical officer. He'd opened up another storefront practice in Ware, but it was hard to find new patients, and his old patients had scattered. The *Republican* reported that Segur had "declared recently that he was prepared to settle with the state for his dual loss, his property and medical income, at a reasonable figure but to date has reached no agreement and believed he would be forced to go to the courts to receive satisfactory compensation."[5]

What the *Republican* did not know, or did not say, was that Dr. Segur was an inpatient at Boston Deaconess Hospital, about to have part of his leg amputated—either from untreated diabetes, some vascular condition, or as the rumor mill had it, walking over the train tracks in Ware without knowing the train was running early.[6]

Segur died of his illness in Boston on January 27. "The taking away of his property and the taking away of his business hit him hard," said his son, Bill. "It hit a lot of people hard. A lot of people died of heartbreak. He was a strong man, but it hurt him badly. I think he felt that whatever remuneration was given him, it didn't make up for 40 years of hard work and the establishment of a home."[7]

Three days later, Frank Winsor, the Commission's chief engineer and architect of the entire Quabbin project, died of a massive heart attack in Boston. He was sixty-eight.

Winsor collapsed on the witness stand around 2 P.M. as he was testifying in a Quabbin contracting claim case at Commission headquarters. According to the *Boston Globe*, "the nationally known hydraulic expert was stricken with a heart attack . . . He slumped to the floor and died while medical aid was being sought . . . Attorney Francis T. Leahy, counsel for the Arthur Johnson Company, which has a claim against the Metropolitan District Water Supply Commission for $400,000 for work done on the Quabbin project, was examining Mr. Winsor when he collapsed."[8]

The *Boston Daily Advertiser* provided more detail: "Attorney Francis Leahy, counsel for the contractor, produced a copy of what was purported to be a memorandum by Winsor ordering the substitution of false data for the real information. When the paper was produced while Winsor was on the witness stand, the latter agreed it contained his signature.

148

Leahy asked Winsor to read it. After Winsor turned pale, but did not reply, Leahy repeated the question. At that point, the engineer suffered a fatal heart attack and died on the witness stand."[9]

Winsor's son, Edward, was particularly incensed at the *Boston Herald* and at the Commonwealth's reaction to his father's death. The *Herald*'s headline to the obituary read, "Highest-Paid Employee of Commonwealth Dies." The Commonwealth mailed Winsor's January paycheck to the family with no note. "What really wore my father down was trying to keep Governor Curley's influence out of the project," Ed Winsor said later.

Equally incensed at Winsor's treatment was Nellie Brown. She kept a copy of Winsor's obituary in her valley scrapbook, and next to it wrote, "Not True! He was a good man!!" in angry, spindly handwriting.

Winsor's funeral was held in the Boston suburb of West Newton, at the West Newton Congregational Church; Winsor had lived for many years on West Newton Hill, a neighborhood of mansions high above what was to become the Massachusetts Turnpike. About seven hundred people attended, including officials of the state and the Metropolitan District Commission and the superintendent of the MDC police. Pallbearers included the three commissioners Eugene Hultman, Davis Kenniston, and Karl Kennison. Winsor's trip to the cemetery was led by an escort of honor composed of MDC policemen. [10]

R. Nelson Molt was the only Commission official at Dr. Segur's funeral. But that service, with hundreds more mourners than Ware's East Congregational Church could accommodate, was an expression of raw grief not just for the loss of this beloved man, but for the whole world he embodied.

At the church, one hundred floral arrangements donated by well-wishers surrounded Segur's casket. Mourning wreaths plastered the sanctuary walls. The minister read Tennyson's poem "Crossing the Bar":

Twilight and evening bell,
And after that the dark!
And may there be no sadness of farewell,
When I embark.

Segur's coffin was carried from the church between lines of his medical associates, who flanked the stairs down to the walkway, and into the tearful crowd.

Nearly a thousand people came for the doctor's farewell. Hundreds stood for more than an hour on the sidewalk in the January weather, dirty, icy snow piled on the curb, so they could pay respects as Segur's coffin was placed in the hearse on its journey to Aspen Grove Cemetery in Ware.

A funeral procession of at least three hundred autos followed the hearse. Ware Police Chief Batholomew Buckley had to order a special police detail to handle the traffic.

The *Springfield Republican* called it "the largest funeral service held in Ware in many years" and "a remarkable tribute to a country doctor who spent nearly a half century caring for the thousands of citizens of the Swift River Valley." [11]

Quabbin Park Cemetery was already open, but Dr. Segur wouldn't be buried there. "He could have gone to Quabbin Park, and had a lot for us all," said Bill Segur, "but I think he was so bitter he went to Ware and bought a lot in Aspen Grove. My mother was buried there, and I will be." (Bill Segur is buried at Quabbin Park.)

A Cold Welcome

Many Swift River refugees had moved to the neighboring town of Belchertown. To welcome them, town officials decided to host the "Belchertown Church Reunion," a ceremony in Belchertown Memorial Hall on the town common. An invitation was sent out to all new Belchertown residents, on heavy white card stock with embossed script, as if for a wedding:

> *You are cordially invited to attend the reception to the former residents of the Swift River Valley tendered by the people of Belchertown. Tuesday evening, January thirty-first, nineteen hundred and thirty-nine at seven-thirty o'clock in Memorial Hall.* [12]

January 31 was two days after Dr. Segur's funeral, and people were in no mood to be entertained. Around a hundred showed up regardless, both whole families and older couples whose children had moved away. At least before the welcoming ceremonies started, there were few smiles. Among the attendees were two engineering families—the Spinks and the Farleys—outsiders, newcomers, and the source of destruction, but just as bereft.

The program included two piano duets; a popular comic monologue of the time called "Her First Ride in an 'Ottymobile'"; an original poem called "Welcome to Belchertown" (*"You have brought from out the valley / Houses whole or cut in two / Or the cash to put up new ones / And make over not a few"*) [13]; greetings from the sponsoring Methodist and Congregational Churches; a group song; and a short play depicting the coming of the first settlers. Clearly the sponsors had worked hard putting this production together and wanted only the best for their new neighbors. [14]

It was cold inside Memorial Hall before the show started. Probably the setup committee began heating the building when they arrived, but audience members, packed together on benches, were still wearing winter coats and even winter hats. The children looked bored, as they might at any adult civic event—plus it was a school night. The adults looked as if they didn't even want to be entertained: It was dark, and snowy, and their new houses still were not homes; Hitler had just given a speech to the Reichstag on the sixth anniversary of the Nazis coming to power; and someone in the US government had leaked that Franklin Roosevelt was considering military involvement in Germany. [15]

And did they warm up at all? The Belchertown newspaper put the best spin on it: "There was no standing in line for a formal reception. Instead, William French, cracked all the inside ice formations with 'electric shocks,' laughing contests, etc. Not only did 'electric shocks' shoot around the hall, but the refreshment committee sent around a battalion of men to pass to those seated, refreshments of sandwiches, cake, coffee, etc. It was a good evening."

The Lab Burns

Soil engineers Norman Hall and Robert Stevens, both of whom had worked on the project since the early 1930s, were sitting down to lunch in the kitchen of the Barlow House testing lab. Snow still covered the ground this last week in March, and the building's heat was on. As they ate, the men watched the controlled brush fires visible across the valley basin.

Then Hall and Stevens smelled smoke—not from the controlled burns outdoors, but from right above them. They ran upstairs to the main laboratory room and found the old chimney leaking, and their lab up in flames.[16]

They yelled for help. Someone telephoned the Commission fire department at the dam. All the engineers in the building grabbed soil and water samples, photographic prints, and laboratory equipment, but the fire was moving faster. They raced out of the house with what little they could carry and fled to the warehouse next door, used as a temporary parking structure for their own cars and Commission trucks. Perhaps the engineers' own building could not be saved, but a row of vehicles on fire would be much worse.

Across the abandoned street was Donald Rowe's house and gas station. Rowe himself no longer lived there, but his property—house and former gas station, garage, and office—were being used as a warehouse by the Coleman Brothers clearing contractors. Coleman also had trucks full of gasoline parked at the old gas station.

By the time the engineers had moved their own vehicles, the Commission fire department had arrived. It was too late to salvage the Barlow house and the adjoining shed. But the Rowe property, separated by the wide street, could still be saved. The Commission called the Ware Fire Department, and the Ware Fire Department, unencumbered by anything human in the valley, was able to arrive quickly.

Engineers abandoned their work at the Chandler and the main dam site to assist the fire department. Laroy Harris, now stationed at the dam, organized a salvage crew. Enfielder and Commission employee Emory Bartlett, along with engineers Homer Briggs, Joseph Riley, William Chevalier, Herbert Spink, Carl Crawford, and Harold McLeod, drove the Coleman Brothers vehicles to safety and helped where they could. Commission Special Agent Roy Kimball briefed the quickly arriving local journalists. Karl Kennison, who had replaced Winsor as chief engineer less than two months prior, and designing engineer William Peabody happened to be at the dam that day and thus were present when the Barlow house collapsed in flames. Embers flew across the street to the roof of the Rowe property, but the dozen firefighters on the scene were able to save it.

Nearly everything at the Barlow house was lost. The equipment alone was worth $15,000—about $275,000 in today's dollars—including "special motion tanks, testing apparatus, hydrometers, more than 1000 glass graduates, and thermometers." Also destroyed was a brand-new piece of "consolidated apparatus," a seven-foot-tall Terzaghi-designed wooden frame attached to a lever and pressure gauges, which was used to determine the settlement, pressure, and permeability of soil. The engineers were so proud of it that they had photographed it when it arrived in January. The engineers also lost all the personal property that had been left in the lab.

Worst was the loss of more than a decade's worth of water and soil samples, which could never be duplicated; composition of both earth and water had been changed irrevocably by the work of building the dams, dike, and tunnel.[17]

The Commission was on a hard deadline; the waters had to rise on schedule. So the engineers moved fast. Salvaged records and equipment were moved immediately to the Chandler House. They hammered together benches, shelves, and cabinets; they built extensions to the Chandler's water piping and electric lines so that testing could be resumed March 25—just two days after the fire.[18]

Even this setup was temporary. The Chandler House was scheduled to be torn down early the next year and the soil lab moved to the basement of the new brick Administration Building, where the engineers could begin purchasing new instruments, shinier and more modern than anything they'd worked with before. But they were angry and resentful; the Commission had no insurance on the Barlow house or anything inside it.

Wreckage

In the first three months of 1939, loggers, bulldozers, "treedozers," and controlled burns dominated the valley landscape. Commission photographers created extensive documentation of the process, including filming it, sometimes in expensive Technicolor (1939 was the release year of *The Wizard of Oz* and *Gone with the Wind*, both of which were filmed in Technicolor, a crowd-pleasing rarity even for feature films). In one dramatic clip, fire and smoke, perhaps fifteen feet high and one hundred feet long, billow from a huge controlled burn, darkening the sky so much the camera perceives it as night. A man runs up to the side of the conflagration, a large flaming torch in his hand. As he reaches a few feet from the fire—probably close enough for him to be uncomfortable, if not in danger—he hurls the torch sidearm into the branches that have not quite caught alight and sprints off in the other direction. Another film clip shows a treedozer pushing its way through a glade of white birch, snapping each trunk in turn and depositing it to the side.[19]

In the rush, mistakes were made. Quabbin contractor Ken Cross recalled how "A foreman said to me, 'Go up to Greenwich Common'—it was where the Rabbit Run was, but it was all dirt then—'are there trees on the common? If so, push 'em over—we're going to burn them on the midnight shift.' I was pushing them until 11:30 or so—I had a hell of a while. Well, the guys came, and got the fire going—and I kept pushing.

It was really cooking, so I had them all pushed together, where the fire was going, and then I backed up and left. The next morning, the foreman said, 'Did you see my car anywhere? I left it here last night because it had a flat tire.' Turns out I'd pushed it right in the fire!"[20]

Over several days, bulldozers flattened grassy Enfield Common and mechanized tree removers yanked up the soon-to-be-flowering shrubs in front of the cellar holes of the grand houses. Trees that had preceded the white settlers piled up like bodies after a battle. The best wood would be transported by truck to another location and cut into lumber; the rest, burned. Toppled trees crashed awkwardly down the hill where the town cemetery had stood and fell into the middle of Enfield Center. Above the cemetery the trees still grew; after the water rose, that tree line would be the banks of the Quabbin Reservoir.

Enfield Town Hall, windows smashed out, stood alone on a flat, smoking empty plain as if on a prairie after a grass fire. Then the town hall was demolished into a pile of bricks, to be transported out in trucks by the contracting company that had purchased it at auction the previous September.

Enfield Center was no more. Two empty streets crossed into flat empty space. The Commission filmed that vacant intersection for its promotional reel with the chirpy caption, "Enfield Has a Changed Appearance after Clearing Operations."[21]

A few remaining houses in Greenwich were being removed also—mostly intact, and by truck. The Ellis Thayer family decided to remove their home this way, except, by necessity, in halves: In a Commission photo, an old Model T truck pulls half a house—the trim has been removed from the front door; the back half, or perhaps the right side, of the house is missing. The truck drives slowly up a small incline on a barren, cracked country road at the end of winter. Wet, late-season snow covers the grass. All the trees in the foreground have been cut down; one sapling, perhaps a property marker, remains. It, too, will be leveled soon.[22]

Both reporters and rubberneckers were eager to get down into the valley for a look at what might today be called "destruction porn." The

Commission was gradually setting up barriers around the watershed, with gates and guards, to prevent vehicles from entering. (These gates still exist; in fact, areas with paths into the Quabbin watershed are referred to as "gates.") Former residents were given no more entrance privileges than outsiders.

One reporter, allowed through the gates in early April, saw nothing but devastation and woe:

> As far as one can see in every direction, every tree is down, below the future high-water mark of elevation 530'. What really surprises one is how small Enfield really was. With trees and buildings gone, it seems only a few steps from one point to another.
>
> It is almost a desert from there to Greenwich. Here and there, everywhere, are little groups of workers picking up and burning rubbish. There is not one building of any kind left from Howe's store in Enfield until one comes to the William Douglass place in Greenwich Plain . . . All the trees and shrubbery are gone, the house is partly dismantled, and looks like a dump . . . Everywhere fires are going, tended by small groups of workers. One can count hundreds of smoke columns.
>
> Everything [in Dana] has been wrecked; nothing has been cleared up. Trees are being chopped up or knocked down. Slash is everywhere. Where the houses and churches and stores stood, are cellar holes filled and surrounded by rubbish, from broken laths to tin cans . . . what an unhappy, unkempt, hopeless sight it is![23]

"Ghost Towns"

Evelina Gustafson had not been to Enfield since the September auctions. As one of the wealthy tourists who came "too little, too late" to the valley, she still felt passionate enough about its loss to self-publish what became the first post-flood book, catchily but misleadingly titled *Ghost Towns 'Neath Quabbin Reservoir*. Gustafson's source of historic information was *Quabbin: The Story of a Small Town with Outlooks on Puritan Life*, but hers was suffused with modern sentimentality ("What a busy life our early settlers spent! The women had their share of work. No afternoon bridge or movie for them").[24]

Throughout 1939 Gustafson insinuated herself the good graces of R. Nelson Molt and Roy Kimball so that she could make her way unimpeded into the valley, which had become "tenfold more desirable, since I was refused permission to enter." After sweet-talking Kimball into providing her with an open pass, she drove in through one of the gates and found herself "in a veritable wilderness . . . methinks I could see the spirits of the Red Men engaged in a great pow-wow rejoicing that now, the white men who drove them from this beloved territory have, at last, been forced to leave themselves!"[25] This was a common theme during the last days of the valley; after 250 years the descendants of the first settlers were getting what they deserved: being chased from their ancestral homes by a political force more powerful than they could fight.

By May, the valley was a massive tourist draw from across the state. The destination for Sunday family drives was the nearly completed dam and the smoking remains of Enfield and Greenwich. The state deployed a whole police force to keep trespassers out of the deserted areas. Special Sunday-duty traffic cops were stationed on Route 9 near the Administration Building to keep people from parking on the highway. A new parking lot had been set up near the building in order to spot wayward cars down in the valley proper, but no one was actually arrested once they'd circumvented the police.[26]

A surprised beneficiary of valley sneak-tourism was the owner of the Prentice store in Greenwich, which, prior to the influx, was about to be torn down. Now its demolition was on hold as long as possible. Mr. Prentice's trick? Like fellow Greenwich storekeeper Stanwood King (they may have been the same man—reporters sometimes got a little sloppy), somehow obtaining "a quantity of relics of the dismantled village, which always attract purchasers whether the object be a piece of board a century old or an old clock picked from the ruins of a demolished home."[27]

Valley families regularly showed up at their old properties regardless. One multigenerational Greenwich family—parents, grandparents, and two teenage daughters—took snapshots of themselves in their springtime Sunday best around their empty home site: bemusedly holding a large piece of corrugated iron that might have been part of a shed or chicken coop; standing next to the flattened foundation of their home, stone retaining wall and circular dirt driveway still intact; striding down their abandoned, denuded road with a Commission tractor parked over on the shoulder. [28]

In April, the Commission dismantled and moved the last private home in Enfield. The Martindale farm was high on Great Quabbin Hill, almost outside the watershed, and the Commission had given dispensation to the heirs, a pair of aging sisters named Martha and Mary, to live there until they moved voluntarily or died. Mary had died; Martha had decided to go live with her nephew in Springfield. The house was purchased from the state by a Polish immigrant in Ware, who planned on using it for parts. Today, the foundations of the Martindale farm are easily accessible, just off Route 9 near the Goodnough Dike, and easily recognizable as a large farmhouse on the hill with trees and a number of outbuildings.

Overall, the Commission collected nearly one million dollars in 1930s money for rentals, sales, and salvage of property. [29]

Once all the trees and foliage were removed from the valley, workers began stripping the fertile loam from the ground. Anything that would be touched by water must have no organic material in which living things could grow. The entire valley basin was stripped to subsoil. The loam was carted off to be sold, or for the Commission tree nurseries, or to fill in the ground at the cemetery—the living soil helped to rebury the dead, leaving in its wake literally a dead world.

The clearing crews of 1938–1939 were older and more professional than their woodpecker predecessors, but the local newspapers still managed to have some gallows-humor fun with them. The *Ware River News* ran a satirical "Manual for Prospective Quabbin Brush Cutters," including a helpful "Glossary of Terms" for the clearing work:

BURNING . . . Quabbin connotation—rushing from brush pile to brush pile with a can of oil on your back and a torch in your hand and lighting the brush. TORCH—Person lighting fires. YELLOW SLIP—Synonym for fired, bounced, canned, ejected, laid off. PUSHER—A gentleman whose duty it is to see that assigned work is done as quickly as possible; called, among other things, "foreman." NEW MAN—Person with new gloves, light shirt, and clean overalls. VETERAN—employee usually of a couple of weeks.[30]

There was little humor for those who had grown up in the valley, or whose families had owned land there for generations. Valley native Lenox Bigelow said, upon seeing his birthplace for the final time, "There is no Enfield. There is only a sluggish dirty stream poking along under the bridge on the old road to Ware. There is only a big, formerly ornate mansion on a knoll to the southeast and another ramshackle house across the highway. There is not even the foundations of the homes that lined the village street . . . nothing but dirt, seared grass, and in one spot, a disconsolate bunch of golden glow left standing near what had been a home for someone . . . [G]rubbers . . . cut and and piled all the growing things and then fired them. A black van filled with wooden boxes was left behind. A car [was] carrying the remains of bodies taken from one of the last cemeteries to be uprooted and taken to a new resting place. Human vultures! The only consoling thought . . . is that someday . . . those barren wasted acres will be mercifully covered, with water whose surface will hide that scene for all time."[31]

Flooding, Burning, Blowing Up

That "some day" began August 14, the day the diversion tunnel was sealed, except for "a portion that would allow 20 million gallons of water a day to flow through the dam." The bathtub drain was plugged. The banks of the three branches of the Swift River could no longer contain it. Flooding began, at a rate of 500,000 gallons per day. But before that, the fish had to be moved out of the lakes and streams. A crew from the State Department of Fisheries and Game arrived with big nets and removed the valley's beloved fish to ponds outside the watershed. [32]

That summer, the East Coast had suffered a drought intense enough for Massachusetts state officials to worry whether the Quabbin would continue to provide sufficient water to the Boston area. While the drought continued in some capacity until 1944, there was a moment of reprieve in late August, when the rain fell hard for several days, speeding up the flooding process. The Belchertown-Enfield road—"the first macadam highway in the entire valley"[33]—was now pronounced unusable, even though Commission trucks, at least for a while, powered through the flooding to get to the Chandler mansion.

On September 1, Nazi Germany attacked Poland. France, Australia, and the United Kingdom declared war.

The "Howe Block" was called that for a reason: the telephone exchange, post office, and general store were all controlled by one family and located in one building. But the Howes, too, had sold out to the state, and finally, in October, the Enfield telephone exchange was shut down. There were no buildings for the calls to be placed to, and telephone poles were being blown up across the valley. The single phone line that remained was a direct line between the Chandler House, the dam headquarters, and the Administration Building.

Two weeks later, the last bridge connecting Enfield Center to the west was dismantled. But there was little news coverage. Local journalistic interest was moving elsewhere—the US was increasingly on a war footing, including building the nearby Chicopee Air Base; the dam was nearing completion; the valley was drowning; and everyone was exhausted.

It was already time for second-guessing. The *Christian Science Monitor* wrote an editorial, "Quabbin Cost is More than Boulder Dam," which was full of praise for the latter and hand-wringing about the former. The *Monitor* asked, at thirty million dollars more than the Boulder Dam, was Quabbin a mistake?

> Quabbin is a big project, but an engineering commonplace. It is neither highest, longest, or largest. It will irrigate no land, it will produce power only over the last ditch stand on the electric utility companies [this never came to pass]. It will simply supply Boston and the Metropolitan District with water. It will be pure water. It should be. An 80-mile system of hard rock tunnels and concrete pipe is bringing the water to Boston. The big hitch appears to be that it will bring more water, much more, than Boston has any hope of consuming.
>
> If all the words in the charges and counter charges uttered about Quabbin were added together, they might look like a typewriter picture of Halley's Comet.
>
> This situation arose, for the most part, from the fact that soon after Quabbin got fairly under way the Depression moved in, and from that time on it became difficult to decide whether Quabbin was a water project or a relief project. There was scandal about the way contracts were given out, criticism of allocation of jobs by politicians, storms of protest about moving people out of ancestral homes and plowing historic towns under.
>
> But the work was accelerated, rather than slowed, through all this barrage of words, and despite the innuendoes of graft the solid fact emerges that the Quabbin Dam and aqueduct were built for $13M less than the original $65M appropriation.[34]

The remaining members of the Enfield Engineers Club of 1928 were disbanding. Some were working on the new leg of the aqueduct, this time as supervisors rather than grinds; some were moving on to other parts of the state government, or back to their home states. Jerome Spurr had moved his family to Wellesley, MA, which was his home base until his death in 2005, so he could supervise the section of the aqueduct that would end at Norumbega Reservoir in neighboring Weston. He also became involved with local universities, particularly Northeastern, where he was a lecturer in the engineering department and the head instructor at the Northeastern ROTC—a job he'd been anticipating since he himself was a ROTC cadet at MIT.[35] He too was expecting war, and expecting to go fight in it.

Spurr also gave lectures to the public on the building of the Quabbin. In December 1939, the *Boston Globe* announced:

> Jerome L. Spurr, assistant state civil engineer, will present a lecture supplemented by colored motion pictures at a meeting tonight at 9:15 at Northeastern University . . . Spurr will discuss the preparation and discussion of the new Winsor Dam in the Quabbin area, on which he worked for several years as an engineer.[36]

Quabbin was now something that could be discussed in the past tense. Moving forward, there was water, and war.

SEVENTEEN

Preparing the Path to Boston— And to War: 1940–1941

The end of 1939 was the end of anything normal in the valley. The diversion tunnel—the stopper of the valley basin—had been plugged, and the millions of gallons of water flooding down the Swift River and rising up the denuded hills would soon become billions.

Before the reservoir froze for the winter, a group of engineers rowed into the water to collect samples; the water was at 416 feet above sea level, and their home base building would be dismantled in the next couple of months. No one wanted to go out to the isolated Chandler House anymore if he didn't have to, including the administrators, and so, early in the winter of 1940, the young, new engineers had the Chandler and the surrounding abandoned land to themselves.

The college graduates of 1939 had spent half their lives in an economic depression and were facing the prospect of being sent off to war. For the college graduates of the 1920s, the Quabbin project probably felt a little like the early days of a modern startup. Nineteen forty would be the year the company was being sold to a larger entity—it was no longer exciting; the work had been completed, and the even the name of where they worked—the Swift River Valley—would be obsolete.

So the engineers had to make their own fun. Six of them took a car onto the ice, directly above the lowest part of Enfield, on the "banks" of the Chandler, and took photos.[1] Presumably they tested the ice for safety first. But, as with any group of high-spirited, stir-crazy young men with a camera to play with, hijinks ensued.

One bright snowy day, they slid down a hill in snowshoes while drinking bottles of gin. They pretended to be asleep, with their feet on their desks. One engineer posed on the side of the abandoned, and absolutely straight, Belchertown-Enfield road holding a traffic sign that said "Curve." Another stood outside the side door of the Chandler, pretending to unbuckle his pants as if for a hurried trip to an imagined outhouse (the house had indoor plumbing). Another picked up the town direction signpost at the Dana-Petersham Road right out of the ground and hugged it.

The Chandler House—home away from home for so many engineers—was torn down and burned by the end of January 1940. The Commission had hoped to save some of it, but the water had risen faster than they expected; the Commission was a victim of its own engineering success, and a break of lucky weather. Also, it was in bad shape. It had been used hard for twelve years.

And so Enfield ended its earthly life, and the water was left to the keepers of the Administration Building, the reporters who begged to hitch a ride in Commission boats, and the wildlife that was already making itself visible.

In the spring of 1940, while there was still land where the Chandler had stood, Commission photographers took regular photos of the encroaching waters, lapping ever higher against the overgrown grass where they used to park their cars and go outside for a smoke. In the captions, they listed the water heights, hundreds of feet above sea level and rising every day.

While the public could no longer get past the Administration Building or any of the other guarded gates, local reporters could still bum onto a Commission boat and satisfy public curiosity that way.

A reporter persuaded Metropolitan Special Agent Roy Kimball, who was also persuaded by Evelina Gustafson, to give him a ride in a Commission motorboat. Even by this point, the reporter noted, wildlife had begun to encroach on what had been the valley basin. A pair of woodchucks were trapped on what had suddenly become a "small island a short distance below the former site of the Enfield Headquarters of the Commission" and would have to be rescued before they would be "forced to swim the quarter mile to land." The reporter also wondered at the "several hundred Canadian geese and as many ducks" inhabiting the Quabbin's "desolate stretch of water, and fish abound[ing] in the lake in spite of the removal of thousands from the smaller ponds and brooks feeding into the reservoir."

The Quabbin, he said, was now "lapping at the foundations of the mansion used for the past 10 years as headquarters . . . Only a brick vault is standing, and this will soon be 40 feet underwater . . . Everywhere are mute evidences of former human habitation: roads leading now to nowhere except into the water; small stretches of farm roads ending where there were fields, barns, homes, and here and there in the higher sections foundations which once were parts of houses, churches, and other buildings."[2]

Another news story concurred: "The water level in Quabbin is now 476.7 feet above sea level. When full it will be 530 feet above sea level, with a capacity of 400 billion gallons. It is not approximately one-fourth full.

"In terms of old landmarks, the water is just now over the foundations of Frank Hall's store in Greenwich Village; nine feet over the dummy at the four corners in Greenwich Village; over the railroad bed of the Athol branch where it crossed Sunk brook, northeast of Quabbin Lake, at William Walker's spruce lot, and is well up on the terraces of the sidehill cemetery at Enfield."[3]

The Commission, however, was unhappy with the quality of its single boat. According to the *Springfield Union*, after an official trip, "The brief experience officials of the Quabbin Dam have had with the 20-foot motor boat used to patrol the large expanse of water in the reservoir has satisfied them a much larger craft is necessary for safety and comfort. Chairman Eugene C. Hultman of the Metropolitan Water Commission said today he had contacted an engineering expert at the Massachusetts Institute of Technology who has agreed to draw the plans for a 40-foot boat which will be used to patrol the 60 miles of water, carry at least 20 or 30 persons in addition to the crew and a fire pump and several hundred feet of hose to battle forest fires. The craft will contain a cabin to afford comfort to fire fighters, and a radio to contact Quabbin headquarters."[4]

Hultman, however, "expressed satisfaction" with the two flocks of sheep that had just been sent from Boston to provide organic cleanup of the grass at the dike and on the downward slope of the dam—just as had been done at FDR's White House. The sheep were from the "zoo" maintained by the Commission's Middlesex Fells Division. Chairman Hultman "jocularly named Division Engineer William Peabody 'shepherd' of the flock." Wool from the sheep would then be sheared and the profits would go to the Commission.[5] A photo shows sheep grazing in what looks like a tree-lined springtime meadow, minded by their official Commission shepherd; on the other side of a long white rubber tube being used as a dividing line, Hultman and Associate Commissioner Edward J. Kelley, dressed in suits, watch with amusement.[6] Chances are that fifteen years prior they had stood in a similar spot and watched a grazing flock of local sheep as they mapped out the dike's dimensions.

The Commission received the twenty-six-foot *Greenwich*, its first patrol boat, in June 1940. The *Enfield*, designed in cooperation with the MIT marine architect, was sent to the Quabbin in early 1941. This forty-six-foot boat could travel at "twelve statute miles per hour,"[7] but no one could figure out how to get it into the water on the day it was delivered.

Ellis Barbier's set of photos from April 16, 1941, called "Unsuccessful Attempt to Launch the *Enfield* Reservoir Service Boat," reveals that the Commission had not entirely considered how to launch such a large boat into the still relatively shallow water.

The *Enfield* had been delivered on the type of truck usually reserved for transporting automobiles, and the rig's driver was backed perilously close to the end of what remained of the Belchertown-Enfield road, in front of the Administration Building, before the road dropped precipitously into the water, trying to nudge the boat into the Quabbin. Before they realized the seriousness of the problem, one Commission administrator and one engineer were on site, trying to guide the boat down to its makeshift asphalt dock.[8]

But the boat didn't slide. Sometime later, the crowd around the boat included Hultman, Kelley, and Kennison, in suits and hats, all of whom probably had expected to be passengers on the *Enfield*'s maiden voyage that afternoon; five despairing engineers, one crouched on the grass holding a lit cigarette; the captain of the *Enfield*; three laborers with slumped shoulders, including the driver of the rig, baring a terrible apologetic grimace; and four boys in knickers and patterned sweaters who had suddenly appeared to watch the debacle.

Twenty-four probably very tense hours later, the engineers had come up with a solution: they hoisted the boat on skids and attached it to a network of slings and pulleys, almost as if it were a stone in a giant slingshot. Standing atop the rigging is a single engineer, probably the setup's mastermind, pipe in his teeth and looking pleased and the littlest bit smug.[9]

That same day, just a few hundred yards away, the pedestal for the Winsor Memorial was being set atop the completed dam.

In 1941, the *Enfield* and the *Greenwich* had national-security duties added to their patrols: making sure that no German spies, cars, or aircraft could sneak in and blow up the dam or contaminate the Quabbin water supply.

Other patrols were stationed at the Wachusett. Nervous American security officials didn't think that more than sixty-five miles from the Atlantic coast was too far away for intrepid Nazi bombers to strike; the Hoover Dam, by far more inland than the Quabbin, was similarly guarded. Nearby, area air defenses were preparing at the new Chicopee Air Base (now Westover Air Reserve Base) in Chicopee, MA, an hour's drive southwest of the Quabbin.

The Chicopee facility broke ground in April 1940, and was intended to be built fast to "protect the industrial northeast in case of war,"[10] which people now assumed was coming, official US neutrality or no. Planes flew overhead for the ceremony; hundreds of guests, including state dignitaries and members of the military, sat in winter coats on folding chairs as speeches were given over a military loudspeaker. The sun was bright but chilly, and the ground under their feet was bare dirt, ready for the steam shovels. With the hills in the background, this could have been the Swift River Valley. R. Nelson Molt was the official representing the Commission, and his increasingly estranged wife, Olive, took photos.

The Molts were also involved in memorializing the Valley to metropolitan Boston, taking the exhibit on the road. Nelson showed the Commission's promotional films to organizations including the Brookline Kiwanis Club.[11] Olive's paintings were part of a retrospective called "Story of Quabbin Valley in Songs and Pictures," held at the Pilgrim Women's Club of Dorchester. In this "unique and dramatic presentation of the vacating of the Quabbin Valley region by its former inhabitants . . . [s]ome of the former residents of the valley who were forced to seek new homes will tell in music, song and short dramatic sketches the story of their transference to other localities."[12]

William Nickerson, former superintendent of the valley consolidated schools, sang a baritone solo, accompanied on the piano by John Bone, "both formerly of Dana and now of Athol." Nickerson also presented a dramatic sketch called "The River Rises"; Mabel Jones, half of the pair of authors of "Letters from Quabbin," performed "Fleeing the Flood," and her daughter, Mary, performed "Childhood Days." Jessie Mabel Prentice, wife of the Greenwich store owner who went down in a blaze of glory the previous year selling "found" artifacts from the valley to intrepid tourists, read a poem called "Good Bye Old Cherished Haunts."

All Quabbin survivors had been invited to attend the performance; it is unclear if any of them were willing to make the trip to hated Boston. But Olive Molt herself was probably thrilled to be counted as one of the "former residents," particularly as the Molts lived in a fine brick house on a good street in Worcester.[13]

Meanwhile, the members of the Quabbin Club wrote to the US post-master general, asking him to create a Swift River Valley stamp "memori-alizing the valley." Nellie Brown edited the draft letter, pushing the idea in her notes to the group that the Quabbin Club could add the "national defense" angle to their pitch.[14] Since Brown did not include a response from the postmaster general in her extensive Quabbin-related papers, she probably did not receive one.

Brown then used her considerable social capital to ask Eugene Hultman if the Commission would consider erecting a statue of Chief Quabbin at the Quabbin Park Cemetery. Hultman said that such a statue would be prohibitively expensive for the state unless the funding were from "public subscription." On the other hand, he found the idea of a postage stamp of the yet-to-be constructed fire tower intriguing, and told Brown that she should contact Molt for suitable design ideas to be sent to the US Post Office.[15]

The Faucet Is Turned

By October 22, 1940, Quabbin water, hundreds of feet above sea level and close to one hundred feet above the valley in spots, was ready to be released into metropolitan Boston. The reservoir was about one-third full; even at that level, abandoned paved roads could still be seen rising out of the water. The following day, incoming governor Leverett Saltonstall, an old Yankee Republican of the Brahmin variety, and members of the

Commission, grateful to no longer have a populist in the state house, held a grand ceremony.

The commemoration began the day at the Quabbin, and the motorcade traveled the path of the aqueduct, first to the Wachusett, then to Southborough for the dedication of the new Hultman Aqueduct, which was to carry water from Southborough to Weston, and then on to metropolitan Boston.

Hultman, along with other members of the Commission and the group of engineers who built the tunnels, stood in rain jackets and boots inside the still-dry tunnel for a photo op.[16] Then, "by a simple movement of his hand," pulling a chain hoist to lift a huge valve, Governor Saltonstall "opened a sluice gate 280 feet below where he was standing and started 150M gallons of water from Quabbin reservoir flowing into the new Norumbega reservoir in Weston."[17]

The party then drove along the path of the Hultman Aqueduct—the tunnels, according to the breathless *Boston Globe*, "large enough to let street cars pass" (although the Quabbin Aqueduct was larger in diameter)—to Weston, where they met other state officials for a 1:15 luncheon and speeches at 2:00, after the ceremonial opening of the Norumbega discharge gate. The afternoon's events were radiocast over New England's Yankee Network.[18]

Hultman gave a speech about the history of the Boston water supply. Then Governor Saltonstall spoke. This system, he said, was "a far cry from the old town pump" and that it "stagger[ed] the imagination when I think of what it means when I open this valve . . . an enduring symbol of the peace we enjoy and the way of life which we cherish in this country.

"Here is the product of man's genius." he said, "created solely for the greater comfort of his fellow men . . . Here is a huge network of earthworks, concrete walls, tunnels and engineering marvels, not laid out for gun emplacements and air raid shelters, but to make us healthier and happier people.

"Here was a vast engineering feat which created a lake 39 square miles where dry valleys lay. Inhabitants of six villages had to be uprooted from their homes. Yet this upheaval of the landscape, this transplanting of human lives, proceeded without a protest, without a hitch, because the objective was the common good and the decision was the will of the people. We are determined to preserve it so long as these reservoirs and mighty tunnels through the hearts of our hills shall stand."[19]

No representatives from those people who left the valley "without a protest" were on the guest list for the event. Nor were any engineers who had dug the rock tunnels hundreds of feet in the earth, turned the direction of the river, raised the dam, and lived with those who had suffered real heartbreak.

The *Boston Globe* cautioned that "no water from the new 405-billion-gallon Quabbin Reservoir passed into Boston mains today, but theoretically, at least, water from the Ware River did."[20]

Preparing for War

Everyone, everywhere, across the US was aware that war was probably coming. The Commission boats on the Quabbin now were for surveillance as well as science.

By the end of the summer of 1941, the Commission posted twenty-four-hour guards "at all power plants, pumping stations, and dams under its control in the state."[21] Visitors to the reservoir were forbidden to enter any structures. "We know of no attempts to destroy or damage any of our plants," said Karl Kennison, "but . . . it is a precautionary measure similar to that taken by utilities and other large companies throughout the country." Police were stationed at the Administration Building's outbuildings; the state police still have a presence there today.

In his January 2, 1941, inaugural address, Governor Saltonstall recommended that the Quabbin watershed be used as an artillery and ammunition proving ground for the British military, which had made the request, although he would have to check with the State Department to make sure that such use would not violate the pre–World War II Neutrality Act. Nevertheless, the Republican governor said, while he believed in a "national government strong enough to protect us in this or any other emergency . . . we must insist upon the independence of our local and State governments."[22]

The Commission exerted its independence by flatly refusing to consider the governor's suggestion. The US Army got its way in the end, even if the British military did not, and was permitted to use two sections of the watershed for gunnery ranges. According to J. R. Greene, "Bunkers and platforms for one of the ranges are still visible at the end of Gate 52 road, near the southern shoreline of the reservoir. Other gun platform foundations are still visible just above the shoreline between the West Branch of Fever Brook and the peninsula near the site of North Dana. A fire-spotting tower built on the northeast shore of the reservoir (along old Route 21) by the air force was still standing (but not in use)."[23]

The fire tower atop Little Quabbin Mountain, which is still open to the public today, was one of the last new contracts before the war. The Springfield *Union*, already in war mode, described it as a "lighthouse" and lauded its fortress-like appearance ("built of a shaft of reinforced steel and concrete covered with fieldstone from every part of the valley"), shiny tech (equipped as it was with "many electrical devices, two-way radio, telephone, sleeping quarters for the observer, and copper-covered steel entrances strongly barred with foolproof locks"), and far visual reach (with a telescope, the viewer could see "an expanse of territory that reaches into Maine, New Hampshire, New York State, Connecticut and Vermont)."[24]

Ellis Barbier "photographed the building of that tower! And that was started in the fall and built during one of the worst winters we ever had! They had to do it that way because it was a PWA project and it had to be started at such and such a time. They made an enclosure with tarpaulins—they had two boilers with 48 steam radiators up there to keep it warm enough to build it up there." Stuart Pike had left the project by that time to find better work and sign up for the war effort, so Barbier was left on his own both in the field and in the darkroom. He'd even learned to type on the negatives instead of handwriting the captions.[25]

Chet Chetwynd was an inspector on the tower contract. The Springfield *Union* took a nice posed photo of him with Designing Engineer William Peabody in the observation booth. It was his most prominent photo in front of the camera before he went to war.[26]

The Administration Building had been finished also, and it had a dedicated darkroom. "The facilities were good," said Barbier, "but the Commission would never buy any equipment. I still went around with a tripod and a 5" x 7" view camera. They were way behind the rest of the world. They wouldn't spend any money on photography. It was primarily an engineering outfit, and they looked down on us—They knew pictures were important, but it was so hard to get anything out of them.

"We got a lot of good comments on the photography. The Boston office used to say, 'Don't make these pictures look so good!' because the people wanted twice as much money for them when they saw the pictures."[27]

Despite the end of Curley's machine, the Commission was still full of pork, and occasionally populated with people who didn't find hard work especially necessary. "We had a man named Donald Sampson—he was from MIT," said Barbier, "and there was a Mayor Cousins of Waltham who lost his job, so Mr. Peabody put him on Construction Division, because it was a pork barrel—you could put anyone on. Anyway, he came into the office the second morning, and Mr. Sampson said, 'We're in the habit of getting to work on time around here!' and the mayor said, 'Don't worry about that—I can call the head man right up on Beacon Hill!' and Sampson said, 'The telephone's right there.' So he came to work on time after that."[28]

It's Official: The Winsor Dam

The June 1941 dedication of the Winsor Dam and the unveiling of the memorial to Frank Winsor at the dam's apex was a surprisingly low-key event. According to the Commission's annual report, "This memorial was erected by Mr. Winsor's many friends and sponsored by the Boston Society of Civil Engineers and the Northeastern Section of the American Society of Civil Engineers. It was presented on behalf of the engineers by George T. Seabury, a lifelong friend of Mr. Winsor and Secretary of the American Society of Civil Engineers, and unveiled by Edward Winsor, Jr., a grandson. It was accepted for the State by His Excellency, Governor Leverett Saltonstall, and Chairman Eugene C. Hultman of the Commission accepted its custodianship. About 250 officials and guests attended the dedication, following which they were served luncheon in the Commission's seaplane hangar in the Administration Buildings and were conducted on a tour over the work."[29]

The Boston papers did not cover the event. Commission photographs show a small crowd of adults and children in summer dress clothes watching the speakers, who were congregating around a small outdoor table along with Mr. Winsor's widow, children, and grandson.

It's possible that Saltonstall might not have shown up at all—June was a busy month for him, with more than one event per day—but he was already in the area to be awarded an honorary doctorate at Amherst College and give the commencement address at nearby Williams College, where he talked about the long-term risks of centralized government: "I firmly believe that," he said, "if we are to survive, we must preserve the town-meeting principle. The trend toward concentration of authority in a central government is exactly opposite to that conception. No emergency can justify the surrender of our people's free will or the silencing of their voice."[30] (Coincidentally or not, the Boston *Globe* headline in the next column over was "Ex-Gov. Curley Given to Oct. 6 to Pay Judgement," in which a district judge informed His Excellency that he owed the city a judgment of $42,629, and His Excellency reassured the judge that he could sell his Nevada silver mine, "which he values at $2,000,000," before the due date."[31]

The group quietly dispersed when the speeches were over, and did not linger to socialize. The dedication was a sign the dam was finished, work on the reservoir was completed, the water was rising, and it was time to move on. It is unclear if any former residents of the Swift River Valley were invited to attend the event.

⸺

Water began to flow east from the reservoir shortly afterward. For this small ceremony in the fall of 1941, guest of honor Mrs. Hultman turned the spigot—really a six-foot version of a regular tap—at the West Boylston head house to prepare the Quabbin water to move freely from the Quabbin Aqueduct through the Hultman Aqueduct and on to Boston. Hultman himself, accompanied by a group of MIT students, turned another crank.[32]

The reservoir was now fully functional. But the forest around it still needed to be rebuilt. The new forest would be a complete ecosystem, and the forested watershed would prevent pollutants from reaching the water supply. Thousands of foot-high European larch transplants and hemlock seedlings were moved to Quabbin Mountain, and Norway spruce transplanted near the dike. Orderly lines of white pine, white spruce, rock maple, black walnut, and hickory dotted the mangled fields and former farms of the new Quabbin Park reservation. The Norway spruce seedlings planted in 1936 were now nearly human height, and the red and white pines planted in Prescott in 1935, were now above the engineers' heads.[33]

At the former Wendemuth property in Prescott, a "plantation" of red and white pine had grown to five feet. The Wendemuths, along with the Griswolds, also of Prescott, were the last two families left to fight the Commission, staying as late as 1939. Because they were far away from the reservoir itself, they claimed there was no objective reason for them to be forced out of their hilly, rocky farmsteads on the Prescott Peninsula, homes without rich land, electricity, plumbing, or easily passable roads. But the land was all they had, and they argued bitterly to keep it.

In their anger, the Wendemuths had left their detritus behind, and the effects were uncanny. A photo shows a pile of twisted metal, wire cable, and posts, evocative of a crashed alien spaceship, sitting in the middle of an abandoned farm field. Behind the wreckage is an engineer dressed in a "detective-style" fedora and overcoat, holding a placard that says "12." Behind him are hundreds of five-foot-high pine trees, and behind those, the forest. Without the Stuart Pike's neutral title ("Reforestation, red and white pine, planted spring 1937, looking northwest from Mabel L. Wendemuth property"), the photo would be open to all sorts of conspiratorial interpretation.[34]

Guarding the Reservoir

"All days off for Metropolitan District Police have been canceled, and Commissioner Eugene Hultman will go before Gov. Saltonstall today to ask appointment of 20 additional men from the Civil Service list, Supt. Edward M. Woods announced last night. Special guards have been set up at the Wachusett, Quabbin and Chestnut Hill reservoirs—a sergeant and nine men at Wachusett and a lieutenant and three men at Quabbin. Orders are to arrest all suspicious persons and to allow no one 'within throwing distance' of a reservoir."[35]

It was December 8, 1941, and the US had just been catapulted into war. The country had no more protection from its nominal neutrality. Every piece of national infrastructure was theoretically in danger.

By December 10, a list of nearly fifty police officers and firefighters across the state had signed up as "eligibles" to help the existing patrolmen guard the reservoir. Twenty-five of them were hired within the week. (This was all very public security, as opposed to the combination of overt and covert surveillance of the Quabbin after the 9/11 attacks.) Quabbin was closed to all visitors for the duration.

Engineer Jerome Spurr left the Quabbin project in the fall of 1941. He'd already quit his daily duties in January, "by reason of military leave of absence without pay,"[36] to become an assistant professor of military science at MIT and to head engineering ROTC companies at both MIT and Northeastern. An MIT ROTC cadet himself, he'd been on the project for fourteen years. Spurr was the most prominent member of the engineering staff to join the military, but he was far from the only one—more than 250 engineers volunteered for military duty during the Second World War.

At the end of the year, the Commission's soil testing lab was discontinued. All the soil they had been testing daily for more than ten years was now underwater.

EIGHTEEN

The War and After: 1942–1946

The final Chief Engineer's Report, in 1948, concluded with the "Honor Roll" for the "Commission's employees who joined the Armed Forces in World War II"[1]—a list of nearly 140 names. Around thirty of those were current or former workers on the aqueduct, dike, and dam.

Jerome Spurr had been disappointed more than a decade earlier when he'd been taken off working in the field to sit at a desk, so his initial wartime desk job may have been just as disappointing. He was certainly homesick. While stationed at Fort Belvoir, VA, in 1943, Jerome Spurr wrote to Nellie Brown:

> *Anne forwarded your kind note of last Sunday to me and I am taking the opportunity to thank you for your loving help and inspiration to us both . . . It doesn't seem so long ago even now to Enfield days and the memory of those years and those that have followed must now serve as a storehouse of memories to brighten the days ahead, together with hopes for a happy reunion some time.*
>
> *Anne agrees with me that entwined through our years together, since we first met in front of your home, has been the thread of*

your friendship, which has been of so much help to us. Please know
that we appreciate all you have done for us. I hope we can finish the
duty that lies ahead, and in that time we can cherish the hope of peace,
and once gained resolve to keep it. With much love, Jerre.[2]

The war was an opportunity for recently married Chet and Rosalind
"Bud" Sawyer Chetwynd to get out of Bud's parents' house in Ware. Home
life was tense at what the Sawyers called "Ample Manse"; Chet was quiet,
polite, and hard-working, and Bud and her family were loud, intellectual,
and cantankerous. Roland B. Sawyer, Bud's father, had voted against the
building of the reservoir, and it's unclear whether he approved of her marriage to an engineer. Bud had stopped working after she and Chet got
married; Chet, although he had been promoted to inspector, was let go by
the Commission when the reservoir had filled. Then, at age thirty-four,
he was drafted into the navy, where he became a carpenter, then chief war-
rant officer, and was stationed at Camp Peary in Virginia with the 101st
Construction Battalion, then on to Port Hueneme in California and then
to Hawaii.[3]

After Chet left, Bud hung around with some of the men from the
project as well as her childhood friends. In 1942 she joined the war effort
by becoming a nurse at Mary Lane Hospital in Ware and collecting for
the Red Cross. Gradually her letters to Chet refer less and less to anything
Quabbin-related—although after he mentions in a letter that he's been
playing baseball on the base, she replies, "you hitting a double reminds me
of the Commission's picnics!"[4] It had been a very long decade since he had
been on the Enfield Engineers team.

Bud had a tumor removed from her kidney, and then a hysterectomy,
in 1944. After her recuperation in Florida, she wrote near-daily letters to
Chet, whom she also called "Bud"; handled the sugar and gas rationing for
their 1929 Ford; and tried to live with her mercurial and opinionated father,
with whom she often fought. After she found a place for herself and Chet
in Rhode Island, her father offered some used furniture. "NOT WITH
STRINGS ATTACHED!" she screamed back.[5]

Throughout, Chet politely wrote to Sawyer at Bud's request, trying to entertain his increasingly erratic father-in-law with interesting news from Hawaii.[6]

Ellis Barbier enlisted in the Navy. "I didn't have to," he said, "but I kind of wanted to get out. I was in the first battalion of Seabees—we were ready to embark, and they landed us up in Norfolk, Virginia, on a cold day in March, I guess it was—1942—and this whole battalion was ready to go, and the chief officer hollered out 'The followin' men fall out!' And my name was the first one." Later, Barbier put his Quabbin photography skills to good use: "I joined the Air Force and they put me in the South Pacific, and I took pictures down there—thousands of 'em."[7]

Bill Segur was living with his mother and sister in Ware in 1940, doing his best to keep his family together after Dr. Segur's death. Segur enlisted in the military in 1942 and found himself in the Coast Artillery, Anti-Aircraft Units.[8] Illness and disease hit him hard: In early 1944 he spent time in the hospital for a perineal infection; that fall he was back in the hospital with malaria. In 1945 he was in the hospital yet again, and then was discharged from the army.[9]

Closer to home, the Quabbin area was on high alert for German spy or artillery airplanes. Engineer Fred Farley and his wife, Marion, were members of the official "ground observer corps" at the Quabbin, climbing the newly built fire tower and spending hours scanning the skies with binoculars.[10]

During the war, the Quabbin watershed itself became enlisted; its temporary title was the Quabbin Reservoir Precision Bombing and Gunnery

Range, used by Army Air Force and later US Air Force planes taking off from both Westover and Hanscom airfields. Planes also used the reservoir's narrow, crumbling roads as practice airstrips, with plenty of raw ground and high grass for emergency skids.

Beginning in May 1941, convoys of darkened military trucks rolled up and down the hills and around the sharp curves of Daniel Shays Highway for many nights between 9:00 P.M. and 12:30 A.M. This was to train the drivers to function without lights. All homes and businesses along the route were asked to stay dark during those hours, and state police stood guard at entryways to the highway to prevent civilian drivers from entering.[11]

During the day, Westover Air Base pilots flew practice missions over the Quabbin, and the watershed was used for gunnery practice, part of a long-negotiated agreement between the Commonwealth and federal officials. The military wanted to use the watershed, said the Springfield *Union*, because it was "one of the largest uninhabited sections of New England."[12] Four years earlier, that "uninhabited" area had hosted a dance for three thousand people.

For those who had relocated to Belchertown and Ware, the disconnect between past and present became even more dramatic once the war began. In the valley, they had gotten uneasily accustomed to seeing large machinery on the ground. But warplanes?

Ware residents began receiving warnings they'd be hearing bombing practice at a distance. Twenty-six bombers would be taking off from Westover Air Base for exercises. The bombing terrain, said the *Ware River News*, would probably be bounded "by Salem Depot on the north, Prescott Peninsula on the southwest, and Dana on the east." Nevertheless, Ware would be safe from errant bombs and strafing, the newspaper reassured readers, because the target areas "now consist of cleared land. As the reservoir fills, the terrain will be under water, interspersed here and there with small islands . . . Targets will be set up on these islands for the bombing planes, and isolation will increase the control."[13] In other words, planes would fly over Dana to drop bombs over Enfield, Greenwich, and the stone foundations of the Griswold and Wendemuth farms in Prescott.

It was fascinating, if horrifying, viewing. The *Ware River News* recommended "the terrace of the administration building" as a good place to see the planes in action: "A Ware man saw one of the preliminary practice tests the other day. He says the plane started from a mile or more up in the air, seemed to dive almost straight down, and to flatten out just in time to escape diving into the water, meanwhile releasing a bomb." So far as it was known, the paper added, there was "nothing secret about the practice."[14]

By mid 1942, military officials had determined that Quabbin was such a high-value target that the public was banned from the entire reservation "for the duration," including the administration building, fire tower, and roads over the dike and dam. (Post 9/11, "the duration" for private vehicles traveling over the Winsor Dam and the Goodnough Dike is ongoing.) But trespassers had had a couple of years to become experts in sneaking into the reservation, past the gates and police guards. Some got cocky. According to the *Ware River News*, "an occasional [trespasser] gets to the administration building and views the filling basin." Woe to the amateur Quabbin photographer: "Anyone getting in with a camera has it taken away and if there is an exposed film, the camera and film will be kept for a time, at least."[15]

Was all this "security theater," to use twenty-first-century parlance, necessary? The *Ware River News* wondered dryly, acknowledging that while "there is always a possibility of sabotage and the Met. commission will take no chances, the Wachusett reservoir would be much more apt to be the mark of bombers or saboteurs, for so long as the Wachusett is operating, the system can spare the use of Quabbin for considerable periods."[16] The Department of War did not ask the editors of the *Ware River News* for their opinions on wartime security.

Eventually, the war was over. The Commission men, and one woman—stenographer Frances E. Donovan of Springfield, who enlisted in the WACs in 1944[17]—came home.

Jerome Spurr returned to Wellesley, where he and his wife, Anna, had purchased a home, but only used it as a pit stop before fighting in the Korean War, then moving to Alaska, then moving to Turkey until his retirement from the military in 1958.[18]

Back from the South Pacific, Ellis Barbier asked for his old job. But the Commission—now disbanded and folded back into the MDC had moved on to other construction projects. "I went down to Fred Gow," Barbier said, "and he said, 'If you want to stay I'll let you, but you have to move to Boston.' So I took photographs—thousands of pictures, mostly underground—of the sewer system from Framingham through the entire metropolitan Boston area, with two big plants—one is in Deer Island and one on Nut Island—to take care of the sewage processing plant for the greater metropolitan area."[19] It was a project Barbier enjoyed so much he worked there until he retired, augmenting his salary with piano gigs at resorts around the state and buying a "little home" in Monson, MA.

Chet Chetwynd came back from Hawaii and took a job at the Navy yard in, ironically, East Greenwich, RI. Bud found herself a childless housewife; to keep herself busy she wrote letters, took long walks with their puppy, Taffy, and did volunteer work. Rev. and Mrs. Sawyer had a de facto separation; Mrs. Sawyer lived with Bud's sister, and Rev. Sawyer moved full time to New Hampshire.[20] The war and the exigencies of daily life—and the physical distance from the valley—severed their connections to the Quabbin, and it fell into increasingly vague totality of the prewar years.

Some engineers returned to their previous profession, and even to the MDC; others moved in different directions:

Quabbin inspector Ray Bunker, who had participated in ROTC training while at Harvard, was stationed in the South Pacific during World War II and continued to serve in the army after the war until his retirement.

Paul Radasch became a first lieutenant in the 333rd Engineer Regiment, stationed in India. When he returned he finished his degree at Worcester Polytechnic on the GI bill, then moved to the Mountain West where he became an insurance broker.

Edmund Carey served as a navy lieutenant. He returned to work at the MDC as a senior civil engineer and was profiled in the 1950 *Journal of Public Health*.

Lloyd Crumb had worked on the Quabbin as a Northeastern University co-op student, where he majored in civil engineering. After graduating in 1941, he was enlisted in the Twelfth Air Force Fifty-Seventh Bombardment Wing in Africa and Europe. After the war, he worked as a civil engineer throughout the eastern half of the US.

Crumb's son, Lloyd K. Crumb, had no idea his father had worked on the Quabbin project: "My father hated the office. As his reputation as a project engineer grew he was able to pick and choose projects simply to learn more about the different specialties in civil engineering. Like the world's largest twin-span suspension bridge where he was field engineer in charge. Also, toward the end he worked for the Royal family of Saudi Arabia building universities and sea ports."

The Quabbin story also prompted Crumb Jr. to remember something about his father's life: "He represented a valley containing a network of small farming communities in Central New York, where he grew up, that would have all been destroyed if the Army had been allowed to build a dam. The valley won and a dam was not built. Perhaps his early work on the Quabbin project . . . had a bearing on his later effort." [21]

Not every Quabbin engineer came home. Henry LaFrance was killed in action in World War II; his niece remembers that "before Quabbin was filled he drove us through the reservoir on Sunday afternoons. I was eight years old at the time. He was a civil engineer with a degree from Norwich U. in Vermont." [22]

World War II also marked the deaths of Mr. and Mrs. Howe—she in 1942 at age 82; he in 1943 at age 83. After two centuries as members of the one of the valley's most prominent families, they died, like many less illustrious valley elders, of "short illness" and broken hearts.

The Spillway Runneth Over

By 1946, the pines seeded at the Harry Reed property in Prescott were now twenty feet tall and the area had begun looking like a forest again. On June 22, seven years after the waters began to rise, the reservoir was so filled that the first water was released over the Winsor Dam Spillway.

Frank Winsor's widow attended the opening ceremony. So did the new MDC commissioners and some of the long-time engineers, who were now middle-aged. They stood on a walkway above the rushing water and posed for Ellis Barbier's photos.[23]

At 2:30 P.M., the "stop logs" holding the water in place were lifted by MDC associate commissioner Louis B. Connors, assisted by two local war veterans who had also worked for the Commission. Tons of water roared into the years-dry basin of the west branch of the Swift River and poured down 150 feet.[24] Gerry Albertine was already taking photos at the foot of the spillway.

The spillway's scale was astonishing. The manmade waterfall poured through the huge brick arch and tumbled down the rocky hillside into the Swift riverbed. Hundreds of men in shirtsleeves and women in bright summer dresses hung over the edge of the bridge. Some of the braver ones picked their way down the steep hill to get closer. A father, crouched in the grass, pointed out something to his open-mouthed young daughter. A man sat defiantly on the concrete shelf right next to the water. In the grand panorama, each one of them was insignificant, almost too small to be seen in comparison to the millions of gallons of pure, drinkable water cascading onto the rocks.[25]

"I recall being at the opening of Quabbin when the water first came over the spillway, and it was quite a thrill," Quabbin supervising engineer Harold Willey said in 1981. "We were standing on the spillway bridge, and the water came over the spillway dam, and right on down into the Swift River. And then you could see the result of many years of work and the labor of a great many people—and the heartbreaks of a great many people—finally ending up in an accomplishment—a real engineering feat."[26]

The chief engineer's write-up of the event was subdued: "The visitors spent the afternoon in viewing the reservoir from various vantage points along the scenic highway, and particularly the new and beautiful waterfall created by a plunge from the upper to the lower levels of the spillway channel against the background of the 41-foot masonry arch span which carries the highway across the channel."[27]

The water's release, said the *Boston Globe*, more triumphally, "brought to a climax the dream of a mighty reservoir to supply water to eastern Massachusetts."

And it was a time of triumph: The war was won; society was celebrating its return to normalcy; technology was the key to a fulfilling future; and, at long last, Boston's thirst could be quenched. "It was the salvation of Massachusetts," decided Harold Willey,[28] who was one of the remaining few who had seen both sides of the story.

NINETEEN

Conclusion:
Modern "Letters" from Quabbin

Under Quabbin

In 1998, UMass Amherst biology professor Ed Klekowski led a series of
dives under the Quabbin Reservoir, assisted by divers with the Massachusetts State Police and the Massachusetts Department of Conservation
and Recreation, the first underwater exploration since the reservoir was
constructed. The dives, which resulted in the 2001 PBS documentary
Under Quabbin,[1] revealed how much inorganic infrastructure had been
abandoned in the depths.

There were no church steeples, as some people still steadfastly
believe—the Commission's engineers were tasked with leaving no structure
standing—but in the gloomy green postapocalyptic landscape one hundred
feet beneath the water's surface, Klekowski's team found schools of fish
swimming around the remains of the Hell Huddle bridge in Greenwich
and Crawford mills in North Dana; water pipes and the bases of streetlights

from the Dugmar golf course; old bottles, cans, and tires along the banks of the Swift River; empty foundations of homes with "the skeletons of bushes preserved under water—a black clump of stems that might have been a lilac bush growing at the corner of the house."

Then Klekowski found the cemetery behind the Enfield Congregational Church.

"I knew it was the cemetery," Klekowski said, "because one of the divers picked up a piece of marble tombstone. At first, I thought we were wasting our time. We saw nothing. And then, as we were swimming along the top of one of the terraces, some stonework materialized out of the gray water. The stonework consisted of a series of granite curbings surrounding a family plot.

"As I swam around, I wondered whose family plot this was. And then one of the divers discovered a name. The name was Underwood. To find *Francis Underwood*'s family plot . . . was just unbelievable."[2]

The Underwoods were not the only families with stonework left behind. The dive team found no caskets, but uncovered numerous intact marble headstones from the nineteenth century and fragments of slate headstones from the eighteenth. The headstones looked as if they had been stacked up and forgotten. Perhaps they belonged to people whose families had chosen to bury them elsewhere, and there was no reason to remove them. Perhaps workers had run out of time.

Not far from the stack of tombstones, the divers discovered the remains of a road. "That road," said Klekowski, "led up from the church to the cemetery proper. Along the road we could still see the granite posts with their iron bolts. This was the road on which horse-drawn hearses would have carried coffins from the church to be buried on the hillside."

The divers also found a pedestal that at one time may have supported an obelisk. Further along they saw "other remains of monuments scattered on the bottom of the reservoir. Bits and pieces of tombs. Pedestals that had been broken off. And occasionally we would just see a lone granite shaft. On other places were just scatterings of broken granite blocks. These, again, probably outlined family plots, piled up, ready to move, and then just abandoned."[3]

An Alternate Timeline

Many folders down inside a CD-ROM filled with Quabbin-related articles, a parting gift from the estate of Bob Wilder handed out to Quabbin researchers at the Swift River Valley Historical Society in New Salem, is a Word document purporting to be the draft of an article from the April 5, 2006, issue of the *Boston Globe*.[4]

"The Swift River Valley—Still Here: Western Massachusetts valley celebrates its 75th anniversary of its new lease on life," by Al Winter, is an alternate timeline fantasy of how the Swift River Valley could have flourished.

In this telling, in 1931, the Massachusetts State Legislature, prodded by the "intense and almost unanimous pressure from the people of central and western Massachusetts," refused to continue the study of the valley as the sole source of drinking water for metropolitan Boston. Instead, the story goes, the state created a "state-of-the-art system of watershed protection, water filtration and aqueducts which keep the area well supplied with clean drinking water. Some of this water comes from the Swift River, via an extension of the Ware River Aqueduct, since the Valley residents were happy to send the flood flows from the river to help Boston with its water needs, as long as the Valley remained intact."

Instead, a highway, I-590, was built to include the valley in the state's prosperity. New factories and office buildings began to appear; a valley-wide public high school was built. The Pioneer Valley Transit Authority extended its bus routes into the valley, and faculty and students from the Five Colleges began living in Prescott because of its harsh beauty and cheap rents. Many folks from the eastern half of the state built summer cottages. Bed-and-breakfasts and the antique trade thrived. So did small family farms.

The reporter, Al Winter, visits the home of a relative newcomer, Jon Melick of Prescott, who serves as a guide to the modern valley. "The Valley," Melick tells Winter, "is a symbol of the need to conserve our natural resources, instead of constantly moving out further and further to exploit the natural resources of those who lack the ability to resist effectively. We're very lucky to have the Valley to enjoy, today. I'm sure that the reservoir would have been a very beautiful place, with all that water, all those wooded hills and islands and all the wildlife that would have flourished there. But then, we wouldn't have all this."[5]

This article from the *Globe* never ran, because it never existed. There is no such reporter named Al Winter. In fact, this is an unpublished story by Jon Melick, himself an interpretive Quabbin historian. He is one of many who have longed to create an alternate history around the Quabbin, and has written a number of stories in which everyone wins.[6]

It could have happened that way, said Bun Doubleday in 1981, "but of course there was no organization like we have today in cases like that, and of course there was no necessity for environmental impact statements or anything like that. There were no environmental societies to protest it. So the legislature just voted to go ahead with it, and that was that."[7]

A Town Meeting

Massachusetts Governor Michael Dukakis declared 1988, the fiftieth anniversary of the disincorporation of the Swift River Valley towns, a "Year of Remembrance." Dukakis signed a proclamation with survivors gathered around his desk, and encouraged eastern Massachusetts residents to learn about the history of their drinking water. Dukakis was running for president that year, and so news organizations, including the *New York Times*, found themselves covering this bit of Massachusetts local color.[8] Survivors and their children attended a formal fiftieth anniversary "Farewell Ball" at UMass Amherst; attendees included eighty-three-year-old Jerome Spurr, who walked with the members of the newly formed Friends of Quabbin nonprofit in a re-creation of the original ball's Grand March.[9] Spurr's granddaughter, Tricia Spurr Thompson, then a recent college graduate, attended as his guest: "In my head I knew they were survivors or descendants of survivors," she recalled, "because my grandfather made me walk in the procession with him. I remember going and sitting, and being introduced to a lot of people. You didn't say no to him."[10] Ellis Barbier played jazz piano at the pre-ball cocktail reception.

On the ground, the view was quite different. A 1988 *Boston Herald* article describes a town meeting in Athol, the former northern terminus of the Rabbit Run, where two hundred residents gathered to complain about night restrictions at Quabbin Park and the reservoir. The MDC (now the Massachusetts Department of Conservation and Recreation) worried that overuse of the wilderness area for hiking, hunting, and fishing might contaminate the reservoir's water. To local residents, the MDC, and metropolitan Boston in general, were still interlopers—taking the area's few resources and then acting patronizing toward them, telling them how to conduct their daily activities. But these issues really functioned as proxies. The fundamental question was who, really, controls the Quabbin?

"'If the people of Boston are so concerned about water, let them put a dam across the Charles [River] and drink that,' one man said. He was followed by a young blonde mother, who told the crowd, 'It's time for everybody to watch your backs. There's a possibility that one day nobody will be walking in the Quabbin, and that will be a sad day.'

"It was a middle-aged fisherman in a nylon jacket who set the tone for the evening, issuing a stern warning: 'This is no longer the 1930s, when the state could get the residents to go along with anything.'"[11]

What, realistically, would the Swift River Valley have looked like today without the Quabbin? A guess is to examine the small towns just outside the watershed.

A large percentage of Enfield and Greenwich residents migrated to Belchertown, to the southwest of the reservoir. Today, Belchertown retains its common, which looks very similar to Enfield Common, Dana Common, or any of the other small surviving New England town commons. Belchertown has a little more than 15,000 residents, a household income of around

$81,000, an average age of nearly forty-two, and a poverty rate of 10.5 percent. It is overwhelmingly but not completely white.[12] Belchertown has supermarkets, strip malls, antique stores, and coffeehouses; it is gradually becoming absorbed by the neighboring Pioneer Valley. It voted 65 percent Democratic in the last presidential election, the Massachusetts state average.[13] (The only town in central Massachusetts that voted Republican in 2020 is Ware, perhaps due to its dying small-industry base.)[14] Would Enfield have turned into Belchertown, or would it have been more like the tiny neighboring towns of Pelham and Shutesbury, which, too, are absorbing the Pioneer Valley's culture (Shutesbury voted 88 percent for the Democratic ticket in 2020)[15] but retain their rural character?

Ultimately, the Swift River Valley was no different than other rural New England communities. The artifacts held at the Swift River Valley Historical Society in New Salem did not belong to people who were particularly wealthy or cultured: What those people left behind shows devotion to church, family, history, land, community. Not much more was necessary.

Rather, the valley is notable in the circumstances of its end. For a hundred years, outsiders have imbued the Quabbin with the pathos and romance of any premature demise. During the valley's dying decade, the natives had no time for romance; they were struggling to survive the upheaval of what had been their predictable, mostly happily circumscribed world.

The engineers were not romantics to begin with. They may have descended into the valley basin with grander ideas than making a living, but those too were blown up and worn down like the rock and soil, washed away like the water that dominated their lives. By the time the Winsor Dam rose hundreds of feet above what had been a farm worked by successive generations of the same family, there was little idealism, let alone romanticism, remaining in the engineering ranks. What was left were the edifices themselves: "the highways running to the water's edge, the mountains appearing as mere islands, and the water."[16]

For those engineers who wanted to forget what had happened there, the Second World War was a far larger canvas for their energies. The few others who stayed connected—even to the point of being buried at Quabbin Park Cemetery, in the section nearest the monuments of the old towns' commons—found ownership and pride in their work, which, in many cases, extended for years after the flood, and sometimes for the rest of their lives. There is no explicit rationale for which engineers took which path.

For the people left behind, the abortive history of the Swift River Valley has become its own mythology. Two and even three generations removed, views on the events have hardened. Today's keepers of the history know their parents' and grandparents' stories, and many live within a short drive of the reservoir and the gates that lead into wilderness and ruin.

In 2012, a volunteer at the Swift River Valley Historical Society refused to believe that there had been any intermarriages between young valley women and Commission engineers, even when presented with the contemporaneous evidence from "Letters from Quabbin." "Those people are lying," the volunteer said. "That never would have happened."[17] Another volunteer would not let researchers handle the nineteenth-century tintype photographs crammed together without protection in an archive box "because they're not your family," but were willing to have Commission photos hand-scanned "because they're just the engineers." [18]

Typically, these descendants aren't part of the larger Pioneer Valley's ultra-liberal culture—for the last several election cycles a disproportionately large number of signs for Republican candidates have been planted outside the modest homes around the Daniel Shays Highway. For students of the valley's past, this political and cultural intransigence, the resentment of being an outsider and an afterthought in one's native home, makes complete sense.

Memorial Day

Historical societies across central Massachusetts and descendants of the valley towns hold a Memorial Day commemoration at Quabbin Park Cemetery every year, lately organized by the town of Belchertown. The ceremony is nominally for war veterans, but it is also an annual living memorial to what was lost.

The ceremony begins with a parade. In front of a crowd of often more than a hundred, banner-carrying children, grandchildren, and great-grandchildren, nieces and nephews of the valley, march to the front of the cemetery, where the artifacts from the destroyed town common now live. A representative from each town lays a wreath on one of the objects. Then a state representative or member of a local civic organization gives a speech about Memorial Day and how it connects with the memorializing of the Swift River Valley:

"Last summer my wife, younger daughter and I walked out to Dana Common . . . There was a group there, but I lingered a little bit, until I was on Dana Common alone, looking at the cellar holes. Dana Common is something you need to do alone, because when you hear the wind whistle through the trees . . . you begin to realize the heritage and the sacrifice of people in Dana, and in Enfield, and Greenwich and Prescott."[19]

The towns around the Quabbin don't even drink its water.

The Quabbin was an engineering marvel for its time, and the men who worked on its construction believed in both its technical wonder and its utility, even though they often had to look away when they saw how the local communities were being affected.

People in power still look away, or find ways to justify destruction and displacement, just as the members of the state committees tasked with finding more water for Boston claimed that the valley—land and people—were stony and inhospitable to progress. Despite better community organizing, as well as better communications and better environmental studies, and despite a heightened awareness of the effects of community destruction, areas world-wide and even in the US are being sacrificed because of water—through flooding, drought, dams, and other changes in the land.

Quabbin is unique in how its creators interacted with the local population. Engineers who constructed the Hoover Dam are not buried in the
new cemetery built in 1935 when old cemeteries were dug up to make way
for Lake Mead.[20] Engineers are not buried with the thousands of reinterred
graves in the new Tennessee Valley Authority cemetery.[21] What makes the
Quabbin different?

Perhaps, despite its relative size, Quabbin was an intimate project.
Few things are so familiar, so close to the earth, so vital, as the water we
drink. In the Swift River Valley, destroyed and destroyer lived amongst
one another as one community for over a decade. The suffering of those
who claimed to prefer to drown in the Quabbin than leave their homes is
well-known, as are the people who died of sudden ailments probably caused
by despair and broken hearts. Forgotten is the fact that the engineers who
made the valley their home also grieved when they left. Their individual
sacrifices have been left out of the historical record but their imprint is in
every drop of water held in the reservoir, in the bald eagles that nest in the
trees of the new Quabbin forest and the wildcats that slink along its forest
floor, in the stone fences and foundations rising out of the hillside, and in
the reverence and curiosity of those who come to experience them.

TWENTY

Coda: Their Own Words

"I just like to go back to the old place and walk around. It's got trees, forty feet tall, in my front yard, in my back yard. Down the steps, down to the place where we hung clothes, the well stones. The foundation is bulldozed in. I find it interesting to go along the old stone walls—you take a stone wall until you know where you are.

"If you didn't know about the history of the people who had to move, you'd stand out there and say, 'What a beautiful spot.' You look at the water and the trees, and think it's beautiful. It's beautiful to the eye. But I know what was there. So I've got two beauties—one to remember, and one to look at."

—Eleanor Griswold Schmidt, Prescott

"A lot of the old-timers died of broken hearts. Because they had to give up a home, like my grandfather . . . for generations, three or four generations of people lived in that farmhouse. And it was just very hard for them to give up . . . when you've lived in one place for years and years and years, it's really hard to pull up your roots and make a home somewhere else."

—Trudy Ward Stalbird Terry, Enfield

196

"There were people who would have been happy to blow Boston right off of the map so they wouldn't need it."

—Sally Parker, Greenwich

"If they were going to take it, they were going to take it. We couldn't fight city hall. Now, Boston politicians can only think of Boston, and they spell it 'B-O-S-S,' in capital letters and 't-o-n' in small letters, because we sure are bossed by them."

—Herman Hanson, North Dana

"Levi Lincoln probably took it as bitter as anyone in the whole area. He just about worried himself into the grave, ten years too soon. And Harry Haskins was cryin' like a baby. When you see a man well in his seventies, maybe early eighties, standing under his own porch, when they tear down his house, it kind of makes you bitter."

—Herman Hanson

"I think they sort of expect you to be bitter. And I think they honestly would like to hear you say that. I don't feel bitter."

—Ruth Ward Howe, Enfield

"What have I lost? Well, really probably not too much, except I cannot, for example, take my children or my grandchildren back there, and say, 'This is the house where I lived when I was your age'—there just isn't any house there. All I can do is point into the water and say, 'That's where my home was.' I think that's the biggest loss I have suffered. Of course, if my old friends and neighbors were still there, why, I'm sure I would want to go back and call on them, socialize with them . . . but I know it's impossible so I just don't dwell on the fact at all. I wish that I could go back and see my old home as it used to look, but after fifty years it probably wouldn't look the same today as it did anyway. It doesn't do any good now to get yourself all stirred up about it—there's nothing you can do about it, certainly, so you just have to accept it. It's all water over the dam."

—Warren "Bun" Doubleday, Dana

"Many people were very unhappy about the whole thing because they'd lived their whole lives in the valley, and taking them out of the valley really did something to them. They never was the same. They went to Ware and Belchertown and practically all the towns, all the way up to Northampton. In Palmer, and in the Brookfields, they married and have big families of their own, I know a great many of them. It was a great joy to go to the Belchertown fair, where we met a lot of the former residents."

—George Boynton, Enfield

"There wasn't too much to do when Greenwich closed. They just said it was closed. And then Roy Kimball, he come up through, and he gathered up all the stuff that had belonged to the town—the snowplow and stuff like that—selectmen up in North Dana, they had their guns and badges. Roy Kimball and them took all the authority away, and that's about all there was."

—Stanwood King, Greenwich

"There were a good many unhappy people, giving up property that had been owned by several generations. It did not come easy, although some people had payments that would allow them to start fresh in some other area, but it must have been a traumatic experience for many of them, especially the older people."

—Jerome Spurr, engineer

"There was a story that a man put a row hook outside the Congregational Church windows so that when the water came, he could row it away."

—Ruth Ward Howe, Enfield

"I would rather be taken out in the field and shot than to have to leave the old home."

—Wallace Hunter, Enfield

"Frankly, I hate to see it go. I have been here so long I am a real country man."

—Norman Hall, engineer

Acknowledgments

This is a project that was initially conceived in 1999, then put aside for more than a decade. Maybe the idea goes back as far as 1994, when a couple of months before our wedding, my husband-to-be and I drove out from Cambridge to the Quabbin in his yellow Jeep and I was stunned—stupefied—to discover there was a whole lost world down there. There is a black-and-white photo of me literally with my hands in my hair on being told that what looks like water and some islands is actually a valley where people lived until the 1930s—and then being disappointed when I found out that no, there are no church steeples under the water. There would be no book without my husband, Simson Garfinkel, who has provided patience, ideas, and resources over the course of eight years.

Researching and writing this book has been a years-long stop-and-start process and has required much patience from many people. Jessica Case, my editor at Pegasus, has been such a kind, positive force and really made me delve into technical and logistical specifics I would have glossed over otherwise. Thanks also to my agent, Jeanne Glasser Levine at PubZone Consulting, who believed in this project and helped me find voice and order.

ACKNOWLEDGMENTS

I'd like to thank the many keepers of Swift River Valley and Quabbin history, many of whom tolerated my coming back to them, repeatedly asking the same questions and asking to see the same materials over and over. This admittedly incomplete list includes the Swift River Valley Historical Society and Dot Frye, who let me in the church building in the middle of winter; the Friends of Quabbin, especially Gene Theroux, who has been so kind and patient and who gave me access to the digitized oral history interviews; Sean Fisher, the keeper of many engineer secrets and who headed the amazing job of digitizing the Commission's photographs and uploading them to the Massachusetts State site, Digital Commonwealth; Clif Read and Maria Beiter at the Quabbin Visitor Center; J.R. Greene, without whose books this one would have been prohibitively difficult to write; and the staffs of the MIT Archives, the University of New Hampshire Archives, UMass Amherst Archives, Massachusetts State Archives, Springfield, MA, Archives, New England Historical Society, and Belchertown Historical Society/Stone House Museum.

I'd also like to thank Lloyd (Ken) Crumb, Alice Dragoon, Marjorie Stalbird Fierst, Paul Godfrey (FOQ), Nancy Huntington (DCR), Phoebe Kiekhofer, Ed Klekowski, Cliff McCarthy, Jon Melick, Mateo Rachansky, Michael Strong, Tricia Spurr Thompson, the late Bob Wilder—and, of course, my children—Sonia, Draken, and Jared Garfinkel—who probably now don't remember a time before their mother's historical preoccupation and wanderlust, and were all kind enough to attend college in Massachusetts so I'd have all the more reason to come up and do research.

Amherst, MA

A Quabbin Timeline

M uch of this information was compiled from two sources, with additions and confirmations from the author: The Friends of Quabbin Chronology page (https://www.foquabbin.org/chronology.html) and Mark T. Alamed's Quabbin Chronology page on his "Exploring Western Massachusetts" website (http://explorewmass.blogspot.com/2007/02/quabbin -chronology-index.html). The author thanks both profusely.

10,000 BCE	Swift River Valley carved from retreating glaciers.
4,000 BCE	Nipmuc Indians already living in Swift River Valley.
1634	Boston Common becomes America's first public park.
1652	Water Works Company is incorporated to bring water into Boston. Boston's population: 18,000.
1675–1678	King Philip's War, the conclusion of which allowed white settlers to move into the valley.
1736	Massachusetts General Court makes grant of 1,000 acres of land for the Quabbin territory.
1744	First church in Swift River Valley built in Greenwich Plains.

1745	First valley saw and grist mill built in Greenwich.
1749	Quabbin becomes incorporated as a parish.
1754	Greenwich incorporated.
1770	First dam constructed in valley, for use as a sawmill in what will become Enfield.
1761	Towns of Belchertown and Ware incorporated.
1788	Enfield Congregational Church built.
1786–1787	Shays' Rebellion.
1795	Boston Aqueduct Corporation is created to supply Boston with water from Jamaica Pond in Roxbury. Boston's population: 20,000.
1799	Sixth Massachusetts Turnpike is built, connecting the Swift River Valley to Amherst and Worcester.
1801	Dana incorporated.
1810	Greenwich Post Office opens.
1812–1813	Dam and cotton mill built at what will become Smith's Village.
1816	Town of Enfield is incorporated from sections of Greenwich and Belchertown.
1821	Swift River Company is established in Enfield, manufacturing cotton products.
1822	Town of Prescott incorporated; post office opens.
1822	Boston incorporated as a city. One hundred gallons of water are used daily by each family.
1823	Dana Post Office opens.
1825	Francis Underwood born in Enfield.
1825	Minot Manufacturing Co. begins operations in Enfield, making satinet fabric.
1830	Swift River Valley total population: 3,250.
1832	Swift River Hotel built in Enfield.
1848	Water from Long Pond (now Lake Cochituate) in Natick reaches Boston Common for the first time. The city holds a grand celebration.

1870	Water from the Sudbury River is added to Lake Cochituate due to demand from Boston.
1872	Sudbury Reservoir approved.
1873	Construction of the "Rabbit" train completed, connecting the town of Athol with the City of Springfield through the Swift River Valley.
1878	Sudbury Reservoir completed.
1880	Framingham reservoirs added to metropolitan Boston water supply.
1884	Enfield Town Hall built.
1893	Massachusetts Board of Health chooses Nashua River as a new water supply for Boston.
1893	Underwood's *Quabbin, The Story of a Small Town with Outlooks Upon Puritan Life* is published.
1894	Underwood dies.
1895	Establishment of Metropolitan Water District, made up of Boston and ten other Massachusetts towns, now a total of more than a million people.
1895	Wachusett Reservoir construction begins.
1895	Metropolitan Water District begins first survey of Swift River Valley.
1897	Quabbin Club founded.
1899	Commonwealth announces proposal to consolidate twenty-six cities and towns into one water supply and sewer system.
1900	Swift River Valley total population: 2,697.
1900	Wachusett Reservoir approved.
1908	Wachusett Reservoir completed. At the time it is the largest water supply in the world.
1919	Commonwealth creates Joint Board, with members of the Metropolitan District Commission (MDC) and Department of Public Health. It is tasked with finding new sources of water for metropolitan Boston. City of Boston's population: 748,000.

1920	Massachusetts enacts "pure milk" laws, ruining the livelihoods of many valley dairy farmers.
	Swift River Valley total population: 2,024.
1921–1922	The Metropolitan Water and Sewer Board, headed by X. Henry Goodnough, proposes a reservoir in the Swift River Valley.
1924	Prescott Post Office closes. People who live in Prescott pick up their mail in Greenwich.
1926	State Legislature passes the Ware River Act, allowing construction of a twelve-mile-long aqueduct from the Ware River to the Wachusett Reservoir. Metropolitan District Water Supply Commission (MDWSC) is set up to run the project. Frank E. Winsor is appointed chief engineer.
1927	April 26: State Legislature passes Swift River Act, appropriating money to construct a reservoir in the Swift River Valley.
	June: First wave of new college graduate engineers arrives in the valley.
	September 26: Ware River Diversion Project begins.
1928	MDWSC assumes administrative operations for the town of Prescott.
	Chandler House becomes Commission's Enfield headquarters.
1929	U.S. stock market crashes, ushering in the Great Depression.
1930	Swift River Valley total population: 1,378. This includes engineers living in Enfield.
1931	U.S. Supreme Court rules in favor of Massachusetts in *Connecticut v. Massachusetts*, ending the final chance for the reservoir project to be halted.
1932	MDWSC names reservoir "Quabbin."
1933	Quabbin aqueduct completed.
	Quabbin Park Cemetery dedicated.

Swift River Diversion tunnel already bypassing water around the dam area.

Dike construction begins.

1934   MDWSC has purchased 60,000 acres to date for the Quabbin project.

Democrat James Michael Curley elected governor of Massachusetts.

1935   Last run of the "Rabbit" train through the valley.

Daniel Shays highway (Route 202) opens.

Last active factory in the Swift River Valley closes.

Total Swift River Valley total population: 1,119. This includes engineers and their families.

1936   March: Flood of 1936 submerges parts of New England.

April: "Woodpeckers" arrive.

Construction of Greenwich baffle dam begins.

Construction of reservoir dam begins.

Swift River Valley Historical Society is formed.

August 1: Enfield Congregational Church burns down.

November: Most woodpeckers leave valley.

Curley loses Massachusetts senatorial election. Democrat Charles F. Hurley replaces him as governor.

1938   February 14: Greenwich final town meeting.

March 7: Dana final town meeting.

March 25: Order of the Eastern Star holds a farewell dance in the Town Hall.

March 28: MDWSC takes remaining unbought valley land by eminent domain.

April 8: Enfield final town meeting.

April 12: Quabbin Club final meeting

April 27: Farewell Ball held in Enfield Town Hall.

April 28: Enfield, Dana, Greenwich, and Prescott disincorporated.

May 30: Quabbin Park Cemetery dedicated in Memorial Day ceremony.

June 16: Enfield and Greenwich Granges disincorporate.

June 22: Enfield School final graduation ceremony. Seven students graduate.

September 10: MDWSC holds auction of remaining assets and property in valley.

September 21: Devastating hurricane hits valley.

November 8: Leverett A. Saltonstall, a moderate Republican, elected governor of Massachusetts.

December 28: Contract for pressure aqueduct, which will connect the Wachusett and Norumbega Reservoirs, is awarded. This will bring Quabbin water as close as Weston, within what is now I-495.

1939   Last families leave the valley.

Quabbin Administration Building finished.

January 14: Enfield Post Office closes.

January 27: Dr. Willard Segur dies.

January 30: Frank Winsor dies.

March 9: Karl Kennison takes over as chief engineer of Quabbin project.

March 23: MDWSC water and soil lab burns down.

August 14: Diversion tunnel is sealed. Quabbin Reservoir begins to fill.

1940   March 21: Chandler House torn down. The only buildings left in the valley basin are at the dam site.

October 23: Governor Leverett Saltonstall (R) opens Quabbin's tap to Eastern Massachusetts at a ceremony at the Norumbega Reservoir in Weston.

1941   Quabbin Tower completed.

Prescott Peninsula is closed to the public, used for bombing practice by Army Air Corps.

	September 17: First Quabbin water sent through the Quabbin Aqueduct to Wachusett Reservoir.
1945	Dam and dike area opened to the public.
1946	Quabbin Reservoir fills to capacity. MDWSC holds ceremony to open spillway.
1947	Metropolitan District Water Supply Commission becomes part of the Metropolitan District Commission.
1949	Prescott Historical Society purchases Prescott Methodist Church building from the state. It will become the first permanent building of the Swift River Valley Historical Society.
1951	Donald Howe publishes *Quabbin: The Lost Valley.*
1961	Swift River Valley Historical Society purchases the Whitaker-Clary House, its second permanent building.
1967	Drought lowers Quabbin water so low that visitors can see street grids and trotting park.
1969	Radio Astronomy telescope built on Prescott Hill.
1972	State legislature passes Kelly-Wetmore Act, which defines public access to the Quabbin and permanently closes Prescott Peninsula to public.
1982	First release of bald eagles at Quabbin.
1984	Water Resources Act passed. It establishes the Massachusetts Water Resources Authority (MWRA).
	Friends of Quabbin nonprofit founded.
	Quabbin Administration Building opened to public as the Quabbin Visitor Center.
1985	MWRA assumes operations of water distribution and sewer systems.
	Prescott Methodist Church is moved next to the Whitaker Clary House in New Salem and becomes permanent home of Swift River Valley Historical Society.
1987	Governor Michael S. Dukakis (D) declares 1988 the official "Year of Remembrance" for the fiftieth anniversary

of the disincorporation of the four Swift River Valley towns.

1988   "Year of Remembrance." Events include Remembrance Ball at UMASS Amherst, Winsor Memorial Rededication, Dana Commemoration, time capsule burial at Quabbin Park Cemetery.

1990   State declares a water emergency and considers using the Connecticut River as another water resource. Resulting conservation efforts decrease water waste by more than 17 percent and the Connecticut River proposal is shelved.

1999   UMass Professor Ed Klckowski, his wife, Libby, and a dive team explore the Quabbin under water and record it.

2001   Winsor Dam and Goodnough Dike permanently closed to vehicular traffic after 9/11 attacks.

2003   Governor Mitt Romney (R) merges the Metropolitan District Commission and the Department of Environmental Management to form the Department of Conservation and Recreation (DCR).

2013   Dana Common added to National Register of Historic Places.

People Mentioned in This Book

The Engineers and their Families

Albertine, Louis (Gerry) (1908–1998) Eventually worked for the MA Fish and Game Commission.

Barbier, Ernest (Ellis) (1912–2007) Worked in his father's Springfield jewelry store until his father's death in 1935 and then decided he wanted to work outdoors. Was a roving piano player after his retirement from the MDC; in his later life he and his partner "bought a fabulous little house in Monson."

Briggs, Charlotte Muriel Feindel (1904–1980) Daughter of Joseph Feindel, Dana town doctor. Married Homer Briggs. Born in Nova Scotia.

Briggs, Homer B. (1905–1970) Member of Enfield Engineers baseball team and Masons.

Bruce, Joe Member of Enfield Masons.

Burbank, Benjamin B. (1901–1979) Photographer of Enfield Engineers Club. Graduated from Bowdoin College. Left Commission work after several months and went to work as a technical engineer at Technicolor Corp.

Chetwynd, Charles "Chet" B. (1906–1994) Immigrated to US from Newfoundland. Was a senior warden of the Enfield Masons.

Chetwynd, Rosalind "Bud" Sawyer (1906–1982) The Chetwynds retired to Las Vegas.

Cross, Kenneth A. (1914–1998) Quabbin contract employee. Worked as a sand hog, grave digger, and truck driver on various contracts.

Crumb, Lloyd P. (1918–2013) One of the youngest workers on the Swift River component of the Quabbin; came out to work in Enfield during his co-op at Northeastern University. Later became the supervising construction engineer on the Cross-Bronx Expressway and Delaware Memorial Bridge.

Farley, Frederick D. (1886–1964) One of the early, pre-Commission engineers to arrive in Enfield.

Farley, Marion H. (1893–1981) Daughter Nancy, born in 1928, was one of the first engineer babies born in Enfield.

Fielding, William K. (1917–1997) Although he had grown up all over the world, as an adult he never left Ware. Copyrighted a number of songs and was published in several literary magazines.

Gow, Frederick W. (1898–1970) Became chief engineer of the MDC in 1950. Tufts graduate. Led work in Quabbin tunnels. Had a farm outside the watershed and collected Quabbin artifacts.

Hall, Norman D. (1905–1989) Began work for the Commission in 1927; worked for it and its successor, the MDC, until his retirement in 1968. Co-chair of the Final Ball. Buried at Quabbin Park Cemetery.

Hall, Wilma S. (1905–1970) Member of Quabbin Club. Buried at Quabbin Park Cemetery.

Hammond, N. LeRoy (1887–1963) Assistant division engineer in charge of the Enfield office. Left Quabbin project in 1936 to work for the State of New York.

Harris, LaRoy G. (1894–1969) Moved back to Rhode Island to continue his engineering work. Became a minor press celebrity when a news wire picked up that, in 1956, he found a turtle with his initials carved on the back, done when he was thirteen years old.

Jackson, Richard W. (Dick) Member of Enfield Engineers baseball team and Enfield Masons.

LaFrance, Henry A., MAJ (1896–1944) The only member of the Quabbin engineering staff killed in action during World War II.

Knight, Anna Eliza Rice (1880–1955) Had her own radio show in Worcester. Member of the Quabbin Club.

Knight, Charles S. (1873–1943) Commission representative for the town of Enfield; made sure that all inhabitants evacuated.

McLeod, Harold Member of Enfield Engineers baseball team and Enfield Masons. Was on-site for the soil and water lab fire.

Pike, Stuart D. (1910–1978) Member of the Ware Craftmen's Guild. Was written up in a 1939 issue of *Popular Mechanics*, where he showed reporters the Commission's films, some of which he had filmed himself. Member of Enfield Masons.

Putnam, Preston M. (1902–1954) MIT graduate. Member of Enfield Engineers baseball team and on the Finance Committee of the Enfield Masons. Married Janice Allardice, daughter of one of the early Quabbin designing engineers.

Radasch, Paul E. (1894–1990) Graduate of Worcester Polytechnic. Member of Enfield Masons. Had surgery on his leg just before the Farewell Ball; photos show him with a tuxedo and a cane.

Remington, Carl A. (1902–1982) Early Quabbin photographer. Graduate of Worcester Polytechnic.

Sheffield, Edward N. (1880–1971) Published an article in the August 1916 issue of *Concrete* magazine called "Three-Hinge Highway Bridge Built in Place at Low Cost." One of the early, older engineers.

Sheffield, Grace C. (1887–1904) Graduated from Mt. Holyoke College in 1909. Member of Quabbin Club.

Snow, O. Russell (1902–1969) Buried at Quabbin Park Cemetery. Botanist and coach of the Enfield Engineers baseball team. Was a Worshipful Master of Enfield Masons.

Snow, Grace E. (1904–1997) Buried at Quabbin Park Cemetery. Was part of the Enfield Engineers' band with her husband.

Spink, Amy A. (1893–1982) Coauthor of "Letters from Quabbin."

Spink, Herbert E. (1898–1948) Supervised Quabbin Aqueducts. Worked on Wachusett Reservoir.

Spurr, Anna Chase (1906–1986) Final president of the Quabbin Club.

Spurr, Jerome L., LTC (1905–2005) The last surviving principal engineer for the overseeing and construction of Quabbin Reservoir. Was a valley Boy Scout leader and Treasurer of the Enfield Masons. During the last years of her life she suffered from dementia; her husband refused to bring her to an assisted living facility and took care of her until her death.

Stalbird, James A. (1901–1958) Left the Commission in 1936 to work as a sanitary engineer in Saranac Lake, NY, and became the head of the Milk Sanitation Department for the New York State Department of Health. Was on the chess, swim, and tug-of-war teams at MIT. In Enfield Masons and Grange.

Thornquist, Barbara (1913–1998) Born Barbara Sheffield, Engineer Ed Sheffield's sister. She and Russ Thornquist were married in Enfield. Lived in Enfield in 1936. Member of Quabbin Club. Buried at Quabbin Park Cemetery.

Thornquist, Russell (1909–1976) Buried at Quabbin Park Cemetery.

The Politicos and the Administrators

Coakley, Daniel H. (1865–1952) Member of the Massachusetts Governors' Council during Governor Curley's time in office and his enabler, particularly for bringing the "woodpeckers" to the reservoir site.

Curley, James Michael (1874–1958) Boston mayor, Massachusetts governor, and Massachusetts representative, and convicted felon. During his time as governor (1935–1937), he used the Quabbin project for graft and patronage.

Duckert, Audrey R. (1927–2007) Professor of Linguistics at UMass whose interest in dialect and regional variations led her to be the first interviewer in the Quabbin Oral History project.

Goodnough, Xanthus Henry (1860–1935) Developer of the MDC's "Goodnough Plan," which created the Quabbin Reservoir. The Quabbin's Goodnough Dike is named after him.

Hultman, Eugene C. (1875–1945) MIT alum. Was Boston police commissioner before being appointed to the Commission. The aqueduct that starts at the Wachusett and runs east is called the Hultman Aqueduct.

Kennison, Karl R. (1886–1977) Buried at Quabbin Park Cemetery. President of the Boston Society of Civil Engineers, and started a scholarship trust. Chief engineer for the New York Board of Water Supply in the 1950s.

Keniston, Davis B. (1880–1954) First chairman of the Commission, appointed in 1926. Was a Boston Ward Chairman, later a judge in Boston. In 1949, Kennison presided over a case where a Yiddish-speaking teacher charged with "concealing horse-race betting slips under his patriarchal beard."

Kimball, Roy (1893–1970) Special agent to the Commission. Buried at Quabbin Park Cemetery. Superintendent of the Quabbin in the 1950s. His father had been the chief engineer of the Massachusetts State House. Won a "bravery award" during WWI for repairing telephone wires under enemy fire.

Peabody, William W. (1870–1955) Division engineer initially in charge of the Coldbrook-Swift Division. Was from Providence, RI, and worked on the reservoir there, so probably knew Frank Winsor.

Molt, Olive S. (1900–1993) Was teaching art at Belchertown High School in the 1950s. Remarried to J. Lewis Johnson.

Molt, R. Nelson (1893–1966) Worked for the MDC until his retirement. Never remarried.

Winsor, Frank E. (1870–1939) The Commission's chief engineer. Son is Edward Winsor, who recorded an interview with Quabbin historian Lois Barnes.

The People of the Valley

Barnes, Lois Doubleday (1920–2012) Part of the Doubleday clan and Quabbin historian.

Bartlett, Emory H. (1891–1964) Poultry breeder.

Brown, Inez Walter Brown's wife; member of Enfield Town Council and the Quabbin Club.

Brown, Lyman [dates unknown] Left college to work on the reservoir.

Brown, Nellie E. (1865–1954) Valley gadfly, early feminist, and developer of kindergarten in Maine. Kept voluminous scrapbooks on Quabbin life, which she donated to the Belchertown Historical Society.

Brown, Walter Nellie Brown's brother.

Curtis. Rev. John S. Minister of the Enfield Congregational Church.

Doubleday, Warren ("Bun") Worked at the soil lab. Participated extensively in promoting Quabbin history.

Downing, Iola (1861–1947) Librarian, reporter, and member of the Quabbin Club. Some people said that she was so broken by her displacement that she entered a mental hospital.

Felton, Charles Enfield businessman.

Glass, Grace Nellie Brown's live-in companion.

Gustafson, Evelina Author of *Ghost Towns 'Neath Quabbin Reservoir* (1940).

Hanson, Herman Mechanic in Enfield. His grief in leaving became widely known as part of the 1980 "Rural Lives" broadcast.

Heidel, Emil Took over Enfield meat market. Lived with his family in the old Enfield Parsonage.

Heidel, Geneva (1882–1958) Member of the Quabbin Club and friendly with valley's richest resident, Marion Smith.

Heidel, Norman (1917–2014) Was at the final ball. Worked for Monsanto for much of his life. Served in the army in the Aleutian Islands in WWII.

Howe, Annie (1889–1942) Co–founder of the Quabbin Club and matriarch of the Howe family.

Howe, Donald W. (1915–2006) Author of *Quabbin: The Lost Valley*.

Howe, Edwin Jr. (1898–1959) Enfield postmaster. Married to and divorced from Ruth Ward Howe.

Howe, Edwin Sr. (1859–1943)—Patriarch of the Howe family. Responsible for post office, telephone exchange, general store, and movie night in Enfield.

Jones, Mabel (1888–1974) Coauthor of "Letters from Quabbin."

King, Stanwood R. (1899–1983) Greenwich storekeeper and town official.

King, Walter J. (1914–1991) Born in Greenwich, and also participated in its destruction. Before he was drafted, he had moved to New Hampshire to work for a contractor there.

Marsh, Rev. Burton E. Last minister of the Enfield Congregational Church. Chaplain of the Masons.

Newbury, Robert A. Member of Masons and one of the eccentric Newbury clan.

Rowe, Donald Garage owner and car dealer in Enfield.

Sawyer, Roland B. (1874–1969) The "sockless stateman" and lone vote in the Massachusetts Judicial Court to prevent the reservoir. His daughter Rosalind married engineer Chet Chetwynd.

Schmidt, Eleanor Griswold (1913–1994) Was instrumental in the start of the Swift River Valley Historical Society and a chronicler of Quabbin life. Her gravestone at Quabbin Park Cemetery is a stone from her family's property in Prescott.

Segur, Willard, Sr. (1866–1939) Valley doctor and member of every civic group.

Segur, William (1912–1998) After returning from the war, he opened a shoe store in Ware.

Smith, Marion A. (1862–1944) Heir to the Smith's Village textile fortune. Never married, she lived alone in a mansion at the edge of the village and either her presence or her money were involved in all aspects of valley life.

Terry, Gertrude Ward Stalbird (1909–2000) Younger sister of Robert and Ruth Ward. Married engineer James Stalbird. Married Randall Terry in Saranac Lake, NY, after Stalbird's death, and after Terry's death, returned to western Massachusetts as the subject of historians' interviews and an overall goodwill ambassador between the valley and the wider world.

Thayer, Ellis (1869–1943) Owner of the Greenwich home that became a symbol for Quabbin displacement as it was driven on a truck to its new location. Also the auctioneer as valley-owned objects were sold.

Ward, Robert (1901–1936) Older brother of Ruth Ward Howe and Trudy Ward Stalbird Terry.

Ward, Ruth L. (1907–1990) Married to postmaster Edwin Howe, but divorced him after a stillbirth and contentious marriage. Spent some years in California before moving back to Massachusetts and working at Amherst College until her retirement. Buried in Quabbin Park Cemetery under her birth last name.

Webster, George Grandfather of Bob, Ruth, and Trudy Ward. Farmer, vaudevillian sheep trainer, and bringer of electricity to his section of Enfield. The foundations of his farm are easily accessible to Quabbin hikers on Webster Road.

Wendemuth, Julia A. (1896–1985) Musician daughter of Prescott family that refused to leave.

Wilder, Robert (1933–2015) Fierce chronicler of valley history. His extensive collection of Quabbin articles and memorabilia was donated to UMass Amherst.

Zappey, J. Frederick (1883–1956) Proponent, along with his wife Marian, of bourgeois activism in the valley.

Zappey, Marian (1882–1972) Very involved in works for the poor.

Endnotes

ONE: BIRTH OF A VALLEY: PREHISTORY TO 1900

1   Underwood, Francis H. *Quabbin: The Story of a Small Town with Outlooks Upon Puritan Life.* Boston: Lee and Shepherd Publishers, 1893, p. 1.
2   Underwood, p. 2.
3   Underwood, p. 7
4   Florentine Films, *The Old Quabbin Valley*, 1981, length 29:26. Accessible via https://www.dropbox.com/s/ifc97bgdmu8xxmt/OldQuabbinValle.m4v?dl=0. Ken Burns is credited with "Additional Cinematography."
5   Underwood, p. 147.
6   Underwood, p. 24.
7   William Segur, interview by Friends of Quabbin, October 10, 1986. https://bit .ly/3sV4sCA.
8   Black and white postcard, addressed to Mrs. Rose Wylie, Malden, MA, and postmarked August 23, 1907. Collection of the University of Massachusetts at Amherst Archives.
9   Underwood, pp. 134–135.
10   Underwood, pp. 103–104.
11   Undated flyer advertising investment in Smith's Village (prob. ca. 1900). Collection of UMass Amherst Archives.
12   Underwood, p. 361.
13   National Park Service, "Dana Common," accessed April 2021. https://www.nps .gov/places/dana-common.htm.

TWO: A LONG, SLOW DECLINE: 1880–1920

1   "Growing Up in Greenwich." *Chickuppy Magazine*, May 1986.
2   Clark, Walter E. *Quabbin Reservoir*, with a New Introduction by J.R. Greene. Originally published 1946 by Hobson Press, New York, New York; Reprinted by Athol Press, Inc., Athol, MA, 1994, p. 18.

3   "Growing Up in Greenwich."

4   Clark, p. 18.

5   Trudy Ward Stalbird Terry, outtakes from interview for "Rural Lives" documentary from WFCR (Amherst, MA), broadcast October 15, 1980. https ://www.digitalcommonwealth.org/search/commonwealth-oai:c247g454f.

6   "Spring in Quabbin," Part 6 of the *Springfield Union* "Letters from Quabbin" series, May 3, 1938.

7   Eleanor Griswold Schmidt, interviewed in "Rural Lives."

8   Lovecraft, H.P. "The Dunwich Horror," first published in the April 1929 issue of *Weird Tales* magazine, pp. 481–508, accessed April 2021, https://www.hplovecraft .com/writings/texts/fiction/dh.aspx.

9   Lovecraft, H.P. "The Colour out of Space," first published in the September 1927 issue of *Amazing Stories* magazine, accessed April 2021, https://www.hplovecraft .com/writings/texts/fiction/cs.aspx.

10   U.S. Census Bureau, Census Information for Smith's Village, Enfield, MA, 1930. Publicly available in 2002. https://www.ancestry.com/imageviewer /collections/6224/images/4607009_00475, accessed May 2021.

11   Friends of Quabbin. William Fielding, interview by Larry Lowenthal, March 12, 1988.

THREE: BOSTON'S THIRST FOR WATER: 1630–1930

1   DeWolfe Howe, M.A. *Boston Common: Scenes from Four Centuries*. Boston: Atlantic Monthly Press, 1910, pp. 48-49.

2   Howe, Donald W. *Quabbin: The Lost Valley*. Worcester, MA: The Davis Press, Inc., 1951, Re-Issued by the Quabbin Book House, Ware, MA, 1999. *The Lost Valley*, written by a member of the prominent Howe family of Enfield, is considered to be the ur-text of Quabbin history and genealogy.

3   Howe, p. 27.

4   Howe, p. xvii.

5   George Boynton, interview by UMass. Professor Audrey Duckert, May 20, 1974. https://www.digitalcommonwealth.org/search/commonwealth-oai:9s167076c.

6   Howe, p. 27.

7   Friends of Quabbin. Edward Winsor, interview by Maria Haas and Lois Barnes (prob. mid-1980s). https://bit.ly/3cXg1TW.

8   Letter from MDWSC to the Massachusetts Governor's Council, Recommending R. Nelson Molt as Commission Secretary, January 25, 1927. Collection of Massachusetts State Archives.

9   Herman Hanson, outtakes from interview for "Rural Lives." 1980.

10   Howe, p. 41.

11   "Recovers $450 for Loss of Job as Newspaper Writer and Librarian— Schoolteacher and Farmers Also Suing for Business Damage in Quabbin Valley Reservoir Taking." *Springfield Union* (prob. 1938).

FOUR: PLANS FOR THE RESERVOIR AND NEW EXPERIENCES FOR THE ENGINEERS:
1926–1930

1   Friends of Quabbin, Jerome L. Spurr, interview by Larry Lowenthal, June 18, 1987. https://bit.ly/3rQ0Xfi.

2   Fielding Interview.

3   Ibid.

4   Ibid.

5   Ibid.

6   Ibid.

7   Ibid.

8   Ruth Ward and Eleanor Griswold Schmidt, interview by Audrey Duckert, March 4, 1974. http://credo.library.umass.edu/view/full/mums756-b001-i002.

9   Photo (prob. by Edwin Howe): Howe General Store, ca. 1910. Collection Swift River Valley Historical Society.

10   Photo by Chet Chetwynd: James Lisk Heirs, Pool Room, Enfield, Mass., April 20, 1928. https://ark.digitalcommonwealth.org/ark:/50959/qr46st461.

11   Fielding Interview.

12   Trudy Ward Stalbird Terry, interview by Audrey Duckert, August 20, 1979. http://credo.library.umass.edu/view/full/mums756-b001-i004.

13   Fielding Interview.

14   Boynton Interview.

15   Fielding Interview.

16   Friends of Quabbin. Norman Heidel, interview by Larry Lowenthal, September 15, 1987. https://bit.ly/3s4SHZ7.

17   "Enfield" (Society Page). *Ware River News*, prob. 1929.

18   Fielding Interview.

19   Ibid.

20   Robert Wilder, "Exodus from Enfield." Lecture. Uploaded to YouTube July 4, 2014. https://www.youtube.com/watch?v=_4FNUvYhEww.

21   Photo by Russell Snow: George W. Newbury Heirs, Enfield, Mass., Apr. 15, 1930. https://www.digitalcommonwealth.org/search/commonwealth:qr46t9926.

22   Friends of Quabbin. Ken Cross and Walter King, interview by Lois Barnes, March 2, 1989. https://bit.ly/3moi1Ih.

23   Friends of Quabbin. William Segur, interview by Lois Barnes, October 10, 1986. https://bit.ly/3sV4sCA.

24   Segur Interview.

25   Ibid.

FIVE: THE ENGINEERS ARRIVE: 1926–1930

1   Spurr Interview.

2   Ibid.

3   Fielding Interview.

4   Spurr Interview.

5   Commonwealth of Massachusetts. "Report of the Metropolitan District Water Supply Commission for the Year 1928," p. 10.

6   Ibid.

7   Ibid.

8   Massachusetts Department of Conservation and Resources: Lecture by DCR Archivist Sean Fisher on the DCR Digital Access Project, Presented at the Quabbin Visitors Center. February 23, 2020. Uploaded to YouTube May 18, 2020. https://www.youtube.com/watch?v=VPvfwkHymOc.

9   Ibid.

10 Ibid.

11 "List of Surveyors for the Ware–Coldbrook Division," 1930. DCR Archive Collection at the Quabbin Visitor Center.

12 Underwood, p. 12.

13 Howe, p. 60.

14 Ibid.

15 "The Engineers," Part 14 of the *Springfield Union* "Letters from Quabbin" series, May 31, 1938.

16 Spurr Interview.

17 Cross and King Interview.

18 Greene, J.R. *The Creation of Quabbin Reservoir: The Death of the Swift River Valley*, 1981, 20th Anniversary Edition with a New Introduction by the author, Athol, MA: Self-Published; printed by J&P Printers, 2001. p. 78.

19 Photo by Benjamin Burbank: "Engineer's Club, Enfield," January 16, 1928. Courtesy of Swift River Valley Historical Society.

20 Fielding Interview.

21 Ibid.

22 Ibid.

23 Spurr Interview.

24 Ibid.

25 Ibid.

SIX: "HUMAN MOLES": 1929

1   "Swift, Ware Rivers Project Progresses." *Springfield Sunday Republican/Union*, date and page unknown.

2   Ibid.

3   Ibid.

4   Ibid.

5   MDWSC undated photos of decompression chambers (prob. 1932). Collection of DCR at Quabbin Visitor Center.

6   "Making Water Run Up Hill to Supply Boston's Needs – Human Moles Have Only to Line with Concrete the 13-Mile Wachusett-Colebrook [sic] Tunnel, for the Headings Have Met." *Worcester Telegram*, ca. January 1930.

7   Ibid.

8   MDWSC Photo, prob. by Chet Chetwynd: "Shafts 6 & 7 - Engineers at a 'Holing Through," October 24, 1929. Collection of DCR at Quabbin Visitor Center.

SEVEN: POVERTY AND WEALTH

1   Trudy Ward Stalbird Terry, outtakes from interview for "Rural Lives."

2   "Growing Up in Greenwich."

3   Howe, p. 302.

4   Ibid.

5   "Growing Up in Greenwich."

6   Warren "Bun" Doubleday, interviewed in "Rural Lives."

7   Audrey Duckert, interview by Ruth Ward Howe, March 4, 1974. Collection of the UMass Amherst Archives. http://credo.library.umass.edu/view/full/mums756-b001-i002. Accessed Mary 2021..

8   Boynton interview.

9   Diary of Flora Wilder for 1934. Available at the UMass Amherst Archives.

10   Ibid.

11   Bob Wilder margin notes in Flora Wilder diary, prob. added 2010-2015.

12   Wilder, "Exodus from Enfield."

13   Gertrude Whitney Ward Terry, interview by Audrey Duckert, August 20, 1979. http://credo.library.umass.edu/view/full/mums756-b001-i004.

14   Heidel Interview.

15   Warren Doubleday, interviewed in "Rural Lives."

16   Eleanor Griswold Schmidt, interviewed in "Rural Lives."

17   Herman Hanson, outtakes from interview for "Rural Lives."

18   Ruth Ward Howe Interview.

19   Group photo at last meeting of Quabbin Club, April 12, 1938, prob. from the *Springfield Republican*.

20   Alice Twible Philips, interview by Audrey Duckert, September 16, 1976. http://credo.library.umass.edu/view/full/mums756-b001-i005.

21   Ibid.

EIGHT: EXAMS AND PROMOTIONS—AND, FINALLY, A NAME: 1931–1932

1   Exam for Massachusetts Assistant Sanitary Engineer Position, May 4, 1931. Collection of UMass Amherst archives.

2   Exam for Massachusetts Assistant Sanitary Engineer Position, January 11, 1936. Collection of UMass Amherst archives.

3   Spurr Interview.

4   Ibid.

5   Ibid.

6   "Report of the Metropolitan District Water Supply Commission for the Year 1932," p. 2.

7 "Our $65,000,000 Baby Has Been Named Quabbin," *Boston Post*, prob. late October 1932.

NINE: "THE BENDS": 1932–1935
1 Photo: MDWSC Engineers baseball team, Enfield, Mass., July 5, 1932. https ://ark.digitalcommonwealth.org/ark:/50959/0z708z498.
2 MDWSC Photo by Stuart Pike: "Sluicing Test Bin," November 24, 1933. https ://ark.digitalcommonwealth.org/ark:/50959/qr46tn686, accessed May 2021.
3 Howe, p. 49.
4 Cross and King Interview.
5 Ibid.
6 Friends of Quabbin: Trudy Ward Stalbird Terry, interviewed by Lois Barnes, ca. 1987. https://bit.ly/3cVc2HJ.
7 James A. Stalbird MDWSC Employment Card. Massachusetts State Archives.
8 "Report of the Metropolitan District Water Supply Commission for 1935," p. 2.
9 "State Names Road after Shays Rebellion Leader." *The Christian Science Monitor*, April 15, 1935, p. 3.
10 "Editorial Notes." *Boston Globe* January 25, 1935, p. 14.
11 "Daniel Shays Highway Pierces Beauty of Hilltop Scenery." *Springfield Union*, prob. 1935.
12 "Community Tree Enjoyed by Whole Town." *Ware River News*, December 21, 1934.
13 Greene, J.R. *Quabbin's Railroad: The Rabbit, Vol. 2, The Boston & Albany Years 1880-1935.* Pepperell, Mass.: Branch Line Press, 2007.
14 Heidel Interview.
15 Segur Interview.
16 Greene, *Quabbin's Railroad.*
17 Ibid.
18 "Old Line of Many Traditions Runs Its Last Passenger Train." *Springfield Republican*, April 28, 1934.
19 Herman Hanson, outtakes from interview for "Rural Lives."

TEN: SOCIAL ORGANIZATIONS AND ENTERTAINMENT
1 Ruth Ward Howe 1974 interview.
2 Ruth Ward Howe (prob. 1980s), interview by Friends of Quabbin. https://bit.ly /39UbPCO.
3 *Constitution, By-laws and Rules of Order, Sciota Tribe, No. 214, Improved Order of Red Men, of Pennsylvania.* Philadelphia, Pennsylvania: Shaw Brothers, Printers, 1886.
4 "The Improved Order of Red Men," Boston Tea Party Historical Society, http ://www.boston-tea-party.org/improved-order-of-red-men.html, accessed April 2021.
5 First Prize Certificate for Enfield Grammar School, Grades 4 & 5, presented February 2, 1935, to Eustace Avery for His Essay on "The Life of George Washington," signed by Grange Master James A. Stalbird. Collection of Swift River Valley Historical Society.

6   Fielding Interview.
7   Barbier Interview.
8   Ray Lego, interview by Audrey Duckert in "Remembering the Grange in the Valley: a Panel Discussion," June 21, 1975. http://credo.library.umass.edu/view /full/mums756-b003-i014.
9   Ibid.
10 Ray Thayer, interview by Audrey Duckert in "Remembering the Grange in the Valley: a Panel Discussion."
11 Dorothy Fittz, interview by Audrey Duckert in "Remembering the Grange in the Valley: a Panel Discussion."

ELEVEN: ALL HELL BREAKS LOOSE: 1936
1   "State to Continue Work on Ware Water Project." *The Christian Science Monitor*, March 28, 1936, p. 9.
2   Barbier Interview.
3   MDWSC Photo by Stuart Pike: Set of Photographs Documenting Flooding of the Swift River, March 19, 1936. https://ark.digitalcommonwealth.org/ark:/50959 /qr46tr28v, accessed May 2021.
4   U.S. Department of the Interior. *The Floods of March 1936: Part 1, New England Rivers*, p. 244. https://pubs.usgs.gov/wsp/0798/report.pdf.
5   "The 1936 Flood That Engulfed New England," New England Historical Society, https://www.newenglandhistoricalsociety.com/great-new-england-flood-1936/, accessed April 2021.
6   "Crowd of Applicants Seek Jobs on Quabbin Project." *Boston Globe*, April 21, 1936.
7   Ibid.
8   Page 2 of Memo from Frank Winsor, prob. to N. Leroy Hammond, April 24, 1936.
9   "Taking Bunk out of Boston Stories." *Ware River News*, April 29, 1936.
10 Howe, p. 52.
11 "Ware Officials Deny Boosts in Food Costs." *Worcester Gazette*, May 8, 1936.
12 "Coakley Finds Clearing Crew Well-Treated." *Springfield Republican*, May 11, 1936.
13 "Robart Goes to Quabbin." *Boston Globe*, May 12, 1936.
14 "Men with Axe, Saw and Brush Hook Descend on Quabbin." Prob. *Springfield Republican*, prob. June 1936.
15 MDWSC Photo by Stuart Pike: "Russ Snow at Thurston Nursery, Enfield – Red and Norway Pine Seedlings," September 25, 1936. https://www.digitalcommon wealth.org/search/commonwealth:qr46tt25f.
16 "Increasing Discipline on Clearing Project." *Ware River News*, prob. June 1936.
17 *Quabbin News*, July 10, 1936.
18 Memo from Frank Winsor to N. Leroy Hammond re: Concession Stand Safety, May 15, 1936. Collection of DCR, Quabbin Visitor Center.
19 Letter from Karl Kennison to Max Grossman on Errors in *Boston Post* article, May 18, 1936. Collection of DCR at Quabbin Visitor Center.
20 "Beacon Hill Merry-Go-Round." *Boston Globe*, May 20, 1936.

21 Series of Memos from Laroy Harris to Clearing Crew Supervisors, June–September 1936. Collection of DCR at Quabbin Visitor Center.
22 "Men with Axe, Saw and Brush Hook Descend on Quabbin."
23 Barbier Interview.
24 "Enfield Folk Fear-Ridden after Indcendiary Fire." *Springfield Union*, August 1, 1936.
25 Ward Stalbird Terry Interview.
26 "Fire Will Not Stop Church Anniversary." *Ware River News*, August 1, 1936.
27 Ward Stalbird Terry Interview.
28 "Enfield Folk Fear-Ridden after Indcendiary Fire."
29 "Fire Will Not Stop Church Anniversary."
30 Program from Enfield Congregational Church 150th Anniversary Celebration, August 9, 1936. Collection of Swift River Valley Historical Society.
31 Howe, p. 115.
32 "So Far 22 Men Have Been Killed on Reservoir Job." *Ware River News*, prob. September 1936.
33 "Leroy Hammond, Engineer, Was 77." *New York Times*, November 11, 1963.
34 "Work at Quabbin Nears an Ending." *Christian Science Monitor*, November 10, 1936, p. 9.
35 "Nearly 4000 State-Owned Tools Missing at Quabbin." *Springfield Union*, November 16, 1936, p. B1.
36 "Yes, They Must Be Disbanding Project Groups." *Ware River News*, November 1, 1936.
37 "Gov. Hurley in Washington Says He Will Not Interfere on Clearing Project." *Ware River News*, prob. January 1937.
38 Ibid.
39 "The Last of the Woodpeckers." Poem in *Hello, Timber!*, January 26, 1937.

TWELVE: THE CALM BEFORE: 1937
1 Segur Interview.
2 Memo from Frank Winsor to MDWSC, announcing resignation of N. Leroy Hammond, November 3, 1936. Collection of DCR at Quabbin Visitors Center.
3 Memo to MDWSC from Frank Winsor re: Staffing and Morale Issues, March 29, 1937. Collection of DCR at Quabbin Visitors Center.
4 Millard Aubey, 1937 Engineer Diary. Collection of Massachusetts State Archives.
5 William Peabody, 1937 Engineer Diary. Collection of Massachusetts State Archives.
6 Stuart Pike, 1937 Photographer Diary. Included in Lecture by DCR Archivist Sean Fisher.
7 Lecture by DCR Archivist Sean Fisher.
8 Barbier Interview.
9 Ibid.

10   Warren "Bun" Doubleday, interview in *The Old Quabbin Valley*.
11   *Ware River News*, March 3, 1937.
12   Untitled Article, *Ware River News*, March 3, 1937.
13   Ibid.
14   "Sturdy Old Homes in Quabbin Reservoir Are Transplanted." *Christian Science Monitor*, September 22, 1937, p.11.
15   Ibid.
16   Heidel Interview.
17   "Big Reservoir Dam Begun in Bay State." *New York Times*, May 23, 1937, p. 37.
18   Ibid.
19   *New York Times*, May 23, 1937, p. 1.
20   Cross and King Interview.
21   Stanwood King, Eleanor Griswold Schmidt, and Dorothy Moult, interview by Audrey Duckert, April 8, 1975. http://credo.library.umass.edu/view/full/mums756-b001-i003.
22   Ibid.
23   Photograph of Enfield Congregational Church Cemetery and Grounds, ca. 1937. Collection Swift River Valley Historical Society.
24   Bill from Schoonmaker & Schoonmaker, Counsellors-at-Law, to the Congregational Church of Enfield, for Services Rendered, December 14, 1937.
25   "Agawam Trucker Sent to Jail for Drunken Driving," *Ware River News*, July 11, 1937.
26   Heidel Interview.
27   "Club at Enfield Begins 40th Year." *Springfield Union*, October 6, 1937.
28   "Quabbin Club Gives 1937-1938 Schedule." *Ware River News*, October 3, 1937.
29   Program for Christmas Exercises, Enfield Center School, December 21, 1937. Collection of UMass Amherst Archives.

THIRTEEN: QUABBIN PARK CEMETERY

1   "Generations Who Lived Since Before the Revolution to Be Mustered There." *Springfield Republican*, prob. 1932.
2   Memo from N. Leroy Hammond to Frank Winsor discussing the Enfield Town Meeting of February 8, 1928. November 10, 1928. Collection of Massachusetts State Archives.
3   Ibid.
4   Letter from R. Nelson Molt to Woodlawn Cemetery Custodian Frank L. Gage, Quoting decision of August 2, 1932. August 25, 1932. Collection of Massachusetts State Archives.
5   MDWSC Photo by Chet Chetwynd: Woodlawn Cemetery, Enfield, September 28, 1928. https://ark.digitalcommonwealth.org/ark:/50959/765376001, accessed May 2021.
6   Anonymous Letter to the Editor of the *Springfield Union*, February 25, 1938.

7   DCR-DWSP Quabbin Interpretive Services (Nancy Huntington), "Quabbin Park
     Cemetery Tour," January 30, 2020. https://storymaps.arcgis.com/stories/538ad13
     4f102458fb94c304cad676346.
8   MDWSC List of People in Each Town Who Knew Graves and Family Histories,
     June 14, 1937. Collection of Massachusetts State Archives.
9   "Five Thousand Dead Will Be Moved Away." *Springfield Union*, prob. 1932.
10   Ibid.
11   Cross and King Interview.
12   "Enfield Will Decorate Quabbin Valley Soldier Graves." *Springfield Republican*,
     May 26, 1938.
13   Ibid.

FOURTEEN: THE END OF EVERYTHING: 1938
1   Photograph of Enfield Congregational Church Cemetery and Grounds, ca. 1937.
     Collection Swift River Valley Historical Society.
2   "Enfield Resident Gasses Up for the Last Time." Clipping from unknown
     newspaper, spring 1938.
3   "Old Swift River Hotel at Enfield Being Torn Down." *Springfield Republican*,
     November 13, 1937.
4   Family in Front of Demolished Store, prob. 1938. Collection of Swift River
     Valley Historical Society.
5   MDWSC Photo: "Inspection Team, 1938." Collection of DCR, Quabbin Visitor
     Center.
6   Commonwealth of Massachusetts, "List of Candidates nominated, to be voted for
     in the town of Enfield, February 7, 1938." Ballot totals. Collection of Swift River
     Valley Historical Society.
7   "Enfield's Last Town Meeting Votes $1800 to Buy Memorial." *Springfield
     Republican*, April 8, 1938.
8   Howe, p. 235.
9   Anonymous Letter to the Editor of the *Springfield Union*, February 12, 1938.
10   Anonymous Letter to the Editor of the *Springfield Union*, February 23, 1938.
11   Anonymous Letter to the Editor of the *Springfield Union*, February 25, 1938.
12   Compiled by Friends of Quabbin. *Letters from Quabbin*, introduction.
     Belchertown, Mass.: 1988, p. ii.
13   *Letters from Quabbin*, "The Exodus," p. 10.
14   Ibid.
15   *Letters from Quabbin*, "The Fishing," p. 23.
16   *Letters from Quabbin*, "The Engineers," p. 40.
17   "Gavel of Quabbin Club of Enfield Will Be Presented to Woman's Club of
     Somerset." *Springfield Republican*, April 12, 1938.
18   Untitled Article, prob. *Springfield Union*, prob. April 12, 1938.
19   Ibid.

20 "The Quabbin Club." From "Letters from Quabbin," Friends of Quabbin compilation, p. 27.

FIFTEEN: TWO DANCES, AN AUCTION, AND A HURRICANE
1 "Water to Dance as Enfield Did; Old Quabbin." *Christian Science Monitor*, March 26, 1938, p. 9.
2 Ibid.
3 "Special Meeting Called April 11, 1938." Handwritten Notes in Notebook. Collection of the Belchertown, MA, Historical Association.
4 Invitation/Flyer for Enfield Farewell Ball. Collection of the Belchertown, MA, Historical Association.
5 Press Photograph of Norman Hall and Muriel Feindel Briggs Serving Cake at Farewell Ball.
6 "Enfield's Last Hurrah – Bittersweet Goodbyes." *Chickuppy Magazine*, June 1986.
7 Greene, J.R. *The Day Four Quabbin Towns Died*. Athol, MA: Self-Published, 1985, p. 45.
8 "Preparing for Fun in Somber Setting." *Springfield Union*, April 26, 1938.
9 Dance Card for Farewell Ball. Collection of the Belchertown, MA, Historical Association.
10 Greene, p. 44.
11 "Enfield's History Ends as Firemen Hold Party." *Springfield Republican*, April 28, 1938.
12 "Enfield Brings Long Existence to Conclusion." *Springfield Union*, April 28, 1938.
13 Announcement of Public Auction in Swift River Valley for September 10, 1938. Prob. *Boston Globe*, prob. September 1938.
14 "Dana and Enfield End Their Careers on Auction Block." *Springfield Sunday Union and Republican*, September 11, 1938.
15 Gustafson, Evelina. *Ghost Towns 'Neath Quabbin Reservoir*. Boston: Amity Press, 1940, p. 104.
16 Ibid.
17 "Dana and Enfield End Their Careers on Auction Block."
18 Ibid.
19 Gustafson, p. 109.
20 "Report of the Metropolitan District Water Supply Commission for the Year 1938," p. 4.
21 Ibid.
22 Spurr Interview.
23 King, Griswold Schmidt, and Moult Interview.
24 Boynton Interview.
25 Howe, p. 45.

26   "Changing Valley." *Fitchburg* (MA) *Sentinel*, October 10, 1938, p. 6.

27   Segur Interview.

SIXTEEN: "LAND OF A THOUSAND SMOKES": 1939

1   *Uniquely Quabbin Magazine*, September-December 2019, p. 58. http://www
      .uniquelyquabbin.com/resources/reduced9-19UQentire.pdf

2   Notice from USPS on Cessation of Mail Delivery to Enfield. Collection of
      Belchertown Historical Society.

3   Photo, prob. by Olive Molt: "Last mail leaving Enfield. January 14, 1939."
      Collection of Swift River Valley Historical Society.

4   "Enfield Postoffice Ends 116 Years." *Springfield Republican*, January 15, 1939.

5   "Town Doctor Hard Luck Victim, Patients Scatter Before Flood." *Springfield
      Republican*, January 13, 1939.

6   Ward Stalbird Terry Interview.

7   Segur Interview.

8   "Frank E. Winsor Dies on Witness Stand." *Boston Globe*, January 31, 1939, p. 1.

9   Greene, J.R. *From Valley to Quabbin: 1938-1946*. Athol, MA: Athol Press, 2010,
      p. 85.

10   Untitled Article about Frank Winsor Funeral. *Boston Globe*, February 3, 1939, p. 19.

11   "Dr. W.B. Segur's Funeral Attended by Nearly 1000." *Springfield Republican*,
      January 30, 1939.

12   Invitation for Belchertown Church Reunion. Collection Belchertown Historical
      Society.

13   Untitled Article Covering the Belchertown Church Reunion. Prob. *Belchertown
      Sentinel*, February 1, 1939.

14   "Programme: Reception to New Residents of Belchertown Who Have Come
      from the Swift River Valley." Collection Belchertown Historical Society.

15   *New York Times*, January 31, 1939, p. 1.

16   "Board's Records, Much Equipment, Lost in Flames." *Springfield Union*, March 23,
      1939.

17   "Records of Quabbin Work Lost in Flames." *Boston Globe*, March 24, 1939, p. 5.

18   "Board's Records, Much Equipment, Lost in Flames."

19   MDWSC Construction Film Compilation. Footage, compiled ca. 1936–1944.
      Collection Swift River Valley Historical Society.

20   Cross and King Interview.

21   MDWSC Construction Film Compilation. Footage, compiled ca. 1936–1944.
      Collection Swift River Valley Historical Society.

22   MDWSC Photo by Stuart Pike: "Moving Part of Thayer House from Greenwich
      out of the Valley," March 21, 1939. Collection DCR, Quabbin Visitor Center.

23   Greene, *From Valley to Quabbin*, p. 91.

24   Gustafson, p. 99.

25   Gustafson, p. 121.

26   "Quabbin Area's Deserted Villages and Big Dam Attract Thousands." *Springfield Union*, May 8, 1939.

27   Ibid.

28   Unknown Family Photos, Spring 1939. Collection Swift River Valley Historical Society.

29   "Last House in 'Lost Valley' to Be Torn Down." *Springfield Republican*, April 9, 1939.

30   Greene, *From Valley to Quabbin*, pp. 99–100.

31   "Quabbin Valley Only Man-Made Wasteland Now." *Springfield Republican*, August 11, 1939.

32   Greene, *From Valley to Quabbin*, p. 102.

33   "Road to Enfield Under Water as Reservoir Fills." Springfield *Republican*, August 26, 1939.

34   "Quabbin Cost Is More Than Boulder Dam." *Christian Science Monitor*, October 14, 1939, p. 9.

35   "Spurr, Buckingham, Leave Technology." *The Tech* [MIT Student Newspaper], August 6, 1943, p. 1.

36   "Spurr to Lecture on Quabbin Project." *Boston Globe*, December 15, 1939.

SEVENTEEN: PREPARING THE PATH TO BOSTON—AND TO WAR: 1940–1941

1   Young Engineers at the Chandler House, prob. January 1940. DCR Collection at Quabbin Visitor Center.

2   "Two Woodchucks Only Animals Living in Huge Quabbin Dam Area." *Springfield Union*, May 8, 1940.

3   "Enfield Vanishing Under Man-Made Flood." *Springfield Union*, January 4, 1940.

4   "Bigger Boat for Quabbin Patrol Ordered Following Official Trip." *Springfield Union*, May 21, 1940.

5   "How do they mow that slope?" Friends of Quabbin Newsletter, Spring 2015, p. 8.

6   Photo: Eugene Hultman and Edward Kelley Standing with Sheep and Shepherd , prob. May 1940. Collection Swift River Valley Historical Society.

7   Greene, *From Valley to Quabbin*, p. 112.

8   MDWSC Photo by Ellis Barbier: "Unsuccessful Attempt to Launch '46 Quabbin Reservoir Service Boat on Old Belchertown–Enfield Road," April 16, 1941. https://www.digitalcommonwealth.org/search/commonwealth:qr46v3194.

9   MDWSC Photo by Ellis Barbier: "Launching 46-Foot Quabbin Reservoir Service Boat on Old Belchertown–Enfield Road," April 17, 1941. https://www.digitalcommonwealth.org/search/commonwealth:qr46v3215.

10   "Army Breaks Ground for New Chicopee Air Base." *Boston Globe*, April 6, 1940, p. 14.

11   Community Notice, *Boston Globe*, May 14, 1940, p. 8.

12   Community Notice, *Boston Globe*, October 18, 1941, p. 5.

13   "Story of Quabbin Valley in Songs and Pictures." *Boston Globe*, October 19, 1941.

14 Undated Draft Letter (prob. 1940-1941) from Quabbin Club to Postmaster General of US, Suggesting a Quabbin Stamp, with Edits by Nellie Brown. Collection Belchertown Historical Society.
15 Letter from Eugene Hultman to Nellie Brown in Response to Her Inquiry about Chief Quabbin Statue, with Brown's Notes Underneath, November 25, 1940. Collection Belchertown Historical Society.
16 Prob. MDWSC Photo: Eugene Hultman, Other Commission Officials, and Engineers inside New Tunnels, October 22, 1940. Collection Swift River Valley Historical Society.
17 "Quabbin Water to Reach Boston Tomorrow." *Springfield Union*, October 21, 1940.
18 Ibid.
19 "Quabbin Water Supply Tunnel Dedicated." *Boston Globe*, October 23, 1940, p. 1.
20 Ibid.
21 "Water Supply of Boston Guarded." *Boston Globe*, August 14, 1940, p. 1.
22 "Saltonstall Pushes Defense." *Boston Globe*, January 3, 1941, p. 1.
23 Greene, *From Valley to Quabbin*, p. 119.
24 "Quabbin Tower, Area's Sentinel, Now Complete." *Springfield Union*, February 8, 1941.
25 Barbier Interview.
26 "Quabbin Tower, Area's Sentinel, Now Complete."
27 Barbier Interview.
28 Ibid.
29 "Report of the Metropolitan District Water Supply Commission for the Year 1941," p. 52.
30 "Gov. Saltonstall Stresses Morale of Main-St. Type." *Boston Globe*, June 17, 1941, p. 5.
31 "Ex-Gov. Curley Given to Oct. 6 to Pay Judgment." *Boston Globe*, June 17, 1941, p. 5.
32 "Quabbin Reservoir Starts Flowing." *Springfield Republican*, September 19, 1941.
33 MDWSC Photo by Ellis Barbier: "Red & White Pine Plantation – Planted in the Spring of 1937 – Mabel L. Wendemuth Prop. – Prescott," November 17, 1941, https://www.digitalcommonwealth.org/search/commonwealth:qr46v447h.
34 MDWSC Photo by Stuart Pike: "Reforestation, red and white pine, planted spring 1937, looking northwest from Mabel L. Wendemuth property, Prescott, Mass.," November 22, 1939. https://www.digitalcommonwealth.org/search/commonwealth:qr46v1531.
35 "Metropolitan Police Guard Big Reservoirs." *Boston Globe*, December 8, 1941, p. 5.
36 Spurr Separation Card.

EIGHTEEN: THE WAR AND AFTER: 1942–1946
1 "Combined Fifteenth, Sixteenth, Seventeenth, Eighteenth, Nineteenth And Twentieth Annual Reports of the Metropolitan District Water Supply Commission," p. 5.

2   Letter to Nellie Brown and Grace Glass from Jerome Spurr, July 8, 1943. Collection Belchertown Historical Society.

3   Letter to Roland B. Sawyer from Chet Chetwynd, May 12, 1944. Collection University of New Hampshire Library Archives.

4   Letter to Chet Chetwynd from Rosalind Sawyer Chetwynd, June 16, 1944. Collection University of New Hampshire Library Archives.

5   Letter to Roland B. Sawyer from Rosalind Sawyer Chetwynd, March 20, 1942. Collection University of New Hampshire Library Archives.

6   Letter to Roland B. Sawyer from Chet Chetwynd, May 12, 1944.

7   Barbier Interview.

8   Ancestry.com, "All Military Records for Willard Segur." https://rb.gy/il5rbd, accessed May 18, 2021

9   Ibid.

10   World War II Hospital Admission Card Files, 1942-1954 results for Willard Segur.

11   "Army Truck Drivers Must Run Nights, in Darkness." *Ware River News*, May 6, 1941.

12   "Quabbin Range Safety Provisions Announced." *Springfield Union*, prob. 1942.

13   Ibid.

14   "Visitors Barred from Quabbin Area." *Ware River News*, August 27, 1942.

15   Ibid.

16   Ibid.

17   Metropolitan District Water Supply Commission "World War II Honor Roll," as part of 1946 annual report.

18   Tricia Spurr Thompson, interview by author, March 19, 2021.

19   Barbier Interview.

20   Letter to Roland B. Sawyer from Rosalind Sawyer Chetwynd, February 6, 1947. Collection University of New Hampshire Library Archives.

21   Lloyd K. Crumb, interview by author, April 7, 2020.

22   Comments Page for "Lost Towns of the Quabbin Reservoir," *New England Today*, June 6, 2017. https://newengland.com/today/living/new-england-history/lost-towns-quabbin-reservoir/#comment-on-post.

23   MDWSC Photo by Ellis Barbier: "First Water Released over Winsor Dam Spillway, 2 P.M., June 22, 1946." https://ark.digitalcommonwealth.org/ark:/50959/qr46v805t.

24   "Windsor [sic] Dam Tapped to Release Overflow of Quabbin Water." *Boston Globe*, June 22, 1946, p. 1.

25   MDWSC Photo by Louis Albertine: "General view below spillway bridge showing first water released from Quabbin Reservoir, looking NE'ly," June 22, 1946. https://ark.digitalcommonwealth.org/ark:/50959/qr46v801q.

26   Harold Willey, interview by Louis Albertine in *The Old Quabbin Valley*.

27   "Report of the Metropolitan District Water Supply Commission for the Year 1946," p. 15.

28   Willey Interview, *The Old Quabbin Valley*.

NINETEEN: CONCLUSION: MODERN "LETTERS" FROM QUABBIN

1   PBS Documentary, *Under Quabbin*, 2001, 57:56. https://www.pbs.org/video /wgby-documentaries-under-quabbin/.

2   Ed Klekowski, quoted in *Under Quabbin*.

3   Ibid.

4   "The Swift River Valley – Still Here," by "Al Winters" aka Jon Melick. Created September 16, 2011. Collection Swift River Valley Historical Society.

5   Ibid.

6   Jon Melick, interview by author, December 8, 2020.

7   Warren "Bun" Doubleday, interviewed in "Rural Lives."

8   "Quabbin Voices," Friends of Quabbin Newsletter, vol. 26, no. 3, p. 6. foquabbin .org/voices_vol26_num3.pdf.

9   Photo by Friends of Quabbin: Jerome Spurr et al. at 50th Anniversary "Remembrance Ball," April 27, 1988.

10   Thompson Interview.

11   "After the Flood." *Boston Sunday Herald Magazine*, April 17, 1988, p. 5.

12   United States Census Bureau, QuickFacts: Belchertown, MA. https://www .census.gov/quickfacts/fact/table/belchertowntownhampshirecounty massachusetts, accessed April 2021.

13   Town of Belchertown, MA: 2020 Voting Results. https://cms2.revize.com/revize /belchertown/Election%20Results/Nov.%203,%202020%20final%20results.pdf, accessed April 2021.

14   "Biden gets near sweep in Hampshire County amid strong voter turnout." *Daily Hampshire Gazette*, November 5, 2020. https://www.gazettenet.com /Local-election-breakdown-37140608.

15   Town of Shutesbury, MA: 2020 Voting Results. https://www.shutesbury.org /sites/default/files/Unofficial%202020%20results.pdf, accessed April 2021.

16   *The Old Quabbin Valley*, https://www.dropbox.com/s/ifc97bgdmu8xxmt /OldQuabbinValle.m4v?dl=0.

17   Author Conversation with Swift River Valley Historical Society Volunteer, August 22, 2012.

18   Author Conversation with Swift River Valley Historical Society Volunteer, September 22, 2012.

19   Author Recording of 2013 Memorial Day Commemoration at Quabbin Park Cemetery, May 27, 2013.

20   "St. Thomas Memorial Cemetery." http://www.usgwarchives.net/nv/clark /photos/tombstones/stthomas2/sttompion.html, accessed April 2021.

21   Tennessee Valley Authority, "Relocated Cemeteries." https://www.tva.com /environment/environmental-stewardship/land-management/cultural -resource-management/relocated-cemeteries, accessed April 2021.